Follow the Son

"I AM THE LIGHT OF THE WORLD, WHOEVER FOLLOWS ME WILL NEVER WALK IN DARKNESS, BUT WILL HAVE THE LIGHT OF LIFE"

JOHN 8:12

Sandie Beckman

Dorrance Publishing Co
585 Alpha Drive
Pittsburgh, PA 15238
Visit our website at www.dorrancebookstore.com

ISBN: 978-1-6480-4089-4
eISBN: 978-1-6480-4901-9

INTRODUCTION

The purpose, vision and desire of *Follow the Son* is written to all those in the Body of Christ and for those who are seeking the Lord and those who do not know the Lord and his love and forgiveness for them. This book's purpose is to bring light to the darkness in a falling world. It is an informative, inspirational tool that will help promote encouragement, comfort, spiritual strength and unity, and will help clarify many unanswered questions people have about the Bible, daily life, and draw them closer in knowing God in a more personal way. It is Biblically based with Scripture, and inspiring, informative articles. This book will focus on spiritual growth, the importance of commitment to God and each other and the world. It reflects God's unconditional love and forgiveness He offers to the world. It invites the truth of the gospel to the needy, lost and hurting to come to God as they are. God wants people to know Jesus died for all mankind and He desires all to come to Him. There is no one person greater, or more important than the other in God's eye. We are all to work together in unity as a team for the kingdom of God, to be a blessing; this is what the book expresses.

We can follow after certain lifestyle principles (to be rich, to be famous, or to be wise) or we can follow a person; we can emulate and desire to be like them. But the Bible, of course, says that first and foremost we must follow Jesus Christ the Son. Since He is the perfect Son of God, and He has created us, and since He knows what is best for us, and since He has prepared a place for us in eternity, doesn't it make sense to follow his direction? To follow Christ we need a willing heart. This means we must think less about what we are leaving behind and more about what we need to pick up in order to follow effectively. If you find yourself compromising your values in order to please those who don't know God, then you are following after the wrong things… the Bible says, "…choose today whom you will serve.. But as for me and family we will serve the Lord," (Joshua 24:15).

It is a tragedy today that so many people are not familiar with the Bible, and if some are, they read it but do not apply it. Many people feel the Bible is out dated, but God says, "For I am Lord, I do not change…" (Malachi 3:6)… "Jesus Christ is the same yesterday, today, and forever" (Hebrews 13:8). The message of God's Word has always been the same; it's all about forgiveness, faith, peace, power, purpose, blessings, God's promises and his love.

Many people are searching for a reliable truth. The Word of God, written in the Bible is the only true authority we have. People ask why have they been born and what is their purpose; is there a heaven, or hell, is there life after death. These questions and more are all answered in the Bible. The Bible is our daily guide! Even if you know the Bible and the love of God, it is such a pleasure to share it with you who know my heartfelt, delight in the Word and the same compassion for the Lord!

Follow the Son leads you to the truths of the Bible. I desire my readers to know what God says that is written to them, not my opinion. This is why I use Scripture in each article, so the readers can know it is the truth and Word of God.

No matter who you are, you are important, loved and valued by God and He wants all mankind to know this, and this is my main reason and desire for this book. I hope you will glean my spirit of seriousness, the love, and concern I have for all who read Follow the Son. I have very much enjoyed writing this book. I hope you will enjoy reading it.

ABOUT THE AUTHOR

The Lord called me into the Family of God in 1975 in just the right time. He is never early or never late! Ever since I have learned and grown closer to the Lord's heart but haven't arrived because there is much depth and wisdom we will not know until his expectant return. But our spiritual journey is never dull. It has its surprising moments, joyous times, and intimate closeness, even its fearful moments, and uncomfortable stretching and challenging, growing spurts. Being a Christian is no walk in the park, but an ever uphill climb to spiritual maturity and a closer intimacy with Jesus as He builds good character, and brings you through to many victories. But the rewards are greater than we can ever imagine!

During my walk with the Lord, He has led me through many dark valleys, trials, disappointments, victories, tested my faith, healed all of my sicknesses as his Word promises and blessed me. Through this growing time with Jesus I learned to trust Him, depend and lean on Him, and learn who I am and who He is. My spiritual walk is not over and I will continue to grow and learn and share his bountiful love and compassionate Word until he calls me home. And I know Jesus is with me every step of the way as He is with all his children.

I feel humbled, but honored that the Lord opened the door for *Follow the Son*" to be able to share with you all the inspired devotions and steps of growth I learned through my time spent with the Lord. My passion of course is Jesus first, and second is to share the unconditional, passionate, merciful love of the Lord and his mighty, living, transforming Word. I am excited each time I have an opportunity to share and witness about our Precious Lord Jesus!

My heart and prayer for all that read this book will not just simply obtain head knowledge, but experience knowing the real Jesus intimately, and the unconditional, deep love He has for you and the blessings for your life which will assure you and be rewarding. Learning to live in God's ways, his love, and his guidance will help you overcome any obstacles in your life as He has promised. This is God's promise for you: "For I know the thoughts that I think toward you, says the Lord, thoughts of peace and not of evil, to give you a future and a hope" (Jeremiah 29:11). That is his part, our part is to seek after the Lord earnestly and with diligent prayer.

Paul prays for the Ephesians in 3:17-19 which clearly expresses my heart as well for you: "I pray from his glorious, unlimited resources He will give you mighty inner strength through his Holy Spirit and that Christ will be more and more at home in your hearts as you trust in Him. May your roots go down deep into the soil of God's marvelous love. And may you have the power to understand, as all God's people should, how wide, how long, how high, and how deep his love really is. May you experience the love of Christ, though it is so great you will never fully understand it. Then you will be filled with the fullness of life and power that comes from God."

I have also included many of my articles written within seven years from the Pathway Outreach newsletter in my book, "Follow the Son."

DEDICATION

I dedicate *Follow the Son* to God for the glory He deserves. Without His guidance and blessings I would not have been able to write this book, for I have learned… "I am the vine, you are the branches. He who abides in Me, and I in him, bears much fruit; for without Me you can do nothing" (John 15:5). It was his desire and hand upon my heart to write this book so I could share his love and Word. I truly want to exalt Jesus for his greatness, mercy, and unconditional love throughout this book, which will draw people to Him, for the Lord promises, "If I am lifted up from the earth, I will draw all peoples to myself" (John 12:32).

I also dedicate this book to my husband, Dennis, for his love and support and the inspiration of hope he gave me, that I might reach many hearts and souls for Jesus.

And lastly, but very importantly, I dedicate this book and my loving appreciation to my good friend Lorraine, who worked countless hours rewriting my messy notes so I could compile them into articles I desired to write.

"I am the light of the world.
Whoever follows We will never
Walk in darkness, but will
Have the light of life."

John 8:12

EACH DAY IS A GIFT

God only knows how many days we have in this world. One does not have to be old to go home with the Lord. We take our days for granted and live them without purpose or value. Some say, "Oh, it's just another day." But is it? The Lord gives each day as a gift to us and within each day there are blessings, but most of us are too busy to notice. But what if we did know our last days would we treat each day different? Of course we would! We would want time to slow up so we don't miss anything. We would look deeper into each day searching for the meaning and the beauty of each blessing that the Lord had given us. We would treat people different without selfishness, but with genuine concern and kindness. We would spend more time talking with the Lord and trusting Him for each moment and getting to know Him more intimately. And we would learn to respect each day; living it to its fullness and regarding it as a precious gift from God! There would be no time for worry, anxiety, anger, because we wouldn't want to waste our precious time that we have left on such frivolous things. Joy, peace and love would be top priority each day! We wouldn't want to argue with our spouse or children, not for one minute. But spending quality time and love would be the most important thing on our mind and each day would be more valuable than gold! Our neighbors would now become a friend we could share with or help. Most of all we would be sharing the Word with everyone we met!

Stop right here! Think about this... Isn't this just the way God desires us to live right now! Isn't this the way we should be viewing each day NOW? We don't know our last day, but we still have time to value each day as a gift from God and live it to the fullness in God's love, peace and joy and live it as it was our last day. Don't overlook God's beautiful tapestry of nature He has given us, or take for granted the time which is also a precious gift from God. Don't say, "Thank God it's Friday," or wish the day away! Each day was meant to be precious, fruitful, with increasing values and importance, opportunities, unique qualities, encouraging, expectant, enthusiastic, significant, and grateful, all functioning to give God the glory! Remember...we are God's beloved children... so enjoy the journey!

"This is the day the Lord has made;
we will rejoice and be glad in it."
Psalm 118:24

SELF-INVENTORY

"Accept Christians who are weak in faith, and don't argue with them about what they think is right or wrong" (Romans 14:1).

We are all weak in some areas and strong in others. Our faith is strong in an area if we can survive contact with sin without falling into it. It is weak if we must avoid certain activities or places in order to protect our spiritual life. We need to take a self-inventory to find our weaknesses and strengths.

In areas of strength, we should not fear that we will be defiled by the world. Rather, from our position of strength we should lead the world. In areas of weakness, however, we need to play it safe. If we have a strong faith but shelter it, we are not doing Christ's work in the world. If we have weak faith but expose it, we are being extremely foolish. We try to steer clear of actions forbidden by Scripture, but when Scripture is silent, we should follow our conscience. When God shows us something is wrong for us, we should avoid it—but we should not look down on other Christians who exercise their freedom in those areas. For example, "But if people have doubts about whether they should eat something, they shouldn't eat it. They would be condemned for not acting in faith before God. If you do anything you believe is not right, you are sinning" (Romans 14:23). God desires us to be in unity as the body of Christ, "May God who gives his patience and encouragement, help you live in complete harmony with each other—each with the attitude of Christ Jesus toward the other" (Romans 15:5).

WE NEED OUR SHEPHERD

Some people perceive God as very hard-faced who drives his church against their will to do things they don't want to do. But that is totally a wrong image. Jesus is called the Good Shepherd. He loves his sheep and cares deeply for them. He knows each of them by name and laid down his life for them. He is a Shepherd who protects and provides his sheep.

In the past there were many shepherds who lived among their sheep. When sheep wandered, the shepherd found them. When the sheep fell, he carried them, when they were hurt, he healed them. The care and concern of a shepherd illustrates God's love for his children. The Bible comforts us about the love and care of our Good Shepherd as well, with this Scripture, "If a man has a hundred sheep and one of them goes astray, does he not leave the ninety-nine and go to the mountains to seek the one that is straying? And if he should find it, assuredly, I say to you, he rejoices more over that sheep than over the ninety-nine that did not go astray. Even so it is not the will of your Father who is in heaven that one of these little ones should perish" (Matthew 18:12-14). No flock ever grazed without a shepherd, and no shepherd was ever off duty. This is also the heart of our Good Shepherd. He is ever with us and guiding us.

Sheep are not smart they have no sense of direction. Out of all God's animals sheep are the least able to take care of themselves. They are defenseless. They will wander into water getting their wool wet which grows heavy and so they drown. They need someone to lead them on the paths that are right. They need a shepherd all the time, just as we also need our Shepherd all the time to keep us from troubled waters and on the right path. We tend to be swept away by waters we should have avoided, "We all have wandered away like sheep; each of us have gone his own way" (Isaiah 53:6). We also have no defense against evil without our Shepherd. We need our Good Shepherd! We have the perfect and faithful Shepherd who loves us, guides us, and protects, provides and heals us and shows us the way we need to go and He knows us by name! Put your trust in Him.

"To him the doorkeeper opens, and the sheep hear his voice;
and he calls his own sheep by name and leads them out.
And when he brings out his own sheep, he goes before them,
and the sheep follow him, for they know his voice"
(John 10:3-4).

THE HAND THAT NEVER LETS GO

"I am the Lord your God, who holds your right hand, and tell you 'Don't be afraid. I will help you.'" (Isaiah 41:13).

The Lord tells us not to long for the absence of problems in our life, for this is an unrealistic goal. John 16:33 tells us, "In this world you will have trouble, but be brave. I have defeated the world." We can be brave because Philippians 4:13 reassures us, "I can do all things through Christ, because He gives me strength." We as believers also can rejoice in our inheritance that awaits in heaven which is; we will be problem free which no one can take away from us! But to expect heaven on earth is unrealistic.

If we begin each day anticipating some problems, or difficulties, but knowing the Lord goes with us and is holding our hand, and He goes before us, we can handle things together. He reminds us to have peace in this: He has overcome the world (John 16:33). With our morning prayer it is good to ask God to equip us for whatever difficulties we encounter throughout the day.

To have this peace we must really trust in the Lord. For everything we can endure can be put to good use: "And we know all things work together for good to those who love God" (Romans 8:28). A trial should not make us bitter...but better. Remember Joseph, he was a prime example of a divine reversal.

So do not fear what the day will bring your way, just concentrate on trusting the Lord. Relax in His sovereignty, remembering that He goes before you, as well as with you, into each day and He will bring good out of every situation you will encounter.

"Even if I walk through a very dark valley, I will not be afraid,
because you are with me. Your rod and walking stick comfort me"
(Psalm 23:4).

GOD WILL LISTEN

You can talk to God because He always listens and takes you seriously. You never need to fear you will be ignored. You do not have to have flowery words; you just speak from your heart. Even if you stammer or stumble God listens to your heart. And even if what you say would not impress someone else; it will impress God! God closely listens to the painful plea of the elderly in the rest homes, and the gruff confession of one that is on death-row. When the drug addict or alcoholic begs for mercy and a spouse seeks guidance, or a businessman needs wisdom God will listen caringly, intently and carefully! The prayers are important and honored by God. Your words will not stop until they reach God's throne. Sincere prayers and heartfelt prayers move God's heart. You may not understand the mystery of prayer, but you don't need to. You just need to speak your heart with the faith and trust and not doubt that God always hears your fervent prayers. Action always happens in heaven when someone prays on earth.

"Anyone who is having troubles should pray. Anyone who is happy should sing praises. Anyone who is sick should call the church's elders. They should pray for and pour oil on the person in the name of the Lord. And the prayer that is said with faith will make the sick person well; the Lord will heal that person. And if the person has sinned, the sins will be forgiven. Confess your sins to each other and pray for each other so God can heal you. When a believing person prays, great things happen" (James 5:13-1).

BLESSINGS FOR THE RETIREE

"If you use wisely what you have you will be given more"

(Matthew 25:29).

Some people are afraid of retirement; thinking their livelihood is over…not so! Yes, everyone wants to feel they are still useful…and they are. Remember when you were working and you said to yourself, "I wish I had more time to myself." I know I did; I was working over 50 hours a week. Then came the age of retirement and I thought, "I'm not ready." I wanted to keep working, but my body was telling me, we have to slow up now and there will be limitations, which I did find out.

I'm sure many of you, felt the same way and thought, "Now what do I do?" But this can be a very special and fruitful time in your life as I too found out. Along with retirement there come blessings…the blessings of opportunities, time and talent and abilities that God has given to us all, no one is left emptyhanded (Eph. 4:11-12). Our goal is to first discover our abilities, then exercise them, and finally channel them toward good, not evil. Remember when you wished you had more time? Well, now you do. You can take down off the shelf the things you wish you could have done. Some of you like to draw, or paint, or sew, or build little birdhouses, or read, or bake, visit people from your church that have been hospitalized go witness to the homeless and lost, or write cards for people's birthdays, or get-well cards, there is so many things you can do to bless others and yourself. Don't allow the devil to steal your personal and valuable time of retirement! The Lord has given each of us a talent to do, and to share and bless others. One could sew lap pads for nursing homes, or help your neighbor and bake goodies for them. For me, now I have time to read and study more, and write articles, and hopefully get my book published this year. I also have more time to write and encourage many souls within the prisons.

There is always something fruitful and fulfilling you can do that is a blessing for you and others. If you are not sure of what you can do, ask the Lord; He knows you better than you know yourself and what you would be happy and prosperous doing. My neighbor John now enjoys making furniture and selling it, my friend Lorraine likes baking for the church.

So don't get frustrated, or unsettled about retirement, look at it as the opportunity to do the things you didn't have time to do before. God has placed talents within you that will fulfill your life, explore and find what is yours and be happy and blessed.

For me…I am happy and blessed for the talent and opportunity of blessing that now fulfills my life and helps me know I am still needed and fruitful in this world. Without God none of our abilities, talents and dreams have any power, or anointing; it is like cups without water, so be sure your heart and motive is for God's glory and He is within whatever you decide to do (2 Corth. 3:5).

TRY KINDNESS

"Be kind to one another, tenderhearted, forgiving one another, even as God in Christ forgave you." (Ephesians 4:32).

These are troubled and dark days in this fallen world. One does not see too many smiling faces, or hear the tone of laughter. So many people are so up-tight that they look as if they would crack and fall into pieces. No one seems to want to give the time of day to anyone. There is just too much darkness, and it is like a cancer, and very contagious. We need to shed some bright light and heal that dark cloud. Church, we can do something about changing this situation! It is called KINDNESS!! Kindness is probably one of the most effective tool Christians have in their kit of virtues. There is no limit to the good we can do if we don't care who gets the credit! Our society seems to be starved for good deeds. As Christians we are to be kind to others because God has been kind to us and commands us to be kind to others (Proverbs 11:17). God promises kindness will nourish the soul. God has shown us his kindness in so many ways and continues to do so, and it's not because of anything good we did. So even though others may not be kind to us, it doesn't matter. What matters is that we as ambassadors of the LIVING CHRIST, are to be kind to others! Kindness is based on the loving heart of the giver, not the loving heart of the recipient. And kindness is never lost; it keeps on going from one person until it returns to you. Galatians 6:7 says, "...whatever a man sows, that he will also reap."

So let's get the ball rolling! I am challenging one and all to focus on doing at least, two or three or more "out-of-the-way-acts of kindness" each week. Also that you all tell your friends to join us in this mission. I also would like to print some of the testimonies to prove kindness makes a big difference in someone's life! I am very excited about this venture and I hope you will be too! We CAN and WILL make a difference! But remember, after the ball of kindness is rolling, it doesn't mean we stop being kind, for the bigger the effort, the bigger the results! Also keep in mind, the right attitude and motive is imperative. We never give, just to get.

So please send in the testimonies or reactions of your kindness shown to others so we can share them in the Pathway Outreach which will be an inspiration for many others as well! We will spread a smile across America, for the newsletter goes from coast to coast! I will be looking forward to YOURS!

THIS GIFT IS FREE

Many people have grown up believing, nothing is free. But even in this fallen world there truly is something that is free… Salvation! God wants to bless us with this wonderful gift. Yet there are some people who are still trying to get right with God. They might think church attendance, church work, giving offerings and being nice is enough, and they say, "After all, we have played by the rules, haven't we?" They don't get it! God's free gift of salvation is for those who realize they can never be good enough, so they depend on what Christ Jesus has done for us at the cross. Only one's faith in Christ will get a person saved.

The truth may be hard to grasp for some people. But do you think it's easier for God to love you when you are good? Or do you secretly think God chose you because you deserved to be chosen? Do you think that some people's behavior is so bad that God couldn't possibly save them? If you think this way, you don't understand the Good News…salvation is free! It can't be earned; it can only be accepted with thankfulness and praise.

Some people haven't yet accepted Christ as their Savior because they don't understand how easy it is to become a Christian. People think it must be a complicated process. But it isn't. The Bible states if one believes in their heart and says with their mouth that Christ died for our sins and He is the risen Lord, and they realize they need a Savior, and ask for forgiveness, they will be saved. Christ paid our penalty for sin. Some people are afraid of change in their life. There is no negative change; only a positive change of the absence and desire to sin, and the assurance of eternity in heaven with Jesus, and a spiritual journey of purpose and value in your life with Christ Jesus at your side!

Everyone comes to the Lord just as they are. Jesus and the Holy Spirit will help change the bad habits and morals. Just trust Him to give you the character you need to live in God's Kingdom. It is by believing in your heart that makes you right with God, not laws and rules. God will enable us to obey and become more like Christ. When we are growing in our relationship with Christ, the Holy Spirit frees us from sins control, and the demands of the law, and from the fear of God's judgment. By trusting in the Holy Spirit and allowing him to help us, we can overcome sin and temptation.

Those of you, who have grown in your spirituality and have learned about the free gift of Salvation, have you passed this truth on to others who haven't learned about salvation, and how much God loves them, and they can come to Jesus just as they are? Explain to them they do not have to fear, feel guilty or condemned…just come to a loving God who has his arms wide open. Believers, we have been anointed by the Spirit of God to witness to the lost. We are responsible to share the Good News, and set the captives free, and snatch the souls from the devil who is deceiving and leading them to hell. Jesus has told us, "Verily, verily, I say unto you, he that believeth on Me, the works that I do shall he do also, and greater works than these shall he do because I go unto my Father" (John 14:12). Remember, Believers, you have Jesus within you and He is greater than he that is in the world. You are filled with the spirit of power. Divine life flows through you and me. No weapon formed against us will prosper. We have overcome. We are victorious! Jesus is greater than all the works of the devil! We are victorious and fearless in Jesus!

THE POWER OF HUMILITY

"Haughtiness goes before destruction;

humility precedes honor" (Proverbs 18:12).

(Shared from *Stories of Faith* by Ruth A. Tucker)

We sometimes think that power only comes through aggressive promotion, but Jesus made it clear that this was not the case. He explained to his disciples that power and authority in his kingdom is based on servanthood.

Dee Jepson, who served as assistant to her husband, a U.S. senator, quickly became aware of the power-hungry atmosphere of Washington, D.C., political wheeling and dealing (always with an eye on gaining influence with high-ranking officials). Jesus' message of servanthood seemed entirely out of place, until one day when Dee observed an honored guest's visit to the city.

"The unimportance of sophistication was brought home to me," she writes, "at a Capitol Hill luncheon for Mother Teresa.... In came this tiny woman, even smaller than I expected, wearing that familiar blue and white habit, over it a gray sweater that had seemed many better days, which she wore again to the White House the next day. As that little woman walked into the room, her bare feet in worn sandals, I saw some of the most powerful leaders in this country stand to their feet with tears in their eyes just to be in her presence.

"As I listened that afternoon, I thought, 'Don't forget this, Dee. Here in this little woman who doesn't want a thing, never asked for anything for herself; never demanded anything, or shook her fist in anger, here's real power.' It was a paradox. She has reached down into the gutter and loved and given. She has loved those the world sees unlovable—the desolate, the dying—because they are created in the image of the God she serves. Ironically, seeking nothing for herself, she has been raised to the pinnacle of world recognition, received the Nobel Peace Prize, and is a figure known to most people, at least in the Western world, and revered by many. She has nothing, yet in a strange way, she has everything."

God gives spiritual leaders to provide order and direction. Be sure to uphold and respect these leaders. Participate in a conversation that always encourages leaders and builds them up, rather than criticizes or demeans them. If you have a legitimate complaint, go directly to the leader before you complain to others.

Humility is not effacing oneself. It is not destroying one's sense of self-worth. It is honest recognition of our own worth, our worth as God sees us. Pride elevates us above others, and often above God himself. But to destroy one's sense of self-worth is also unacceptable, for it denies the value God placed upon us when He created us in his image. Humility is true strength, for it reaches into the Kingdom of Heaven. Pride is true weakness, for it reaches no further than our own ego (Matt. 18:4; James 4:6; 1 Peter 5:5-6).

Acts 20:19 states, "I have done the Lord's work humbly...yes, and with tears." I'm sure Mother Teresa thought the same. It would be easy to do the Lord's work with great pride. After all, his work is the most wonderful work in the entire world. But Paul recognized that doing God's work is serving, which takes humility, and Mother Teresa knew this as well.

THE GOOD GARDENER

"I am the true vine; my Father is the gardener.

He cuts off every branch of mine that does not bear fruit.

And He trims and cleans every branch that produces fruit so

that it will produce even more fruit" (John 15:1).

A good gardener will do whatever it takes to help a vine to bear fruit. The fruit God wants his Children to produce are: love, joy, peace, patience, kindness, goodness, faithfulness, gentleness, and self-control (Gal. 5:22-23). These are the fruits of the Spirit. And like a good gardener, God will clip and cut away anything that interferes. The verb "to cut off" is from the Greek word airo. It has at least two meanings; one is to "cut off" and the other is to "pick up" or "lift up."

Before God cuts a fruitless branch, He lifts up. A good gardener will position the branch so it gets more space and sun. He as a good vine dresser will also stretch the vine along the arbor to afford it to get more air and sun to help it grow much better.

For example, God will at times realign a life and up root a family and transfer them to another place...was it so they could learn to trust Him? Or the person who is healthy suddenly becomes sick...was it to remind him to rely on the Gardener? Or suddenly one finds their income dried up...was it God's way of lifting them out of the soil of self and drawing them to Himself? Leaders with questionable motives and morals are at times elected, is it God's way of stirring people to revival?

God does everything just right and on time. He is never early or never late. God is always the busy and active Gardener who clears the field and removes the stones. He inspects the plants and pulls the weeds...God is the Good Gardener who cares for the vine!

Do you see where God might be pruning, cutting or trimming you to bear more fruit? Allow God to do anything in your life if it will lead you to bear more fruit.

"God began doing a good work in you, and I am sure He will continue it until it's finished when Jesus Christ comes again"
(Philippians 1:6)

"I am the vine, and you are the branches. If any remain in me and I remain in them, they produce much fruit. But without me they can do nothing. If any do not remain in me, they are like a branch that is thrown away and then dies. People pick up dead branches, throw them into the fire, and burn them. If you remain in me and follow my teachings you can ask anything you want, and it will be given to you. You should produce much fruit and show that you are my followers, which brings glory to my Father" (John 15:5-8).

"Therefore, as God's chosen people, holy and dearly loved, clothe yourselves with compassion, kindness, humility, gentleness and patience. Bear with each other and forgive whatever grievances You may have against one another. Forgive as the LORD forgave you" (Colossians 3:12, 13).

LIFE WITHOUT GOD

In the Book of Ecclesiastes Solomon shows how empty it is to pursue life's pleasures in place of a relationship with the eternal God. The search for pleasure, wealth, and success ultimately is disappointing. True happiness does not come from accumulating or attaining honors—we always want more than we can have, and there are circumstances beyond our control that can snatch away all our possessions and achievements. Nothing in the world can satisfy our longing, restless heart. One reason is this is not our real home, heaven is. Everything in this world as material is only temporary, God tells us not to love the world and the things of this world. Look what happened to Lot's wife for her love of the world; she became a pillar of salt. Without God, there is no lasting reward or benefit in hard work. The Bible states everything we do, we should do unto God. Ecclesiastes 11:9-12:8 makes it clear that to live life to the fullest, we must follow God-not in fear that He wants to take away our fun, but in faith that He wants to make our life into something wonderful. Life begins the moment we realize that the world doesn't revolve around us, but around God who made the world and all that is in it. We are in this world to do the work of the Lord, not to live for our own pleasures.

There are some people who are afraid to dedicate their life to God, making Jesus their Lord and Savior because they think they will miss out on all life has for them. They think they can make that decision later on in life...saying, "I'll do it later...tomorrow." They don't realize this is Satan's strategy...this is just what he wants people to think. For many people tomorrow never comes! This tactic works like Novocain. It numbs people and keeps them from turning to the truth when they hear it. Thought patterns become habits; habits become beliefs; beliefs become actions and actions determine our eternity. So don't be afraid that you will miss out on all the fun, because those "fun times" don't last. Most of what the world pursues is shallow and meaningless.

To understand life, we need the wisdom that can only be found in God's Word. His wisdom will spare us the bitterness of ending life without having fulfilled a worthwhile purpose. Work done with the wrong attitude leaves us empty but work accepted as an assignment from God can be seen as a gift.

The final conclusion and wisdom is found in Ecclesiastes 12:13-14... "Fear God and obey his commands, for this is the duty of every person. God will judge us for everything we do, including every secret thing, whether good or bad."

THE SECRET TO TRUE BEAUTY

The world of today has put much pressure on women thinking they are valued by their beauty. So we spend a small fortune on beauty products, facelifts, tummy tucks and whatever is said to guarantee to make you beautiful. The magazines and TV ads tell us to try this diet, and that diet so we can look like models too. But when we cannot measure up we feel like a depressed failure. Why...because we are judging ourselves on our looks.

Ladies, let's be wise; true beauty is not looking like a made-up model which will dissipates as she ages; it is not your outward appearance that counts. Beauty comes from within you, and you can be as beautiful as you want to be! It's all up to you! Of course there is nothing wrong with trying to look your best, but don't allow it to become an obsession.

The secret to true beauty comes from a woman's inner qualities! It's not makeup, or what you wear; it's what you say and how you act. Your inside appearance will overshadow your outward look. Your face takes on a glow from your inner qualities of softness, godliness, kindness, loving, and caring. You even carry yourself with regal bearing. True beauty comes from inner strength of character and cannot be bought, or applied with expensive creams. Inner beauty will last forever, but outward beauty will fade with age. Your character and true virtues are what draws people to you with admiration and praise. Good character and godly virtues are obtained by knowing God and his Word.

A woman who respects God deserves more praise than one who is just physically beautiful! Proverbs 31 has a lot to say about the ideal woman. We all know this Proverb, but now reread it with a different, realistic outlook. She is a woman of strong character, great wisdom, many skills and great compassion. Plus she is a loving, supportive wife and a nourishing, caring mother. Her amazing achievements, however, are a result of the reverence for God. After reading Proverbs 31 (the virtuous woman), do not see her as a total model to imitate in every detail; your days are not long enough to do everything she does! See her instead as an inspiration to be all you can be. Notice, it does not describe her appearance at all; her attractiveness comes from her character. Your success develops from your obedience, devotion, faith and your personal relationship with God which determines your inner-self, which creates a good reputation, moral character, and spirituality, which develops a successful, godly and beautiful woman. You also are beautiful because you were made in God's image. A successful relationship with God counts for eternity, everything else is only temporary. A woman who bases her value on looks is doomed to fail. Keep in mind God is your creator…you were the clay, He was the potter. He thinks you are beautiful, so who are you to say you're not?

"A woman who fears (reverence)
the Lord, she shall be praised"
(Proverbs 31:30).

ARE THE AMISH...AN EXAMPLE?

Have you ever considered how the Amish people live? If you examine their life, one will see they are strong in their spiritual believes. They put God first in their life. They live humble and with just their basic needs. They don't have car payments, loans for things they don't need, or houses they can't afford. They live without TV, radio, movies, magazines, electrical appliances; Sleep Number beds, alcohol, drugs, the need for fancy clothes, or the hairdressers.

They live this way because they know many of these things lead to temptation and then to Idolatry, the "me" syndrome. We ourselves know TV and movies and some magazines are the temptation that can lead to lust, violence and mistrust and fear. They will turn you away from God and purity. The Amish people live to please God and his ways. They are very aware of sin, and confess quickly when they fall into it. Besides being aware they have to be accountable. If they do not repent, they are shunned from the group. Which is Biblical; for the Bible states that one apple can spoil the whole bushel. Also when there is sin in the camp it is to be dealt with. I'm not stating they are perfect, because there are no perfect people anywhere. What I am saying is their lifestyle is conformed around God and his ways.

The Amish are polite and caring to each other, they help each other in their needs and respect each other. That sounds like God's ways to me! They would not think of going to a bar, or a strip joint, or to any place that would tarnish their beliefs. They are too busy with real life, such as planting their own food, making their own clothes, baking and wood working. They make their own and grow their own material and food to sell to make money for their families. They don't have to go out of the country to sell goods or count on other countries for supplies. They discuss matters with respect and know how to come into an agreement that is good for the whole community; there is no arguing or belittling, or fighting. They know the Bible and God and hold their faith in high regards!

I am not saying we all should live as the Amish; which most of us could not do because we are all used to having things we want and immediately when we want it. I am saying; take time to think about your life and how you live. Do you put God first, do you live what you believe, and are you caring, kind, and helpful and sensitive to people's needs. Do you hold the whole Body of Christ in high regards? Do you talk the talk and walk the walk? If not, NOW is the time to repent and start living for God. It's NOT about us...it is all about Jesus; isn't it why you became a Christian?

A MORNING TO REMEMBER

Your eyes are now opened, and your mind is awakening, and your feet have not hit the floor yet, so this is a good time to start your day off by declaring…you will have a great day today. Declare: "I will have a peaceful day (1) and be glad in it (2). Because I live for Christ Jesus everything I do for Him will be fruitful (3 & 4). I will not worry, or fear of any problem (5). I always win because the Lord is with me (6). I will think of good things and not be negative (7). I am grateful for the Lord, and I thank Him for being in my life and He is always with me and for me (8)! My day is successful because I stay in touch with Jesus and His Word (9). I know my day was planned by God and my future too."

If you are a believer, bought by the blood of Jesus and sealed by the Holy Spirit, you have every right to declare your day, because your words are backed up by the God's Words and his Words never return void (10).

(1) "Peace I leave with you, My peace I give to you; not as the world gives do I give to you. Let not your heart be troubled, neither let it be afraid" (John 14:27).

(2) "This is the day the Lord has made; we will rejoice and be glad in it" (Psalm 118:24).

(3) "I have been crucified with Christ and I no longer live, but Christ lives in me. The life I now live in my body, I live by faith in the Son of God who gave Himself to me" (Galatians 2:20).

(4) "I can do all things through Christ" (Philippians 4:13).

(5) "He will not fear of bad news; his heart is steadfast trusting in the Lord" (Psalm 112:7).

(6) "Now thanks be unto God, which always causeth me to triumph in Christ, and maketh manifest the savor of his knowledge by us in every place" (2 Corinthians 2:14).

(6) "But thanks be to God, which giveth us the victory through our Lord Jesus Christ" (1Corinthains 15:57).

(7) "Think on things pure, lovely, just, praiseworthy and of good report" (Ephesians 4:8).

(8) "I will be with you. I will never leave you nor forsake you" (Joshua 1:5).

(9) "This book of the law shall not depart out of thy mouth; but thou shalt meditate therein day and night, that thou mayest observe to do according to all that is written therein; for then thou shalt make thy way prosperous, and then thou shalt have good success" (Joshua 1:8).

(10) "So shall My word be that goes forth from My mouth; it shall not return to Me void, but it shall accomplish what I please" (Isaiah 55:11) "for I know the thoughts that I think toward you says the Lord, thoughts of peace and not of evil, to give you a future and a hope" (Jeremiah 29:11).

Now get up and start your successful day! If you want every day a God-filled, successful day, remember to declare the day with confidence by lining your words with God's.

INTENTIONS ARE NOT ENOUGH FOR GOD

God does not listen to our prayers if we intend to go back to our sin as soon as we get off our knees. If we want to forsake our sin and follow Him, however, He willingly listens, no matter how bad our sin has been. What closes his ears is not the depth of our sin, but the shallowness of our "repentance."

"The prayers of a person who ignores the laws are despised" (Proverbs 28:9).

A WORD FROM BILLY GRAHAM...

FROM UNTO THE HILLS

I have found that the casual Christian has little or no influence upon others. I am finding that it is only the Christian who refuses to compromise in matters of honesty, integrity, and morality who is bearing an effective witness for Christ. The worldly Christian is prepared to do as the world does and will condone practices which are dishonest and unethical because he is afraid of the world's displeasure. Only by a life of obedience to the voice of the Spirit, by daily dying to self, by a full dedication to Christ and constant fellowship with Him, are we able to live a godly life and have a positive influence in this present ungodly world.

Ask yourself...are you an example of faith and love to people around you? Do you have a reputation for being faithful? What attitudes are typical of people whose faith you respect?

PAUL POINTS OUT...

Paul pointed out to Jesus as the ultimate example of servanthood and selflessness. Jesus gave up his rights so that we could be saved. Jesus deliberately stripped Himself of everything—His divine rights and privileges—and crossed the unthinkable chasm between God and man.

Philippians 2:5-9: "In your lives you must think and act like Jesus. Christ himself was like God in everything. But he did not think that being equal with God was something to be used for his own benefit. But he gave up his place with God and made himself nothing. He was born to be a man and become like a servant. And when he was living as a man, he humbled himself and was fully obedient to God, even when that caused his death...death on a cross."

BE UNSELFISH LIKE CHRIST

Jesus knowingly and actively embraced a life of giving, serving, losing, and dying. What was, and is, really hard for Jesus' followers to swallow is that we are called to do the same. To make ourselves nothing...we must believe that as painful as it sometimes feels, descending is the only way to greatness....Jesus obeyed for the sake of love. And we, His followers and recipients of His love, are called to do the same. When asked about the two greatest commands, Jesus replied: to love God and love others. That is what motivated Jesus, and that is what is to motivate us!

God views service and humility as strengths, not weaknesses. What steps in your relationship can you take to show greater humility?

ARE YOU CONTENT?

"My grace is sufficient for you" (2 Corinthian 12:9).

Ask yourself, is God a good Father? Or is He only good when everything is going your way? How would you feel if He didn't heal you, instead He took a loved one to heaven and didn't heal them as you expected, or if you were waiting for God to help you get a particular job but you didn't get it, or you are waiting for a prayer that never got answered because He said, "No," or He won't remove the many problems and troubles you endure. How would you feel? Is God being fair? Is God's grace enough for you if you only were saved from hell?

It is unwise to form a dogmatic conclusion about any of God's ways! Anyway, most of us do not worry about the Father's actions because He loves us and is fair, faithful and just. Plus He has given us his promises to sustain us, heal us, and meet all of our needs (Philippians 4:19) and He is faithful to keep all his promises. So, should we really complain or be content, especially knowing we will one day have every blessing in heaven. Our Father is a good Father and we are blessed in so many ways. But if one is not content and not in peace with God you will not recognize the blessing you do have.

Let's look at why contentment is important. Having contentment means there's a serene satisfaction in that kind of contentment that brings a sense of gladness, gratification, happiness and pleasure and quietude. Contentment in the positive sense means to feel that we have enough that what we have is sufficient. But looking on the other hand, we should be careful not to be at ease that we do not strive for nothing, like godliness. We should not become too content that we become self-sufficient and feel we do not need God. You need to find the balance between contentment that pleases God and contentment that displeases him in a daily quest. When you trust God completely, you will have peace and contentment. Many think contentment is found in money or success. But to enjoy your work and accept your lot in life...that is indeed a gift from God. Stay away from the love of money; be satisfied with what you have, for God has said, "I will never fail you. I will never forsake you" (Hebrews 13:5). Contentment is not depending on wealth, nor does it have to be stifled by poverty. The key is to thank God for what we have and to use our time, talent and resources to please Him! So be content and take to heart... My Grace is sufficient for you. "GIVE THANKS TO THE LORD FOR HE IS GOOD. HIS FAITHFUL LOVE ENDURES FOREVER." (Psalm 107:1-2).

ASTONISHING HONESTY

When the minister asked one of his elders to lead the congregation in prayer, the man shocked everyone by saying, "I'm sorry, Pastor, but I've been arguing with my wife on the way to church, and I'm in no condition to pray." The minister then prayed and the service moved on. Later that day the Pastor thought about that morning, and then vowed to never to ask anyone to pray publicly without first asking privately.

That man had astonishing honesty in a place where hypocrisy would have been easier. But there is a larger lesson about prayer here. God is a loving Father. If a husband does not respect and honor his wife, a cherished daughter of God, why would the heavenly Father hear the husband's prayers? First Peter 3:7 states, "Treat your wife as you should so your prayers will not be hindered."

The apostle Peter made an interesting observation about this. He instructed husbands to treat their wives with respect and as equal heirs in Christ, so nothing would hinder their prayers. The underlying principle is that our relationships affect our prayer life.

What would happen if we exchanged the Sunday smiles and the facade of religiosity for refreshing honesty with our brothers and sisters? What might God do through us when we pray and learn to love each other as we love ourselves?

"Father...You love all your children, but so often we fight and disagree. Help us learn to interact with love and respect in all our relationships so the world will see the difference You make in us. Teach us to pray more, and remind us to realize how important prayer is, and what a precious privilege it is to have an honest and intimate conversation with You, Father."

ARE YOU SOWING SEEDS FOR THE NEXT GENERATION?

"Do not be deceived, God is not mocked; for whatever a man sows, that he will also reap. For he who sows to his flesh will of the flesh reap corruption, but he who sows to the Spirit will of the Spirit reap everlasting life" (Galatians 6:7-8).

Don't look at what you do today as insignificant. The seeds you plant today may grow into a mighty tree...a tree whose fruit may feed the hungry long after you've passed away. But it's important that you sow "good" seed and not seed of evil. What you say today may take root in somebody's heart. What you do today may influence someone far more than what you say. It's important what kind of life you live as a testimony. Every day we get another opportunity to sow a seed and send the right message. It may be a word, a smile, a deed, or a gift. It may be just overcoming an obstacle with grace or conquering a bad habit by leaning on Jesus. Whatever makes people think about God with reverence and gratitude promotes His glory. What you think is insignificant, God may see as very important. You are earning jewels for your crown in Heaven as you live for God day by day. The best preparation for Heaven is the faithful execution of God's will on earth. Don't get so caught up in life's business. Don't let what you want make you forsake what God wants. It doesn't always take much to start something for God. It just takes the first step of obedience; then the next step and the next. What you do may seem small, yet out of your obedience, a work may grow that blesses the world! You may end up influencing someone who takes your seed to the next level. You may have planted a tree, but someone may come behind you and use those seeds to plant an orchard. You may only know your influence when you get to Heaven. You have to ask yourself, "Am I a one-generation person? Will what I do for the Lord glorify God after I'm gone?" We can be sure our seeds will continue to grow for the next generation if we are sowing spiritual seeds instead of the seeds of the flesh. Let's sow seeds now with our words and actions that will feed the hungry generations long after we are gone!

ARE YOU SICK OF A SICK SOCIETY?

"Despise God's Word and find yourself in trouble.

Obey it and succeed" (Proverbs 13:13).

Repeatedly it is being said that our society is sick. Recently a woman wrote to the editor of the St. Petersburg Times: "Is our society sick? I know I am sick—sick of having policemen ridiculed and called 'pigs,' while police killers are hailed as heroes. I am sick of commentators and columnists canonizing anarchists, revolutionaries and criminal rapists. I am sick of being told that religion is the opiate of people but marijuana should be legalized. I am sick of being told that pornography is the right of the free press, but freedom of the press does not include being able to read the Bible or pray in schools. Yes, I am sick of not being free to take my family to a movie without the risk of their being exposed to nudity, homosexuality and glorification of narcotics. I am sick of riots, demonstrations. And I am sick of the personal decline in honesty, integrity and human sincerity!" I would say here is a woman who loves the Lord and is standing up for righteousness and knows the fear (reverent respect) of the Lord and His Word!

Yes, our society, like Jeremiah's, is sick, Jeremiah also lived in a sick society. For fifty-five years his country was ruled by an evil king, Manasseh. Under his rule there was pagan worship, adultery, infant sacrifices, fortune-telling and wizardry (fortunetelling). So many people were persecuted and killed that blood flowed from one end of Jerusalem to the other.

What is the medicine that will cure the illness? The world claims they have the prescription. They claim, that the key is earn...earn more money, because there is nothing that money can't cure. There was a national survey of 250,000 college freshmen. Two-thirds of them said that they aspire to be well off after graduation. They are going to college so that later they can earn high salaries. Why are we going in debt and living beyond our means? Is it not greed? Is life about the abundance of things possessed? But is money the answer? According to Jesus, it is not. He asked, "What does it profit a man to gain the whole world and lose his soul? Many today are shouting that the prescription for our social illness is "learn!" The world says get as much education as you can. But the limitation of learning is that it cannot guarantee or produce character. The obvious assumption of the world is to make people literate and they will not go to jail. But we have many criminals who are smart people! We can be too educated for our own good. Is learning the prescription for getting a sick society well? The answer is in Psalms... "The fear of the Lord is the beginning of wisdom."

So if it isn't earn or learn the world says it must be burn…blast the status quo to the heavens. In other words the best thing to do is to tear it all down and begin anew. Some are actually doing this through violence and terrorism. The nations consider violence the answer. It is not the answer according to Jesus who said, "They who take the sword shall perish by the sword." This is what the world calls the solutions for a sick society and none of these prescriptions can hold water. So what does God say? His word is found in Jeremiah, "If you will turn back to me, I shall take you back and you shall stand before me." This means a full 180-degree turn. It means to turn from Satan to God, from self to Christ, from evil to good if we are to get morally and spiritually well. We need spiritual help from the Great Physician! Jesus said, "Unless you repent, you will all likewise perish." The best reason of all is to humbly turn to God to experience His mercy. "Return to the Lord and you will live, your sins will be forgotten and your spiritual illness will be cured." So the inevitable conclusion is: Our sick society can be restored to health by turning fully to God through Christ Jesus. Who is America? It is you and me. America will not turn to God unless each one of us does by being a living example of the Word. Jesus is our perfect leader. If we truly want Him to lead us and our nation, devotion must be more than talk. Christian believers are given the responsibility to God for witnessing and teaching those we lead, including our own families. The success of our future generations will be in the hands of what we teach are children now about God, His love and his Word!

Iniquity is atoned for by mercy and truth; evil is avoided by reverence for God. When a man is trying to please God, God makes even his worst enemies to be at peace with him (Proverbs 16:6-7).

ARE YOU READY TO STAND UP FOR YOUR FAITH IN GOD

Hello, Christian, do you know where your focus and heart's desire is? Could it be a new car, a new house, a vacation, a new career, or a cruise? None of these are bad, but what comes first, God or your desires?

It seems that one-half of the Christians are too busy with their personal desires and the other half of the Christians are playing church. Or Christian families work so much that Sunday, they say, is the only time they have for family. But what a great way for the whole family to spend two quality hours together, with so much results and reward! Why do I say this? Just look at most of the churches, they are not filled up with the Holy Spirit and on fire for God and His cause, or filled up with compassion for lost souls. Why? This is why; they are not in harmony and not in unity as the Body of Christ? No, they are busy judging each other instead of loving each other, and not willing to accept their faults, as we all have. Do you see a considerable difference in the lifestyle of the Christian and the worldly? If so, it's not enough difference to make the world say, "I want what they have." Our time as Christians has come! We can no longer be stagnate and just stand by and let the unbelievers tell us we can't stand up for what we believe and worship our God. Meanwhile people are dying every day and going to hell.

We do have to be proud of the woman clerk who stood up for her believe in God's Word, who would not marry the same-sex couple, and the football players who prayed before they started their game and the two of the football players who raised their hand to thank God for their victory! That's what it is all about! Are YOU ready to stand up for God? We never know when we will be called upon to stand up for our faith. This is what is going to make a difference to the unbelievers. But if we are not even focused on what's going on because our desires are more important that having compassion for the lost, more souls will be going to hell. The harvest is ripe! The world is fearful and is looking for answers for encouragement, hope, security, peace and protection they can count on. We, as Christians have the answer...Jesus. But we have to be filled with the Holy Spirit, not living by the flesh. There is nothing that can benefit from the flesh (John 6:63). If you don't check your heart and where your focus is, and if you are not feeding your spirit man with the Word and fellowshipping with the Lord, and praying for your family, yourself and others, you won't be ready to stand up for God. Jesus however makes it clear that around us a continual harvest awaits to be reaped (John 4:35). Don't let Jesus find you making excuses. Jesus also said, "My nourishment comes from doing the will of God who sent Me, and from finishing."

You know we reap what we sow. So if we start sowing only those spiritual things we desire to reap, God guarantees that we will bring in the harvest (Gal. 6:7-9). By living under the control of the Spirit and obeying His leading will defeat any fleshly or carnal inclinations we have. This is what will result in Jesus' life being reproduced in us. We must humble ourselves and pray and get direction, believe and seek His face (2 Chron. 7:14)! Then we have the strength and courage and strong faith we need to stand up for God when our turn comes around and it will! If we honor God, He will honor us. If we don't check our heart and where our focus is, and we are not feeding our spirit man with the Word, praying and fellowshipping with the Lord, we won't be ready to stand up for God and we will miss our opportunities to make a difference in this hurting world We won't recognize when God is calling upon us if we are not sensitive to the Holy Spirit. We will miss our chance to show the world we too have a devoted faith in our God that will make others want to know Him too! God is worth standing up for, no matter what! If you are not ready for this important standing revival, get yourself and your family ready!! The whole Christian Body of Christ is needed! This message cannot be candy-coated because it is a serious godly commission! For one day Jesus will ask you, "What have you done with the life I gave you?" How will you answer?

If one man, like Paul in the Bible can turn the world upside down, can you imagine what the whole Body of Christ could do as they come together in perfect unity, one mind and one heart for God's great call! Hallelujah! Praise to our God! It's our time to shine and bring in the harvest!

ARE YOU ON THE RIGHT ROAD?

"I call heaven and earth to record this day against you, that I have set before you, life and death, blessing and cursing therefore choose life, that both thou and thy seed may live" (Deuteronomy 30:19).

The Bible tells us there's been a curse in effect for thousands of years. And the devil is the cause of it, not the Lord God. God gave warning of it in Deuteronomy 30:19. After describing in detail the blessings that fall upon those who followed God and the suffering that would fall on those who separate themselves from Him, He said, "I have set before you life and death, blessing and cursing: therefore choose life, that both thou and thy seed may live." So God has warned us not to travel the road that leads to Curseville. He has warned us there are deadly wages for sin! If we get on the wrong road and don't get off of it, we're going to wind up in Curseville. Is that because God sent us there? He urges us NOT to travel that road.

The vital thing to realize is this: At any point of our journey, whether we are on the road to Curseville or living right in the middle of it...God will save us from it He can take us out of there and deliver us! He will deliver us from diseases, addictions, or anything else that's holding us captive. But the important thing to keep in mind, if we find we are on the wrong road, and see destruction ahead, we MUST seriously, with our heart, REPENT and get back on the right road. By committing our way to Jesus is what will deliver us from being captive. We can begin by praying, "Lord Jesus, I've chosen the wrong road and right now I ask you to forgive me. Today I choose life by choosing Your way. Please deliver me from this bondage and fill me with Your Holy Spirit. Thank You, Lord!"

Remember, no matter what you've done, God doesn't want to GET YOU for it, He wants to forgive you of it. He doesn't want to slap you down, He wants to save you and lift you up. Trust Him and let Him put you on the road of life today!

ARE YOU PREPARED FOR THE COMING OF THE LORD?

"Not everyone who says to Me, 'Lord, Lord, shall enter the kingdom of heaven, but he who does the will of my Father in heaven.' Many will say to Me in that day, 'Lord, Lord, have we not prophesied in Your Name, cast out demons in Your name, and done many wonders in Your Name?' And then I will declare to them, I never knew you; depart from Me, you who practice lawlessness!"

Jesus warns against self-deception, a mere verbal profession of lordship without obedience to the will of God. Each individual has been entrusted with resources of time and material wealth. Everything we have comes from God and belongs to Him. We are responsible for using those resources so that they increase in value. As Christians we have the most valuable resource of all the Word of God. If we believe and understand Him, and apply His Word as good stewards, we are a blessing to others and the value of what we do multiplies. We are accountable to the Lord for the use of His resources.

In Matthew chapter 24 and 25 Jesus uses vivid, prophetic and symbolic language to describe His glorious return, but even Jesus knows not the time of His return, so it is futile for us to know, only the Father knows. But as Jesus' followers, we are to eagerly await the Lord's return by being faithful and responsible in our service to Him and the kingdom. Jesus teaches the necessity of preparedness for His return through the Parable of the Wise and Foolish Virgins (Matt. 25 1:13). We know the Bridegroom is Jesus and the wise virgins are the Christians who know Jesus and His character. They are faithful, dedicated and keeps our Covenant with the Lord. They are "saved" and have the Holy Spirit for their guide and they are not deceived by false prophets. They strive to draw closer to the Lord for when their patience and faith and testimony is tried. They pray, listen for God's voice to do His will and they watch with joy and gladness and eagerness for their Lords return. Watchfulness is not just being idle; it means a faithful discharge of one's responsibilities—the use of our gifts and abilities that was entrusted to us. Being ready for Christ's return, whether it be the Rapture or through the Tribulation ultimately involves one major thing which manifests itself in several areas of our lives. If we are to be ready, we must be born again through saving faith in Jesus Christ. The overall and easily seen thrust of the parable is that Christ will return at an unknown hour and His people must be ready! Whatever it is, we must be about our Father's business. We must be doing it in such a way that we don't have time to "make things right" or get more oil when He comes, like the foolish virgins. The five virgins without the oil represent false believers who enjoy the benefits of the Christian community without true love or obedience to Christ. Their hope is that their association with true believers ("give us some of your oil" of Matt. 25 verse 8) will bring them into the kingdom at the end. One person's faith in Jesus cannot save another. Take the time NOW to fill your lamp with oil!

Also the Parable of the Talents constitutes final warnings and encouragements to be ready. Jesus is reminding us of our responsibilities as stewards to care for the kingdom and the serious consequences of neglecting to understand and apply His instructions. As stewards, we must know the personality and character of our Lord. He expects us to know Him well enough to apply the spirit as well as the letter of His instructions. Those that do are richly rewarded. The others receive severe judgment. The untrusting steward is rejected and punished. The statement, in Matthew 24:13, "But he shall endure unto the end, the same shall be saved." If we believe and understand Him, and apply His Word as good stewards, we will bless others and the value of what we do multiplies.

We as Christians must be prepared for the unexpected delay of the Bridegroom! Jesus commands us, "Watch, be prepared and watch since you know neither the day nor the hour in which the Son of man shall return" (Matthew 25:13). Don't be as the third servant in the Parable of the Talents who was lazy and afraid, did not use his abilities or talent; who also forfeited his reward for committed service in the kingdom or heard, "Well done, good and faithful servant."

ARE YOU PULLING DOWN OR LIFTING UP?

"Bear one another's burdens, and so fulfill the law of Christ"

(Galatians 6):

"Brethren, if a man is overtaken in any trespass, you who are

spiritual restore such a one in a spirit of gentleness…"

(Galatians 6:1).

Sometimes Christians forget their purpose, value or influence they should have, could have, or would have on people, especially people who are hurting. Everyone wants and deserves to be loved, have self-worth and respected, whether they are Christians or not! God loves and wants His best for everyone! Some people may have forgotten what it is to be needy, rejected, hurt or let down. I'm sure you will agree, we are all thankful that Jesus never gave up on us even when we were difficult. He saw us through. Then there are others who may have never had to experience a soul wrenching or physical crisis yet, so they may not understand the impact it has on one's life. But everyone has, or will experience some kind of drama in their life, whether big or small, depending on the circumstance and will want someone that cares to be there for them. As God's Word says, "You reap what you sow."

As Christians we need to be openminded, having insight or praying for insight, and understanding for those around us who are going through hurt, anger problems, or rejection and feeling worthless; not knowing they too have value to God and a great purpose on this earth. Are we too busy to care, or pray for their help, or do we not care enough to be concerned to stop what we are doing to show them there is help, hope and Jesus does have the answer if we don't? We aren't in the Kingdom to pull people down, or avoid them. We are here to lift people up!

Jesus commanded us to walk in love and 1 Corinthians 13:4-5 says, "Love… is not touchy or fretful or resentful; it takes no account of the evil done to it (it pays no attention to a suffering wrong!)." Jesus was a perfect example of His love and Word…as He took the beatings that disfigured Him, had his beard pulled out, a needle point thorn of crowns jabbed into his head, nails pounded into his feet and hands and a sword into his side, and He said… "Forgive them, for they know not what they do." Believers, there are still people who do not know what they do! How many times have we heard or seen people who want to get even for the hurt or rejection they received? The person who says they are a Christian believer has no option to react in this way if they are walking in love as 1 Corinthian 13:4-5 says. And if we are dead to self and we have been crucified with Christ and Christ now lives in us, as Galatians 2:20 states then we can no longer react in the flesh without love toward someone who has hurt us or, toward an angry situation, a disagreement, or rejection from a person who may or may not know better. We have to be quick to forgive and not count the evils done to us, just as Jesus did. We need to be lifting people up, showing them they have value and purpose and a vital part in the Kingdom of God, or show them with love the way to Jesus in gentleness and love! Our patience and effort to walk in love could mean a right decision for heaven and not hell for a person. We have many opportunities to be aware of exercising our walk of love and forgiving almost daily with other Christians and the world. We as Christians have the privilege and honor of serving others and being an example and mentoring others with love who do not know the Lord, His Word and love. Remember, Jesus came to serve, not to be served. The greatest in the Kingdom of God is the servant!

If you are one who has a problem forgiving others, or an anger problem or you are finding fault with others, pray, "In the Name of Jesus, loose me and let me go! I'm putting hostility, unforgiveness and selfishness behind me. I'm going on with God. I'm going to live the life of love!" It won't take a miracle to turn your life around. All it will take for the believer is a decision to desire to reflect the living Jesus Christ within you and a decision to yield to the powerful force of love. For those who do not know Jesus and have not made the decision to make Jesus your Lord and Savior, but desire to, will you pray this prayer and ask Jesus into your heart and life: Heavenly Father, I come to you in the Name of Jesus. Your Word says, "Whoever shall call on the name of the Lord shall be saved" and, "if they confess with their mouth the Lord Jesus, and shall believe in their heart that God has raised Him from the dead, they shalt be saved" (Acts 2:21; Romans 10:9). I take you at Your Word, I confess Jesus is Lord, and I believe in my heart that you raised Him from the dead. Thank You, Jesus, for coming into my heart, and giving me Your Holy Spirit as promised. If you have prayed this prayer, now get into a Bible-believing church, start reading the Word and continue your spiritual growth and discover how much Jesus really loves you and the promises and life He has for you! God Bless You and welcome into the family of God!

ARE YOU HUNGRY?

"The backslider in heart will be filled with his own ways,

but a good man will be satisfied from above"

(Proverbs 14:14).

Are you too busy and stuffed with the worldly food of material things, the love of money, cares, and ways that you are no longer hungry for God? Are you too contented with your daily routine and have no time for God or feel you have no need for Him? Maybe you have been skipping church or not reading the Word. Have you let your prayer time slip?

If you have answered yes to any of the questions, you are in danger of starving! You are starving your spirit and your desire for God is buried under disobedience, ignorance, lack of responsibility to God and the Covenant, and entered into the worldly lust and worry.

Does the word backsliding ring a bell? Backsliding comes easy, for many things can tempt us to abandon what we know right. It can lead us into behavior that is unacceptable to God and is disobedience. Backsliding allows sin to control us and disregard God's commands and authority over our lives. But recognizing the seriousness of backsliding, and sin, is the first step toward changing and repenting and once again stirring up our hearts for an appetite for the hunger of God. Jeremiah two, verse 19, warns us to recognize the sin of backsliding: "Your own wickedness will correct you. And your backsliding will rebuke you. Know therefore and see that it is an evil and bitter thing that you have forsaken the LORD your GOD and the fear of ME is not in you," says the Lord God of hosts.

If you feel you have backslidden, and have a spiritual sickness and lost the hunger for God, humble yourself and ask God to forgive you for being disobedient, self-sufficient and proud. Just as the Prodigal Son was forgiven by his father (Luke 15:11-31), God will forgive you for He is merciful and loves us and wants to bless us. Genuine repentance brings pardon, blessing and restoration.

God knows everything about us and yet He still wants to be a father to us. His thoughts are upon us all through the day. Psalm 139:17-19 expresses God's loving thoughts: "How precious also are your thoughts to me, O God! How great is the sum of them! If I should count them, they would be more in number than the sand; when I awake, I am still with You." Just to know how much God loves us and thinks about us should give us an incredible feeling of worth!

To maintain an intimate relationship with God and stir up our hunger will mean we need to give God daily quality time. God Longs for our fellowship. Jesus requires absolute devotion and rejects lackadaisical, halfhearted followers. Zeal for the Lord is not optional. Avoid lukewarmness; give your love for Jesus first place in your life, and commit yourself both emotionally and intellectually to Christ (Rev. 2:4; 3:15).

Remember, God is only a prayer away!

ARE YOU AFRAID TO GIVE YOUR LIFE TO GOD?

Are you afraid God's going to ask you to do things later on, like be a missionary in another country? Or are you afraid it will change your life and it will become boring and you will lose friends? Friend, let me tell you, the only thing you will lose is your sin and you will have everything to gain, blessings, promises and the abundance of life, plus a valued, unique purpose for your life!

When you give your life to God, there is no half way; it has to be all the way. Unfortunately many Christians, by their attitudes and their actions, tell God two things: they don't really want the benefits and fun of playing on the team (except heaven, of course); and they don't want to contribute their time when other people might need them the most!

God wants your whole life, so he can make something extraordinary out of it. Jesus told his followers, "The thief's purpose is to steal, kill and destroy. My purpose is to give life in all its fullness" (John 10:10).

The Christian life was never meant to be done halfway. You're either sold out to God or sold out to the world. For God to give you "life in all its fullness," you must give your life in full to God. Jesus said, "If you cling to your life, you will lose it; but if you give it up for me, you will save it" (Matthew 10:39). True life comes from serving Jesus and his desires will bring you much honor and eternity, but serving self and self's desires is a dead end with a dead destiny.

Don't worry about what God will ask of you. God knows you better than anyone else does. He made you, and he loves you more than you'll ever know. Because He put you together, and he knows what it will take to make you the happiest and most fulfilled in life! If you choose any other direction, you'll be settling for second best. Don't do it!

God's goal isn't to make his kids miserable. Just take a look at Jeremiah 29:11: "For I know the plans I have for you, says the Lord. They are plans for good and not for evil, to give you a future and a hope. You'll see God wants to lead us in the abundance of life" and "He will perfect what concerns you"(Psalm 138:8). It is not always easy but you never have to face trouble, trials, and circumstances alone.... Jesus is right by your side: "The righteous man shall have many afflictions, but the Lord will deliver him out of them all"(34:19).

You do not have to be afraid to give your life to God for you can be confident in faith that God is committed to his Word and God always honors his Word above His name. God's Word is sovereign; rest in the confidence that God is always working to fulfill his Word.

AMERICA, WHERE IS OUR IDENTITY?

Why as Americans and Christians allowing our culture, beliefs and history to be hidden, or prevented? We are allowing people from other countries and cultures to say they are offended with what we say or do. So we are told not to pray in public, not to praise God when and where we want, not to mention His name in public, or carry or read our Bible when and where we want.

If we continue to allow this as Americans and Christians, we will lose our country's identity. Our country became great because our forefathers believed in God and the Bible and built our country on these principals. This was meant for our way of life each day. This is God's great country and He has called us to His ways and morals so we could be blessed and live a good life. If we no longer follow God and His Word we will no longer be under His protection and blessings.

We as Americans and Christians cannot allow our heritage and history to be hindered or stopped because "It might offend someone." We are in no way trying to offend anyone! We have been living this way since our country was founded on July 4, 1776, and our Constitution was adopted on September 17, 1787, and ratified by the States 1788! The first ten amendments, called the Bill of Rights, was ratified in 1791, designed to guarantee many fundamental civil liberties.

We do not ask others to change their beliefs and culture even though they live in our country. Unless any beliefs or actions would cause violence, and then no matter what culture it is, it would be disciplined. If one should desire to live in America they have the choice to live our culture or theirs.

So as Americans and Christians, we need to stand up for our country's beliefs, our heritage, our history, and our right to pray when and where, and our right to read and carry our Bibles when and where and pray wherever. We do not want to offend anyone!! We are AMERICANS and CHRISTIANS and this is how we live. Prayer is our support and strength and so much more! We also have the right to say "Merry Christmas" instead of "Happy Holidays"! Christmas is not so much a holiday as it is a Holy Day. Also Easter, or Resurrection Day, is our other Holy Day and we want to celebrate it without offense or hindrance.

Americans, stand up for America!

ALLOW THE HOLY SPIRIT TO CONTROL YOUR MIND AND ACTIONS

"The mind of sinful man is death, but the mind controlled by the Spirit is life and peace" (Romans 8:6).

When the Holy Spirit controls your mind and actions more fully, you become free in Jesus and released to become the one He created you to be. Though it might sound like a contradiction to be controlled to become free, but yet, you will feel more alive...more real...more content! Ask the Holy Spirit through prayer; invite the Holy Spirit to live through you and love through you. The Holy Spirit will help you to control your thinking and actions. He lives in the depths of your spirit and He knows you better than you know yourself. The Spirit and the Lord work together in perfect harmony.

Jesus is always pleased when we ask His Spirit to think and love through us. So when you collaborate with the Holy Spirit, the freer you become to live and love extravagantly and know the Lord in an ever-increasing and intimate relationship.

"In the same way, the Spirit helps us in our weakness. We do not know what we ought to pray for, but the Spirit himself intercedes for us with groans that words cannot express. And who searches our hearts knows the mind of the Spirit, because the Spirit intercedes for the saints in accordance with God's will" (Romans 8:26-27).

AGE IS JUST A NUMBER

It doesn't matter how old you are; you can be effective and fruitful. The Lord can use you at any age if you are willing. What matters is what's in your heart, mind and spirit and the love for the Lord. God has limitless ways of reaching people of all ages. As Christians we are the "light of the world" and the "salt of the Earth" and it doesn't require an age limit. No one is too old to be effective or a witness for Christ. So if you don't feel you have the ability to reach others for Christ, think about 76-year-old Ethel Hatfield. Desiring to serve her Lord, she asked her pastor if she could teach a Sunday school class. He informed her that he thought she was too old! She went home heavyhearted and disappointed. Then one day as Ethel was tending her rose garden, a Chinese student from the nearby university stopped to comment on the beauty of her flowers. She invited him in for a cup of tea. As they talked together, she had the opportunity to tell him about Jesus and His love. He returned the next day with another student, and that was the beginning of Ethel's ministry.

Ethel was delighted to share the gospel of Christ with these students, because she knew He has the power to change lives. His gospel "is the power of God to salvation for everyone who believes" (Rom. 1:6). Because of Ethel's age, the Chinese students listened to her with respect and appreciation. When she died, a group of 70 Chinese believers sat together at her funeral. They had been won to Christ by a woman who was thought to be too old to teach a Sunday school class!

Another example of never being too old is Nola Ochs, a student at Fort Hays State University in Kansas, who took a break from her studies recently to celebrate her 95th birthday. She began attending college at Fort Hayes in 1930 but didn't graduate. When she realized she was only a few credits away from earning her degree, she returned to the university in 2006. Nola is not going to let her age prevent her from honoring a commitment over 75 years ago to finish her education.

In Joshua 14 we read that Caleb did not allow his advancing age to prevent him from believing that God would still honor His promise given 45 years earlier (v. 10-12). As one of the original scouts sent into the Promised Land, he saw large cities inhabited by powerful people of great stature (Num. 13:28-33). But Caleb was faithful to God and believed He would help the Israelites conquer the land (14:6-9). At 85 years of age, Caleb was still physically strong and his faith unwavering. So Joshua blessed Caleb with his portion of the land, fulfilling God's 45-year-old promise. Like Caleb, Ethel and Nola, we must not allow age, our personal giants, or yet-unfulfilled promises to prevent us from believing that God still honors His word to us, for every promise of God comes with His personal guarantee.

A THANKFUL ATTITUDE OPENS THE WINDOWS OF HEAVEN

"Open the gates of the Temple—I will go in and give him thanks. Those gates are the way into the presence of the Lord and the godly enter there" (Psalm 118:19-20).

A thankful heart opens the windows of heaven through which spiritual blessings fall freely. And all the Lord requires to rain down those blessings is our gratitude! It seems such a simple choice; yet we seem to stumble over it almost every day. Allowing God to help us to be more grateful, we then will be able to receive his bountiful blessings.

As we go through our day we need to keep these in mind: Throughout the Bible God repeatedly commands thankfulness because it is vital to our well-being. It is crucial for a healthy relationship with God for He is our Creator, our Savior and our King. When we thank Him, we acknowledge how much He has done for us: "It is good to say thank you to the Lord, to sing praises to the God who is above all gods. Every morning tell him, 'Thank you for your kindness,' and every evening rejoice in all his faithfulness" (Psalm 92:1-2). This attitude brings joy to both God and us.

Giving thanks is similar to priming a pump with water so that it will produce more water. Since thankfulness is one of the spiritual blessings God bestows on us, it will increase along with others when you prime Him with thanksgiving.

Remember that He is the God of grace. When we fail in our endeavor to be thankful, we can simply ask God for forgiveness. As we freely receive this priceless gift…thinking about what it cost Jesus, our gratitude will grow. Look up to the Lord and see spiritual blessings cascading down upon you through heaven's wide windows.

"Blessed be the God and Father of our Lord Jesus Christ, who has blessed us with every spiritual blessing in the heavenly places in Christ" (Ephesians 1:3).

"Devote yourselves to prayer, being watchful and thankful" (Colossians 4:2).

"Enter his gates with thanksgiving and his courts with praise; give thanks to him and praise his name" (Psalms 100:4).

A SPIRITUAL BATTLE BETWEEN GOD AND SATAN

Death, disease, and divorce could be called the three Ds of misery. They slice through life like a tsunami, of sorrow, raising doubts and destroying dreams. Consider Job, in a short period of time he lost his children, his health, his wealth and his wife's respect. Job's distress was so great that he pleaded, "May the day perish on which I was born" (Job 3:3). Job wanted God to erase not just a year, but all memory of his existence! He had enjoyed years of success and respect. Now, he questioned the purpose of living (3:20). Job wanted to die and be forgotten, but instead God made sure his name and story would be remembered forever. Rather than give Job what he asked for, God gave future generations what they would need—an inside look at the spiritual battle between God and Satan. The result is a God-inspired document about suffering that has comforted countless people.

When what we fear actually happens, we know, thanks to Job, that God can use it for good!

"Our highest good may come from our deepest suffering."

A LIVING CHURCH

Exercise, eating the right food, and getting sleep and rest make a body healthy. So it is for Christians; they must eat the right "spiritual food," exercise by resisting temptation, enduring trials, serving others and spreading the gospel. Christians rest through worship.

Many Christians are trying to survive on spiritual "fast food." That is, they watch Christian TV, read Christian magazines and listen to Christian music, but they rarely give attention to God's Word. There is only one food that will nourish our soul: reading the Bible. Everything else is only meant to be encouragement and supplement.

We need to be pushed to stay strong. This means spiritual exercise! Temptation and problems test character; serving others stretches our faith; telling people about Christ strengthens our devotion.

Christians rest through worship. Our world has a tendency to tighten us like a rubber band pulled to the limit. Unless we take time weekly (and daily) to recognize and worship God, He won't have the opportunity to minister to our needs...give us our daily bread. We need our sleep, rest and times of vacation to get our physical batteries recharged. In the same way, we need worship to keep us spiritually renewed. Spiritual growth takes time...a lifetime! This means growing in a relationship, not just changing our behavior. Growing into a living Christian church means learning to love the person of Jesus Christ more each day, staying close to Him and getting to know Him better.

When we respond to Christ's love by trusting in Him, his purpose becomes our mission. We should always be seeking to understand more of whom God created us to be and what He wants us to do with our life.

Paul encourages all Christians to make wise, dynamic Christian a living goal. Because God through Christ paid our penalty for sin and forgave us, we as Christians have been reconciled and brought near to Him. We are a new society, a new family. Being united with Christ means that we are to treat each other as family members. We are one family in Christ; so there should be no barriers, no divisions, and no discrimination. Because we all belong to Him, we should live in harmony with one another. We have a responsibility toward each other as brothers and sisters in Christ.

Christ is exalted as the central meaning of the universe and the focus of history. He is the Head of his body...the church. Because Christ is central to everything, his power must be central in us! Our life decisions should be based on who we are as his disciples. God's purpose and eternal plan is for Christians to be a living church for the world to come to know Jesus Christ our Savior! So let us as the followers of Jesus commit ourselves to fulfill God's purpose by doing all that makes us a living church!

A GOOD FATHER REFLECTS THE LOVE OF THE HEAVENLY FATHER

"Honor your father" (Ephesians 6:2).

Father's Day will bring many memories; some happy and some sad. Unfortunately some children have been abused by their earthly father and some might not have ever known their earthly father. Therefore, knowing only pain, desertion, or hate, they will find it hard to except the Father in heaven that truly loves them and wants to bless them and care for them; giving them a life of value and purpose. But the children who have been blessed with a loving, caring, supportive, father with godly values will have the joy of loving and appreciating their earthly father and honoring their number-one Father in heaven.

It is very sad and destructive to have to struggle with a father who left his children to grow up with memories that will change that child's life forever. Some dads just don't realize they are the backbone of their child's future! They are to be the example, the leader, the spiritual guide of knowledge of knowing God the Father and the godly values of life! The father has a great deal of responsibly to their child's wellbeing. It is okay for your children to know their parents aren't perfect, because there are NO perfect people on this earth! BUT there are values, and there is a guide to living the right way...God's way. It's called the BIBLE. Parents have been given the responsibility to teach their children about God, His love and His Word. Being an example of living right, praying as a family, respect for each other, going to church as a family, and most of all loving each other knowing each has value and purpose from God should be supported.

Yes, we all have failed at times, but that's the time to show children we ask God for His forgiveness and theirs as well. We are not to hold grudges, point fingers or criticize. This is the time we need to grow from our mistakes and move on. The best fathers not only give life; they teach their children how to live.

There are many ways to honor our fathers on Father's Day, even if they are no longer with us. We can show respect for the good values they taught us. Also, for those who have been holding on to painful memories...let them go, give them to God, don't take them back, so God can heal you, and ask God to help you to forgive so you are set free! Remember the commandment to honor your Mother and Father and YOU will have a good and long life. There were no "IF" clauses that came with that command: " if they were good," "if they loved you," if...if...if, etc. Just honor them. We don't always understand God's ways, but we are always just to obey. For those without fathers, keep in mind you have a great, most powerful and caring Father who loves you without conditions, He loves you for yourself and He wants to bless your socks off and give you a most wonderful life, if you will trust Him with your heart and life! Always remember, God loved us all before we were born and we will continue to love us after we die. Not one thing can ever separate us from Him! HE IS FOR YOU AND NOT AGAINST YOU! HE IS OUR ABBA FATHER... our DADDY God!

"Blessings come from applying God's Word" (Luke 11:28).

BEHAVIOR

Actions speak louder than words. Our behavior is eloquent testimony to who we are and what we think. Holy thought and corrupt behavior cannot coexist. It is a lie to say we follow Christ if we are disregarding His Word and ignoring Jesus. It is disappointing when we hear people give a clear Christian testimony and yet see they have a questionable lifestyle. The Bible calls us to holy living. We are to make every effort to live according to its guidelines. If we are truly a new creature in Christ (2 Cor. 5:17), then God's Holy Spirit is living within us helping us to want to do what is right. Godly living is an example to unbelieving friends, neighbors, coworkers and family members that we are different. People are attracted to others who are consistently kind, gracious, and loving. When they ask what makes you different, you will have a wonderful opportunity to tell them about God's love. Godly living is a confirmation that you are, in fact, living for God and not yourself. It is a barometer of your relationship with Him. Godly living means that you are emulating Christ who is our ultimate example of how to live.

If we claim to be God's children, we should behave like God's children, "Our lifestyle clearly displays our loyalties. People of God will live as God commands" (Romans 8:15).

We must show love, faith and works. One without the other is incomplete. Faith without works is belief without hands or feet to live it out. Works without faith are hands and feet without divine guidance. Together God's truth, love and our consecrated hands and feet and lips are a dynamic combination that can change the world for Him. Love is a commitment and is willing to sacrifice for the good of others. Our Christian conduct is proof as to whether we love each other, and loving each other is proof that we belong to Christ. God wants us to love Him, not for his benefit, but for ours. He does, however, require that love for Him be complete...with all our heart, soul, mind and strength. All the special gifts and powers from God will someday come to an end, but love goes on forever (1 Cor. 13:8).

BITTERNESS

In the world today we have a very destructive weapon that destroys so many people and their lives and their health, This weapon is called bitterness. Bitterness is anger that has settled in for a long term. It is an anger that has birthed resentment, the feeling that we have been treated harshly, unfairly, or carelessly. Left to eat its way deep into our mind, emotions, and even our soul, bitterness can turn us into hostile, hardened people. The poison of bitterness, left unchecked, can destroy us! And the most dangerous thing about bitterness is that it renders forgiveness inactive, which puts our relationship with God and others on hold. If we allow bitterness to control us, we have allowed anger and hatred to control us.

We become bitter when we demand our way and stop forgiving and forgetting. We would do well to remember that God has forgiven us despite our continual sinful tendencies. We become bitter by forgetting God's grace, which is showered upon us each day.

Intense grief or mourning can produce bitterness of spirit. The bitterness of intense grief, allowed to continue, robs us of the joy our spirits long for.

When we are unjust or unfair in our dealings with others, particularly those who are poor and oppressed, we cause them to become bitter.

There are times when simple forgiveness can relieve a lifetime of bitterness. Recovery from acute bitterness may be as complex as the reasons for bitterness, but it may also be as simple as three spoken words: "I forgive you."

Ephesians four, verses thirty-one and thirty-two, tell us get rid of all bitterness, rage, anger…instead, be kind to each other, tenderhearted, forgiving one another, just as God through Christ has forgiven you.

Believers, we are deeper into the end times, the last of the last days where prayer is so essential and the unity of the Body of Christ…THE CHURCH is a must! We definitely have to put all our differences aside and focus on what God wants. It doesn't matter what our denomination thinks. It matters how God thinks. We have to stop arguing and disagreeing with one another and come together if we are going to be a glorious church! A glorious church is a church where God's presence is revealed in signs and wonders and visible demonstrations of God's miracle-working power is manifested. That's what God wants! Ephesians 5:27 describes us as a glorious church, not having spot or wrinkle. We have to believe God for everything He promised. We can no longer just play Church, or be content to be passive. Yes, the hour is late, so we need to rise up in boldness for RIGHTEOUSNESS AND FOCUS ON GOD AND HIS PLAN! We need to stir up our faith to believe in God's power and glory to manifest in our life and expect to do the works Jesus said we would. We have to destroy the devil's works and minister life and the Truth to people. If we don't, there will be too many souls going to hell, many of whom will be our fault! Let us not have regrets that we did not do our part and responsibility. God doesn't want to just keep people out of hell, his plan is to have a family; sons and daughters He can relate too on his own spiritual level. God wants us to walk in His blessings.

As believers we've been recreated in God's image so that spiritually we are just like Jesus. We are filled with the same Spirit that filled Him. We are not just hanging around on earth waiting to go to heaven. We are here to destroy the lies and works of the devil; undo the results of sin and death, and minister life to people. We have been born into God's forever family and walk in His glory, and do His will on earth as it is in heaven!

Because our world has become so corrupt we as the Body of Christ (the CHURCH) have to unite in love, peace and our spiritual focus, and in prayer. It is our responsibility as born-again believers! We need to be praying together with all our heart, mind and strength and praising God. As we unite and pray together with faith, and believe for a Spirit-led leadership who will boldly, openly, praise God and pray for the rebirth of this nation: ONE NATION UNDER GOD.... God will hear our prayers!

In unity there is power and in prayer there is power...little prayer, little power, more prayer, more power, MUCH prayer, MUCH POWER! Believers, NOW IS THE TIME TO UNITE AND WALK IN LOVE; NOW IS THE TIME TO PRAY FOR ONE ANOTHER AND OUR NATION AND LEADERS! With our prayers of faith, and our love for one another and the help of the Holy Spirit, we can have a brand-new UNITED STATES OF AMERICA!

BE POSITIVE.... HAVE GODLY POTENTIAL!

"In righteousness shalt thou be established: thou shalt be far from oppression: for thou shalt not fear: and from terror; for it shall not come near thee" (Isaiah 54:14).

One does not have to be a Christian to know this nation has a negative attitude. But being a Christian can teach you why one should have a positive attitude. Everyone knows that a negative attitude is caused by negative words which are destructive. Negative words spoken will cause the actions of anger, depression, hopelessness, failure, hate, division, anxiety and discouragement, a broken spirit and so much more. Positive words spoken will cause encouragement, hope, victory, potential, creativity, unity, harmony, courage, peace, fulfillment, accomplishments and character and life happens!

Every day we hear and see negativity from the TV news, newspapers, or magazines about crime, accidents, tragedies, government dishonesty, death and destruction. People don't realize it, but this constant brainwashing of negativity affects people's lives to be drained, and even discouraged on their job, and even causing them to make wrong choices, thoughtless decisions, lacking morality, potential and value. Why? Because a negative, discouraging attitude of failure comes from thinking and speaking negative words which will causes negative actions? If this was NOT true, why would the Lord warn us, "for whatever a man sows, that he will reap" (Galatians 6:7)? Ask yourself, "Do I have a negative attitude, or a positive, godly outlook on life that is fulfilling and encouraging to me and others?" Negative and positive words grow daily without you realizing it and they can become a good habit or a bad habit. The Bible warns us that there is life or death in the power of our tongue and we will one day be accountable for our useless words. Nothing can cause more damage than our tongue! Christians, we are to bridle our tongue (James 3:2). Monitoring our spoken words will help advance righteousness. Criticism, slander, backbiting, gossip, words of doubt, anger are negative, damaging words which tear and divide people and nations down! This is a reality and very evil and NOT from God! Whether you believe it or not, it will remain a fact!

We as a nation and as individuals and families must come to realize that a positive, godly, attitude is healing to our souls and will bring potential in every area of our lives, along with value, peace, unity, progressive accomplishments and the hope for a fulfilling future! God loves this nation and the people and desires for our country to be a leader in godly character, wisdom, beauty, peace.

He wants us to know the potential He has for us to make our country great as well as each individual. But if we stay in a heavy, dark and negative attitude of discouragement and hopelessness, dragging day by day without enthusiasm without changing our words; listening to the words of negative people, we will not change or learn how great and how much potential we really have to make this nation great and our families, our communities, our jobs, and whoever we come in contact with! Stop listening to the lies of the devil and his distracting, destructive tactics! America, let's lift our spirits, pick ourselves up and each other, dust ourselves off, and make a difference! Let's be in the business of putting God first, loving and caring for each other and having value, morals and character. Enforce the Golden Rule... DO UNTO OTHERS AS YOU WOULD LIKE DONE TO YOU! It takes all of us working together in unity to make this nation great! People, shed that evil negativity.... We need to be effective, positive and live with godly potential for greatness! There's power in unity!

BE MOTIVATED BY LOVE

"In this the children of God and the children of the devil are manifest: Whoever does not practice righteousness is not of God, nor is he who does not love his brother" (1 John 3).

When we are not motivated by love, we become critical of others. We stop looking for the good in them and see only their faults. Soon the unity of believers becomes broken. Unity is vital to the Body of Christ! Have you talked behind someone's back? Have you focused on others' shortcomings instead of their strengths? Remind yourself of Jesus' command to love others as we love ourselves (Matthew 22:39). When you begin to feel critical of someone, make a list of that person's positive qualities. Don't say anything behind their back that you wouldn't say to their face. Remember, God created all people, and He loves them too! They might have made wrong choices and decisions, but haven't we all?

It is very hard to keep in mind, when someone upsets us, or hurts us, let us remember, "We do not wrestle against flesh and blood, but against principalities, against powers, against the rulers of the darkness of this age, against spiritual hosts of wickedness in heavenly places" (Ephesians 6:12). Our greatest demands are to discern between the spiritual struggle and other social, personal, and political difficulties. Otherwise, individual believers and groups become too easily detoured, "wrestling" with human adversaries instead of prayerfully warring against the invisible works of hell behind the scenes. It is important to learn and root this scripture in our hearts (Eph. 6:12). It will help us to walk in love and enjoy and except others for who they are. We all have the flesh to deal with, none of us are perfect. Beware of ruining each other by being critical and catty. Our love should be like God's kind of which is directed outward toward others, not inward toward ourselves. Without love for others, there is no value to our faith, or any of our spiritual gifts. All these special gifts and powers from God will someday come to an end, but love goes on forever.

If we say we love God, and we don't show love to others, then we are liars and not of God. He who says, "I know Him," and does not keep His commandments, is a liar, and the truth is not in him (1 John 1:4) and, "But he who hates his brother is in darkness and walks in darkness, and does not know where he is going, because the darkness has blinded his eyes" (1 John 1:11), "He who loves his brother abides in the light, and there is no cause for stumbling in him" (1 John 1:10). Love is a characteristic of light, and hate is characteristic of darkness. Those two are mortal enemies. Therefore, a person reveals the genuineness of his or her relationship with God and their relationship with others. If you say you are a Christian who loves and wants to honor God, be sure your love is being reflected! GOD IS LOVE!

COURAGE

When you read Luke 23:13-25, you can clearly see Pilate lacked courage. He wanted to release Jesus, but the crowd demanded Jesus' death, so Pilate sentenced Jesus to die. It was necessary for Pilate to release one prisoner (being Barabbas) for them during the feast. Pilate did not want to risk losing his position, which may already have been shaky, by allowing a riot to occur in his province. As a career politician, he knew the art of compromise, and he saw Jesus more as a political threat than as a human being with rights and dignity.

When the stakes are high, it is difficult to stand up for what is right, and it is easy to see our opponents as a problem to be solved rather than as a person to be rejected. Had Pilate been a man of real courage, he would have released Jesus no matter what the consequences. But the crowd roared, and Pilate buckled.

When you have a difficult decision to make, don't discount the effects of peer pressure. Realize beforehand that the right decision could have unpleasant consequences: social rejection, career derailment, public ridicule. But when you are tempted to lose your courage and sway before the crowd...remember Pilate.

Courage is the ability to act on what we know is right and good, to dare to do what we should or must. Fear paralyzes; courage is what helps us move ahead. Courage does not conquer fear, it simply renders fear ineffective. It gives us a confident assurance that we can succeed. Christians recognize that they have an extra resource in God's promised help in time of trouble (Psalm 46:1). This should bring a boldness to face any situation that comes our way. It should be noted that sometimes the courageous thing to do is run, if that is what will bring about the greatest good. The Bible speaks of courage to stand firm against evil, to remain strong in our faith, to resist temptation, to do the right thing. The more we learn to rely on God, the more courageous we will become. True courage comes from God, understanding that He is stronger than our mightiest foes and that He wants to use His strength to help us, "... be strong and courageous! Do not be afraid or discouraged. For the LORD your GOD is with you wherever you go" (Joshua 1:9). Change may be part of God's plan for you, but don't fear the change, especially when you know it's from God; for you are headed into joy and satisfaction. To experience fear is normal. To be paralyzed by fear, however, can be an indication that you doubt God's ability to care for you in the face of change (Genesis 46:3-4). We also need courage at times to admit our mistakes and sins. When we do it will open the door to forgiveness and restoration (2 Samuel 12:13). Standing up for what is right can get you in trouble from corrupt people. Failing to stand up for what is right can get you in trouble with God (Luke 23:13-25).

CONSCIENCE-TESTERS

"My conscience is clear, but that isn't what matters.

It is the Lord himself who will examine me and decide"

(1 Corinthians 4:4).

Nearly every day we face questions of conscience. We must choose between doing what is pleasing to God and what appeals to our own selfish desires. God gives us the freedom to choose what we want to do, but we should know the consequences of choosing to sin. Before we act we should think and consider the consequences of our actions. The greatest consequence of sin is eternal separation from God (Rom. 6:23). Faithfulness results in good consequences. We must listen to and obey our conscience or else it will be useless. More than that, it can malfunction if not properly cared for. It can become a flawed witness that may condemn us too harshly or let us off too easily.

As Christians, we face situations in our daily lives that are conscience-testers. They help us to see whether we are serious about the integrity God expects of us. Our greatest protection against making the wrong decision is trusting God to take care of us as we choose to do what's right, regardless of the outcome. Just as Shadrach and his friends made the decision not to bow down to the gold image, they dared to disobey the king because they trusted God (Daniel 3). As we too face matters of conscience, we can do the right thing and leave the consequences with God. When we avoid sin, our conscience has no reason to witness against us and we are then actively nurturing our conscience and keeping it from witnessing against us.

God uses others as well to testify to our conscience so that our conscience may testify against us. As an example, in 2 Samuel 12:13 David confessed his sin to Nathan for killing Uriah and taking his wife. But it condemned him only after Nathan pricked David's conscience.

If our conscience is witnessing faithfully for or against us we will have a strong inner call, a voice of accountability, to do what is right. If you have a reputation for not always doing the right thing, or if you find yourself unmoved by evil, it may be an indication that your conscience has become inactive. If your conscience is witnessing faithfully for you or against you, it will activate your heart and mind so that you know what is right or what is wrong. Conscience is not always an unbiased witness. We may have persuaded our conscience that all is well when it isn't. In a sense, we have "bought off the witness of our conscience. But we can't buy off God. He is the only truly unbiased witness and judge" ("My conscience is clear, but that isn't what matters. It is the Lord himself who will examine me and decide") (1 Corinthians 4:4). Let God through his holy Word develop your conscience in godly ways; then it can speak to you in concert with God himself. Our conscience will witness effectively to us if we truly desire to stay close to God, spend time in his Word, and make an effort to understand ourselves and our tendencies to right and wrong.

CONFIDENCE IN PRAYER

"Now this is the confidence that we have in Him,

that if we ask anything according to His will, He will hear us.

And if we know that He hears us, whatever we ask,

we know that we have the petitions that we have asked of Him"

(1 John 5:14-15).

Children of God may have confidence of free access and boldness of speech in presenting their requests to Him. There is, however, a limitation to the assurance that our prayers will be answered. The New Testament bases the assurance on: 1. asking in Jesus' Name (John 14:13, 14; 15:16; 16:23, 24), 2. abiding in Christ and allowing His words to abide in us (John 15:7), 3. having faith (Matthew 21:22; James 1:6), 4. and being righteous in life and fervent prayer (1 John 3:21-22; James 5:16). Here John says, that we must ask according to His will, which inclusively states the fundamental condition for assurance in prayer. One who abides (to remain; continue; stay; to continue in a particular condition, attitude, relationship, to accept without opposition, endure to submit, to remain steadfast or faithful) in Christ and whose words abide in Him; who prays in the Name of Jesus, that is, in accord with His character and nature; and who is full of faith and righteousness is not inclined to pray anything contrary to His will. But more than how we pray, God wills and cares that we pray. Genuine prayer is not an attempt at precise means of getting God to meet our desires and demands; but rather, in subordinating our will to His, we open the doorway to His fullest blessings being released in our lives.

But what do we do if we don't know God's will? If you are not sure a prayer request is according to God's will, ask Him about it; He can tell you. And don't worry about making mistakes when you pray. Do you think the sovereignty of God will be shattered because one of his children makes a mistake while praying? Isn't it bigger if you do not pray?

If the answer is "no" to your request, the Lord will communicate with you by internal witness of the Holy Spirit. Sometimes the answer may not come immediate. God may be developing your patient trust in His perfect will. A consistent prayer life in your walk with God will help a sensitivity develop between you and your heavenly Father. When God says "no" to a request you make, trust His goodness. Jesus made the point that parents do not give their children worthless or bad gifts when they request something. How much more can we trust our heavenly Father, who always gives us what is good (Matt. 7:7-11). But we need to ask according to His will.

Earnestly seeking God in prayer will lead to our finding spiritual strength and satisfaction. Prayer is the simplest way to communicate with our God, yet so often we approach prayer like a one-way telephone conversation, forgetting that God also wants to speak to us. Just what is prayer? It is an act of humble worship in which we seek God with all our heart. Prayer often is confession of sin. Our prayer must be accompanied by a willingness to obey with actions. Our prayers bring us into God's presence (Psm. 145:18). God honors persistent prayer (Matt. 7:7). God invites us to bring all our needs to Him in prayer. Jesus taught his disciples that prayer is an intimate relationship with the Father that includes a dependency for daily needs, commitment to obedience, and forgiveness of sin.

CHRISTIANS HAVE THE BRIGHTEST HOPE AND A REVERENT FEAR OF GOD

"God will wipe away every tear from their eyes"

(Revelation 7:9-1).

"Serve the LORD with reverent fear,

and rejoice with trembling"

(2:11 Psalm).

We all from time to time wonder what lies ahead tomorrow, or next week and even next year, for it often looks dark and bleak. But when our mind seems to wander down that foggy path we have to bring to remembrance what John, the writer of Revelation shared with us.

When John was on the Island of Patmos he wrote to people threatened with persecution for their faith. To help them, and us face what lies ahead, John painted a picture of our ultimate future. In the presence of God, Christians will "neither hunger anymore nor thirst anymore; the sun shall not strike them, nor any heat" (v. 7:16). And "God will wipe every tear from their eyes" (v. 17). What comfort that holds for us! We can count on God being there for us no matter what we face or what lies ahead of all our tomorrows. Our hope is in God which provides optimism for the future and strength for today and each day! Hope is essential to a Christians perseverance; our getting through the tough times. Without hope we would give up. We as Christians have ultimate, eternal hope, but people who don't know Christ have nothing but their own hopelessness to cling to. Hope does require one thing, though...trust in the One who brings real hope. Hope is trusting God to act in His good timing. Who but God controls the future? Who but God has a home for us that is eternal? Who but God forgives our sins? Who but God can give us a life that lasts forever? No wonder He is our hope! We do not have to fear what lies ahead, "For God has not given us a spirit of fear, but of power and love and a sound mind" (2 Timothy 1:7). We were not meant to live in fear! Fear is not good if it keeps us from doing the things we ought to do. A healthy fear of God is good for it motivates us to strive for holiness. Why do we fear God? It is a healthy fear of God because God is so great and mighty, and He holds the power of life and death in his hands. We are to have a reverent fear of Him for it helps us believers to keep our perspective about where we need to be in our relationship.

CHRISTIAN BARRIERS AND DIVISION IN CHURCH

The freedom to be one's self with our defenses down and a relaxed relief of being totally open and authentic is a wonderful blessing. We can and should feel this way in the presence of the Lord, for we cannot hide anything from Him. He knows everything about us and the Lord desires to have this open relationship with us because He loves us. He already knows our faults, weaknesses, our failures and our victories and the best part is we are still His treasure; He loves us unconditionally! But He does expect us, his children to share our love, trust and heart with Him, and make Him apart of all our troubles, our anxieties, our fears, our good times and bad times. He wants us to depend on Him for our victories, deliverances, health or any circumstance or situation! This is how and what a loving Father does! He wants us to know and believe and trust He is THERE for us, now and forever!

Sometimes in church is the last place where people feel free to be themselves. They cover up with Sunday clothes and Sunday smiles. They even feel relief when they leave because of the strain of false fellowship. Instead of coming together in unity and accepting each other's differences; loving them for who they are in Christ, and how God sees them, they feel threatened to expose their real heart ("He who loves his brother abides in the light, and there is no cause for stumbling in him" (1 John 2:10)). The best antidote to this artificial atmosphere is practicing the Lord's presence at church, allowing your primary focus to be communing with the Lord, and worshiping Him. Then you will be able to smile at others with His joy and love each other with His love.

If one is claiming to be a Christian then their words and actions must line up with the Word of God, not only in church but each day of our life ("He who says he abides in Him ought himself also to walk just as He walked" (1John 2:6). We can't be carnal one day and deeply spiritual the next. Having strife, envy, divisions, criticism, and false pretense is not acceptable for the Body of Christ. The Lord is expecting his Children to grow up and walk in unity and harmony. The Bible extols unity as the highest form of Christian relationship! Unity is not synonymous with uniformity. God has created us differently, which means there will be differences of opinion. But our common goal is the same...to serve God! Unity creates a more beautiful worship experience.

Satan had sent the same spirit of division among the early Corinthian Christians and he is still sending the same spirit among us today. He knows that a house divided against itself will fall ("Every kingdom divided against itself is brought to desolation, and a house divided against a house falls" (Luke 11:17)). He also knows if we all come together in unity of our faith, we'll arrive at the full stature of Christ Jesus (Ephesians 4:15). So he has assigned a spirit of division to operate in our personal lives, our church lives, our social lives and our families' lives.

CLING TO GOD...HE IS YOUR LIFELINE

"For I am the Lord, your God, who takes hold of your right hand and says to you, Do not fear, I will help you" (Isaiah 41:13).

We need the Lord's help every day, and He is always eager to provide it. But He also commands us to love Him with all our heart, soul and mind. Although we do this imperfectly, God still delights in our love just as a mother would when her child brings her a crumbled up flower out of love. Even our obedience is flawed, but we have the desire to obey and God sees our heart.

We should not worry so about all the ways we fall short, but instead focus on what we can do out of love for God. At times our awareness can actually be a blessing to us for it will protect us from becoming self-righteous. We have to learn to depend more and more on the Lord, not ourselves.

We please the Lord when we rely on Him to be our lifeline. He has created us to be dependent on Him, otherwise we may cling on to other things such as, addictions, destructive relationships and other forms of idolatry. The more we depend on the Lord, the better our life will be!

CHARACTER...GODLINESS...VALUES

The thing we call character is...who you are. It's the sum total of all that distinguishes you as a person from everyone else. Your reputation is what other people are saying about you, which is often a good indicator of your character. If two people were talking about you, what would they say? Character is something you are; but it must also be something you desire to become. Ultimately, your character is your mark on society. Those striving for good character, or better yet for godly character, are working toward moral excellence. And Jesus is the ultimate example in moral excellence. We work hard all our lives to become excellent in many areas of our lives. Doesn't it make sense to also work hard at becoming morally excellent, to be known as someone who has mastered the art of living in areas that really matter; like integrity, kindness, love, and faithfulness? To be as God is possible and to seek to build our character traits like the character of God. To be godly should be a high motivation and valued priority. But godliness is more than being like God. It is practicing a closer walk with God. As goodness is more than the absence of badness, so godliness is more than the absence of worldliness, materialism, hedonism (a life of total happiness), and all other "isms." Godliness is the practice of the presence of God in all we are and all we do.

Jesus said that our actions give away our value system. What we do show is what we really believe (Luke 6:45). Do your actions clearly show you are living by the values taught in the Bible? Living by values of Scripture earns us a good reputation and makes us trustworthy. The heart is the wellspring of moral, or immoral, behavior. Conduct is the fruit of character, and character is the fruit of belief. When we build on the foundation of God's Word and yield our ways to God's ways, we allow God to produce in us His good fruits of godliness. A sacrifice is offering God a gift. Our obedience is offering God ourselves. This is one of the clearest indications that we are committed to godly character and desiring excellent morals.

Whether an ancient Israelite or a modern-day Christian, those who are called God's people are special...holy, dedicated to the Lord, and chosen to be His own. This is a special privilege, but also a special responsibility. It must affect the way we live!

CAN DEMONS HAVE ANY INFLUENCE ON BELIEVERS?

"Be sober; be vigilant because your adversary the devil walks about like a roaring lion, seeking who he may devour" (1 Peter 5:8).

If Satan and his forces could have no influence on believers, why would Paul and Peter have written these words: "Put on the whole armor of God" (Ephesians 6:11) and "Be self-controlled and alert. Your enemy the devil prowls around like a roaring lion looking for someone to devour" (1 Peter 5:8). If the devil did not have influence upon believers we would not need the armor of God and we needn't be on alert if the roaring lion has no teeth.

Our enemy does want to devour us. He was brazen enough to attack Jesus, so you can be sure he will shoot his fiery darts at us (Eph. 6:16, KJV). We are still fully accountable for our choices but his influence can be incredibly strong. The enemy can't possess us, but that doesn't mean he doesn't try to harm us any way he can. In fact, sometimes he is so persistent and powerfully attacks us that our souls seem to be tormented under attack. Some call this state "oppression." There are four ways the enemy tries to oppress believers: (1) He causes believers to lose hope (2) doubt their salvation (3) stay discouraged and (4) face continual temptation. But Satan has limits in the lives of the believer. He can go no further than God allows. The Book of Job is the example of God's limitations on the devil toward what he could do to Job.

The enemy tries to oppress believers by accusing us and gives us false messages about ourselves: "You're no good." "God doesn't love you, and nobody else does either." "You're never going to experience victory." "You're wasting your time trying to be a Christian." Messages like these bombard us to the point we lose hope and struggle with believing even God's promises. He also leads us to doubt our salvation, and the doubts consume us. The devil knows the Word as well and he knows a doubting person is "like a wave of the sea, blown and tossed by the wind" (James 1:6). The person who wrestles with doubt often becomes works-driven; that is he begins to do as many works as possible to convince himself of his salvation. When doubts remain it can be accompanied by fear which can be overwhelming. He will also try to discourage us, and the persistent discouragement becomes debilitating. Maybe you have served God but have seen few results from your ministry. Perhaps you haven't seen as many changes in your own life as you want. Maybe you've never found freedom from a particular sin. Discouragement sets in, and the hope of victory decreases. Our joy disappears and it seems like we will never regain it. Satan can also reintroduce sin strongholds in our lives by continual temptation, and we lose our will to fight. So knowing our vulnerability, Satan attacks, entices, lures, and seduces us in those areas. If he can convince us that the powerful temptations will never decrease, we are more inclined to give in and the foothold becomes a stronghold.

This is exactly why we need to put on the whole armor of God every day (Eph. 6:11-18). We need to know and use the Word of God, just as Jesus did in the wilderness against the devil's temptations. Keep your faith strong and your fellowship close and intimate with the Lord and repent as quickly as you sin, and walk in love and in the Spirit every day. Take your spiritual walk with the Lord seriously. Keep yourself built up and stay in an attitude of gratitude toward the Lord with prayer and praise. ("Resist the devil and he will flee" (James 4:7)). If you are walking with the Lord, you have no reason to fear, for fear is also from the devil. Jesus wants us to depend on Him and enter his rest and peace.

DON'T FAKE LOVE

"Let no corrupt word proceed out of your mouth, but what is good for necessary edification" (Ephesians 4:29).

Nobody likes to be criticized. It hurts even worse when it comes from someone who talks about us behind our backs, and especially if they are our Christian friend or our spiritual sister or brother! Tragically, some Christians are guilty of these sins. They wouldn't run people down with their cars, but they willingly "run them down" their words, belittling what they do or say. This is such a cheap and demeaning action! Whisperers are gossipers who secretly spread rumors, and backbiters are those who talk spitefully about a person.

People who engage in these destructive acts don't see the inconsistency of their behavior and haven't taken to heart the words of the apostle Paul: "Let love be without hypocrisy" (Rom. 12:9). Or, another way of translating it is: "Don't fake love."

We need to repent of our gossip and replace it with what John Stott calls "holy gossip." This means, we need to talk enthusiastically about the transforming work that Christ is doing in people's lives. Talk about the great changes you see in someone's life since they gave their life to Christ. How genuine is your love?

Remember, our words have the power to build or tear down!

DEFEAT EVIL WITH GOOD

If you want to change any situation for the better, this is exactly what you need to do…defeat evil with good, overcome hate with love. If you want to, strengthen a relationship, give more compassion toward it. If you want friendlier neighbors, overcome their attitude problem with kindness. If you want more out of your job, apply more of yourself. If you want more out of your fellowship with Jesus, draw nearer, spend more quality time with the Lord, decrease self and increase God. You will get out what measure of love you have given in each situation, "You will reap what you sow" (Galatians 6:7).

It's definitely not the world's way of doing things. It's God's way. His ways are higher than ours (Isa. 55:8). God based the commandants on love. He used love to change the world because "Love never fails" (1 Corth. 13:8). Jesus overcame the works of the devil with compassion. He defeated hatred with love. The love God has and gives is AGAPE love which is unconditional, committed, and undefeatable, and it's unconquerable goodwill, always seeking the highest good of the other person. Compassion doesn't just skim the top of things, it goes to the root. That's why it's always successful.

Don't complain about any situation. You have the power to change it with the authority that Jesus gave you (Luke 10:19) and with love and prayer. God tells us, "Do everything without complaining and disputing" (Phil. 2:14). Learn to apply love to all situations and defeat evil with good. If each of us took the time to show more love, concern, and compassion by meeting the needs of others, or give a genuine hug, or pray for each other, the church would be a power house of love that would radiate a welcome for miles around! Church we can do this!! We would be "The light in the dark world, and the salt of the earth," as God states we are (Matt. 5:13-16). Also, I John 2:5 states, God's love is perfected in us as we keep His Word and, His love has been shed abroad in our heart (Rom. 5:5). God's love inside of us will set us free from fear and we will not be afraid to reach out to others with love. We are God's special children, He told us this in Deuteronomy 7:6. But it's not going to do us good if we confess to be a Christian and continue to growl and complain.

Make a quality decision to commit today. Challenge for yourself and see what a difference you can make in your home, community, job and church just by applying more love to improve a situation for the better. Turn failures to victories with the mighty force of love. Refuse to listen to words that will only cause damage to the problem and refuse to speak words that add fuel to the situation, and refuse to complain or murmur in a situation you have power to change. Trust God to hear your prayers and use your love to release those defeats. God says, LOVE NEVER FAILS and it will put the devil on the run!

DO YOU HAVE A CLOGGED DRAIN?

Everyone has had hurt feelings at one time. Some hurt can be devastating. The gap between knowing you need to forgive someone and actually being able to do it seems like a vast canyon. You can see the other side, but getting there seems impossible.

Have you ever seen a shower drain plugged up with a two-month accumulation of hair...ugh? The water slowly seeps through the molding mass of soapy yuk. No amount of plunging can bring the glob up because it is too deep. So the next solution is usually to apply something like Draino. But sometimes the buildup is too severe. The last resort, of course, is to call a plumber.

Unforgiveness is like a clogged drain. Sometimes it is fairly easy to unclog. Someone hurts us, we then let them know, and they say they are sorry, we then forgive and the whole episode is forgotten. But when unforgiveness collects from years of hurt it becomes similar to what a drain would look like after years of bathing your cat in the sink without cleaning out the drain!

Likewise, our sin can collect and become a gross yucky mass that eventually clogs our relationship with God. Until it is removed, we can't really receive anything meaningful from Him. Jesus came to "unclog our pipes" so God's love and forgiveness could flow to us freely. He died to open the way for the flow of love.

You might have had a devastating hurt, or someone's sin of unkindness came against you, and you feel you have every right not to forgive, but you must put aside that right for a greater goal...you must "die to self." You must forgive the person who did you wrong! Otherwise the clog will only get worse. If say you are a follower of Jesus, and you call yourself a Christian, then forgiveness IS a MUST! Jesus humbled himself and forgave all our sin, who are we not to! The key to forgiving others is to quit focusing on what they did to you and start focusing on what God did for you: "Be kind and loving to each other, and forgive each other just as God forgave you in Christ" (Ephesians 4:32). Understand this, relationships don't thrive because the guilty are punished but because the innocent are merciful.

Forgiveness must be from the heart and must not be dependent upon whether they feel sorry for what they did or not. Forgiving someone is a gift only we can offer. We can't make someone take a free gift; they must reach out and receive it. Though the canyon may look deep and treacherous, the reward on the other side is a clear conscience. To be disciples of Jesus our love for others should have no limits and either should our forgiveness. "Even if he wrongs you seven times a day and each time turns again and asks forgiveness, forgive him" (Luke 17:4). Will you obey God and forgive?

DO WE REALLY KNOW GOD ALMIGHTY?

"God, who made the world and everything in it, since He is Lord of heaven and earth, does not dwell in temples made with hands. Nor is worshiped with men's hands, as though He needed anything, since He gives to all life, breath, and all things. And He has made from one blood every nation of men to dwell on all the face of the earth, and has determined their pre-appointed times and the boundaries of their dwellings, so that they should seek the Lord, in hope that they might grope for Him and find Him, though He is not far from each one of us... (Acts 17:24-27). Truly, these times of ignorance God overlooked, but now commands all men everywhere to repent, because He has appointed a day on which He will judge the world in righteousness by the Man (Jesus) He has ordained. He has given assurance of this to all by raising Him from the dead" (Acts 17:30-31).

One must ask themselves... "Do I really know God?" To really know God we must know his many characteristics. Knowing them is not enough. We must respect them, honor them, love them, and realize how great his marvelous nature is. If we knew the reality of his power and authority we would humble ourselves. If we knew his love for us, we would surely trust Him totally. If we knew Him as our creator and heavenly Father, we would look up to Him and depend on Him as we would our earthly father, but even more. If we knew He is at our side every second of our life, we would not say or do the things that displease Him. When we realized everything we do, we must realize we take Jesus through it too. If we walk in the mud and disrespect ourselves, we muddy Jesus and disrespect Him too. If we realized, really realized, Jesus knows all our thoughts and hears every word we say, we would be careful in what we say or do! When we really know God, love in our heart continues to grow; our central focus is then Jesus! Everything becomes centered around Jesus, and his desires, his ways. Our desire is only then to please and obey Him out of the relationship of reality and the deep love we have for Him! We go out of our way to please Him and show our love by loving others, helping them, praying for them. Why.... Because now we know who God is!

If we don't know God and his total nature, He is taken too lightly! There is no reality of who He really is! What He is not is a heavenly Santa Claus! He is not here for our desires, but his! It is all about JESUS! His traits are not to be disrespected or taken for advantage. How many people say, "Well, it's only a little lie, Jesus will forgive me." A lie is a lie, there is no big or little, it's all the same and not tolerated by God! God hates lies: "A false witness will not go unpunished, and he who speaks lies will not escape" (Proverbs 19:5). God does not lie and He doesn't want us to either. The little things we do at times that we don't think will hurt, actually does! It hurts us and the Body of

Christ since we are all connected spiritually. The Holy Spirit will correct us, but we must listen.

Look at our nation now…is God a reality? Is He being respected, or loved, or honored? Who is in control of the hearts of people, God or the Devil? God is well aware of this destruction and disobedience because He knows everything! He is still in control of this world! But God is so loving He gave us free will of our hearts and minds because He only wants true love from our hearts, not forced love and obedience. If people knew God for who He is, do you think our nation would be in chaos? Do you see where God has been taken for granted and much too lightly? Is God really known for who He is? Where is the humility, love, and the heartfelt trust and faith to please God? Has the "ME" factor taken over? Are people thinking about what God wants?

God is eternal and ever-living. He has no beginning or end. He is a person who is totally self-aware, and totally self-assertive. He is the essence of love, and loving, and He is a righteous judge…totally fair and just! God is the Father of all nations, the Creator of all. He is all-powerful and sustains the universe. He exists in nature, but He is not nature, nor is He bound by laws of nature. He is the source of all nature and everything that is.

This is the truth about our Amazing God and if you find you don't know God's total nature; it's time you really got to know Him personally and intimately. It could change your life and give it much more meaning, value, depth, and a more blessed future. He is the lover of your soul and is desiring and longing to be your all and all! He is waiting with open arms! Just pray and ask God to cause you to know Him and all of his marvelous attributes in a personal way. You will surely find Him waiting in your Bible to talk to you and standing alongside of you all day. God is real…take the time to really know Him then shine your light of truth among the world!

DO NOT GRIEVE THE HOLY SPIRIT

The Holy Spirit is our personal Protector. Our safety matters to Him. Our peace of mind matters to Him. He does not want us to waste our life or time in the wrong places. Our enemies do exist and we must recognize this. Satan assigned people with evil to break our focus and distract you from the will of God. He is clever and deceptive so we cannot trust our own mind we have to trust in the Lord (Prov. 3:5-6). When we listen to the Holy Spirit, we will be protected. The Holy Spirit will often warn us in advance of possible danger.

The Holy Spirit is holy and our conduct and behavior is monitored continuously. He will withdraw His manifested presence when He has been grieved and offended. The Apostle Paul warns us not to grieve the Holy Spirit (Eph. 4:29-32). It is important that we permit the Holy Spirit to correct us and prevent us from saying or doing anything that is grievous to Him. The Holy Spirit gives us the criteria and guidelines for proper conversation: True, Honest, Just, Pure, Lovely, Good report, Virtuous Praiseworthy. The Holy Spirit studies us. Our motives are continuously monitored and evaluated (1 Sam. 16:7; 1 Corth. 312-15). The Holy Spirit has a dangerous side. He can become an enemy to those who persist in rebellion. There are eight facts about offending the Holy Spirit: 1. Ignoring His Word each day (2 Tim. 2:15) 2. Careless and useless conversation (2 Tim. 2:16), 3. Continuous resistance to the Holy Spirit can turn Him into an enemy (Acts 7:51), 4. When we ignore the warnings of the Holy Spirit, there is no other source for help (Heb. 10:26-27). 5. Disdain and contempt in attending the house of God (Heb. 10:28), 6. Developing companionship and relationships with those who are ungodly and rebellious toward truth (Eph. 5:11), 7. Any word that does not edify and strengthen others can become grievous to the Holy Spirit (Eph. 4:29-32), 8. Permitting others to deceive you with error and falsehood infuriates the Holy Spirit (Eph. 5:6-7). The reason the Holy Spirit deals so strongly with rebellion is to bring us into the fear of God (Acts 5:11). Rejection of the Holy Spirit can be fatal, remember Lot's wife (Luke 17:32)? The presence of the Holy Spirit yesterday does not guarantee the presence of God tomorrow. God had selected Saul, and anointed him (1 Sam. 16:14, yet "the Spirit of the Lord departed from Saul and an evil spirit from the Lord troubled him." Always remember, the Holy Spirit may withdraw His manifest presence when He has been offended. Let's pray: "Holy Spirit, forgive me for anything that I have done to offend You and for ignoring Your inner voice. Cleanse, purge and remove anything in me that is unlike You. Reveal Yourself again to me. Heavenly Father, thank You for every blessing You have given us, especially for the Divine guidance through the Holy Spirit. I trust you to guide me into a place of Blessing. Guide me away from any place of temptation, unholy relationships, and where I could fall into error. Guide me concerning my place of business, in my finances, rest in peace and in all decisions. I trust You for You will never disappoint me. I lean on you. My faith is wholly in You and because of that, I rest in peace today. In Jesus' Name, Amen."

DAVID AND JONATHAN

In the Book of I Samuel, we can learn much from the friendship of David and Jonathan. Not only was their friendship one of the valued, and deepest, it was recorded in the Bible. Their devotion and commitment to God and each other and their "oneness" with God, teaches us about true love and friendship, and how to be successful in life, the importance of humility, faithfulness, respect and morality.

When we think of David, we think of a shepherd, poet, giant-killer, king and ancestor of Jesus. But other words could also be used to describe David: betrayer, liar, adulterer, and murderer, David was not without sin, he sinned many times, but he was quick to repent. His example to us is that while he sinned greatly, he did not sin repeatedly and he didn't make the same mistakes. He also learned from his mistakes and accepted the suffering it brought. David believed as deeply as he could that God was loving and forgiving. His confessions were from his heart and his repentance was real. David never took God's forgiveness lightly or his blessings for granted. In return, God never held back from David either his forgiveness or the consequences of his actions. We too should have the willingness to honestly admit our mistakes and accept there are consequences to face. God greatly desires our complete trust and worship. Although David succeeded in almost everything and became famous throughout the land, he refused to use his popularity to support his advantage against Saul who wanted to kill David. David kept his respect for Saul even though Saul was seeking to kill him and Saul had been anointed by God. Saul's popularity made him proud and arrogant, and because of his pride and his disobedience to God, Saul was dethroned. David remained humble, even when the entire nation praised him. Saul looked good on the outside, but he was decaying on the inside. Godly character is much more valuable than good looks. God does not look at the outside of a person. He looks at the inside, at the heart.

When David and Jonathan met, they became close friends at once. They based their friendship on their commitment to God, not just each other. They did not let anything come between career, or family problems. David and Jonathan drew even closer when their friendship was tested. They remained friends to the end.

Jonathan's loyalty is one of life's most costly qualities. Loyalty is the most unselfish part of love. To be loyal, you cannot live only for yourself. Loyal people not only stand by their commitments, they also are willing to suffer for them. Jonathan is a shining example of loyalty. Sometimes he was forced to deal with a conflict between his loyalties to his father, Saul, and to his friend David. His solution to that conflict teaches us both how to be loyal and what must guide loyalty. In Jonathan, truth, always guided loyalty. Jonathan found the source of truth in his relationship with God. He realized that no matter what, he must be loyal to Him. It was this ultimate loyalty to God that gave Jonathan the wisdom to deal effectively with the complications and situations in his life. He was loyal to Saul because he was his father and the king. He was loyal to David because David was his friend. But the loyalty to God helped him see the limits of each of those relationships. The lesson of loyalty is one of the strongest aspects of courage. An allegiance to God puts all other relationships in perspective. God's faithfulness, mercy and unselfish love should inspire us also to be completely dedicated to God as David and Jonathan were.

EVERYONE IS IMPORTANT!

"God created man in His own image; in the image of God He created him; male and female He created them. Then He blessed them…" (Genesis 1:27-28).

Then God said, "Let us make man in Our image, according to our likeness…" (Genesis 1:26).

When God said "Let us" God was not only speaking to the rest of the Trinity, but to the entire host of heaven, and the angels, as well. Our likeness refers to such qualities as reason, personality, and intellect, and to the capacity to relate, to hear, to see, and to speak. All of these are characteristics of God, which He chose to reproduce in mankind. God created man to be His kingdom agent, to rule and subdue the rest of creation, including satanic forces. Man is a spiritual being who is not only body, but also soul and spirit. He is a moral being whose intelligence, perception, and self-determination far exceed that of any other earthly being. These properties imply the intrinsic worth, not only of the family of mankind, but also of each human individual. We should never be pleased to dwell on a level of existence lower than that on which God has made possible for us to dwell. We should strive to be the best we can be and to reach the highest levels we can reach. To do less is to be unfaithful stewards of the life entrusted to us.

Not only was man made distinct from the rest of creation, he was given authority over the Earth and everything upon it (Psalm 8:4-9). Although Adam and Eve sinned and lost this authority, God began the plan to restore the lost perfection. Christ Jesus has taken it back through His death and resurrection! Our ability to exercise authority over the Earth is dependent on our willingness to submit to, serve, and obey the living God who holds authority over us. Our authority over Earth makes us accountable for the Earth. God has also given us free will to choose Jesus as our Lord and Savior out of love and the need to be forgiven and live a life of righteousness as a Christian. To accept Jesus in our life and as our life we become more valuable, for we then become the Body of Christ, his hands, heart and voice to share the Truth, and Jesus has given us the authority over the power of the devil (Luke 10:19). We are to share the Truth, the Gospel.

All creation was created to glorify God. Human beings are unique in their ability to bring God glory because they are created in God's image. Because sin broke man's good relationship with God, each person must look to God for a restoration of that lost fellowship. Only God can reverse the consequences of sinful choices.

God made us in HIS IMAGE or likeness, this is the first sign of the value He placed on us. If God made us valuable and the second sign of value God places on us is that He placed people over all creatures on Earth; who are we to say we are not! God showed us how much value He placed on us by the way He made us (Jer. 1:5). Almighty God thinks wonderful thoughts of us all the time (Psm. 139:17). God values us so much that He watches over us no matter where we go or what we are doing. God loves and values us so much that He allows our body to become a temple in which He lives. He chooses to live in us and calls us His temple and dwelling place.

If God Almighty has placed value on you, then there is no reason (only in hell) that you should think any less of your worth. Don't disgrace or disappoint God by thinking you are worthless! If you have sinned, repent and come back to God; He will be waiting with open arms! If you have not asked Jesus in your life...pray, repent and invite Jesus in your life. Don't ever forget, you were always meant to be highly loved, honored, blessed and valued by God, so accept His love and Word, and believe in who He has made you.

EASTER IS NOT CANDY BASKETS AND RABBITS, IT IS...DEATH TO LIFE!

"For God so loved the world that he gave his only son,
that whoever believes in him should not perish
but have everlasting life" (John 3:16).

How can we allow the devil to direct us to make Easter, Resurrection Day, commercialized? This is a holy day! Jesus died so we could live! If it wasn't for His resurrection we would all be going to hell in a handbasket. The world is focused on the money it makes in candy, stuffed toys and colored eggs. Where is the holy, heartfelt, grateful remembrance of the degrading, suffering and rejection of our Lord and Savior? Jesus did not suffer spiritual and physical torture, pain and humility just for us to celebrate a commercial day! Yes, there is history of the Easter egg, the lily and dogwood tree, but still if there was no Cross, there would have been no miraculous history greater (besides His birth), even to this present day, than Jesus' Death and Resurrection and Life to celebrate!

All humans are sinners. We've broken God's laws, so we stand guilty before God and deserving of punishment. We stand rebellious and defiant of the God who loves us. There are many who do not believe that, but one day we ALL will stand before God for Judgment; it is a true fact, whether one believes it or not, it will happen! We are guilty before God and we deserve his anger and punishment. But GOD took the wrath we deserved, and poured it out on Jesus, on the cross. Jesus took upon himself, our sins, every disgusting thought, or action. Then, in exchange, He poured God's goodness into us, which brought us back to God by the blood of Jesus! As horrible as the physical agony must have been, the spiritual agony of Jesus' transformation from sinless to all sin was worse. Jesus had never been separated from God until now. No wonder He screamed out, "My God, my God, why have you deserted me?" Jesus was deserted by God so that you and I never would have to be! JESUS DIED FOR YOU AND ME! Accepting Jesus is the only way to have peace with God and eternal life. God took the cross of Christ...the single darkest hour in the history of humanity, and turned it into the way of redemption for all people everywhere.

"Once we were far away from God but now we are reconciled by the blood of Jesus" (Ephesians 2:11-21). Reconciliation begins with recognition that without Christ we are lost and separated from God. God never rejects the sinner, just the sin (John 8:1-11). God desires to restore all wayward sinful relationships, but one must believe in what Jesus did for us on the cross and that He was resurrected three days later, and He was truly the Son of God. Jesus lives and reigns today! Also one must ask Jesus for forgiveness of their sins and allow Jesus to come into their heart and change their life, pleasing to God and His ways. Repentance is motivated by the realization that you have taken the wrong way in life. You must admit your sin and repent, making a commitment with God, and depending on his help to change you, if you want to be resurrected from sin and death to life eternal, receiving God's favor and blessings. God has a plan for each of our lives that will give us hope and a future (Jeremiah 29:11-14).

Easter, or Resurrection Day, is a vital, holy day! It could mean the difference between life or death, heaven or hell. Why would anyone want to commercialize this most wondrous, valuable, love gift from God? Parents, have you told your children the real meaning of Easter? Easter is celebrated yearly, but each year we must sincerely hold it holy, grateful and heartfelt; don't become complacent and take it lightly and sin, having a casual attitude. Complacency toward God and sin puts us at great risk! God loves us too much to lose us without a fight! Remember always God's awesome, unfailing love!

DOES YOUR MARRIAGE BRING GLORY TO GOD?

"May God...help you live in complete harmony with each other—each with the attitude of Christ Jesus toward the other. Then all of you can together with one voice, giving praise and glory to God..." (Romans 15:5-7).

Marriage was God's idea from the very beginning. It is as old as Eden yet as fresh as the last wedding. Marriage is ordained by God, a sacred relationship, one not to be entered into lightly. But in the world today, marriage is entered into lightly, and for the wrong reasons, and without a great deal of thought about the value and a lifetime commitment. Many do not take time to get to know each other as friends first, or to find out if they too are a Christian. A couple nowadays do not realize they are to be a united purpose to serve God (Joshua 24:15) and take their marriage seriously as a faithful, devoted sacred relationship that GOD joined together. A marriage under God should teach the couple much about how God relates to his church, "A man leaves his father and mother and is joined to his wife, and two are united into one. This is a great mystery, but it is an illustration of the way Christ and the church are one." Through their vows two people, in a miraculous way, should become one. That is, if they have taken their marriage as a symbol of Christ and the church. God's loving relationship with his people is so similar to the marriage relationship that he uses human marriage to illustrate his covenant with his people in the Old Testament and Christ's love for the church in the New Testament.

Some people think it is fine just to live together, but if they know God's heart, they would know it is not and it is sin. God says, give honor to marriage, and remain faithful to one another in marriage. God will surely judge people who are immoral and those who commit adultery (Hebrews 13:4). Without God in their life or marriage a couple will not understand the importance of faithfulness, trust, commitment, sacrifice, understanding each other's differences, communication and mutual submitting to one another out of reverence for Christ (Ephesians 5:21-33).

Romans 15:1-2 states...We should please others. If we do what helps them, we will build them up in the Lord. A constant desire to build each other up and to enhance each other's value is very important to a marriage. A godly, good husband or wife should bring many great blessings to the other. The next time something irritates you about your spouse, keep in mind the blessings your mate brings to you as well…precious times, trust, satisfaction, fulfill needs, helpfulness and happiness.

The person we marry can build us up or destroy us. The Bible encourages us not to marry an unbeliever, for it is too easy for that person to tempt you away from God (2 Corinthians 6:14).

God compares our marriage with our relationship with him which is based on mutual love, faithfulness, and permanent commitment. If we are taking our marriage as a sacred covenant with total value to our vows to our spouse and with God, we will bring honor and glory to God! Does your marriage line up with the Word of God, does it bring glory to God, or does it need looking into? Does your marriage seem like a battleground or a sanctuary? Try looking at it through God's eyes.

DOES GOD CARE WHEN BAD THINGS HAPPEN IN THE WORLD?

"The wages of sin is death, but the gift of God is eternal life in Christ Jesus our Lord" (Romans 6:23).

There are bad things that happen all the time and there are tragedies every day. At some time in life everyone will experience one or the other. The important thing is when something bad happens to someone do they learn from it? As an example: if a ten-year-old boy darts into the street behind a parked car without looking and is almost hit by the oncoming car, realizing he could have been killed. Did he learn his lesson? He better have, he might not get another chance!

Each situation in life, good or bad is a learning experience. Does God care that we learn important lessons about studying or safety? He cares very much!

You can ask many people who have experienced bad situations if they learned anything from going through them. Then ask what they learned from them. Most people will agree they did learn a hard lesson which they would be aware not to repeat them. Going through tough times is bad only when you don't learn from these experiences.

Unfortunately, no one is immune from what we believe is the ultimate tragedy...death. Even Jesus went through the loss and grief of someone he loved (see John 11). It is the timing of death (especially when someone dies young), and how it occurs (like an innocent victim killed by a drunk driver), that makes us wonder if God really cares.

When Adam and Eve disobeyed God, their punishment was separation from God. This incident also set in motion the life cycle, ending in death. But the good news is that Jesus Christ's death on the cross killed death! Not physical death, but spiritual death. But all those who receive Jesus and his gift of forgiveness will not experience spiritual death. Since the time of Adam, man has discovered many other ways of physical death, such as the nuclear bombs, lung cancer, AIDS, and many more.

Still as terrible as those may be, God knows that spiritual death is far worse that physical death. That's why he focused his attention on taking care of the real penalty for our sin...spiritual death! God also knows how tragedy can point us to Him and his purposes: "And we know that all that happens to us is working for our good if we love God and are fitting into his plans" (Romans 8:28).

Although God is not in heaven pushing buttons to make people die young, He can use any situation the devil meant for bad, God can use for good and for his glory! Remember, whatever happens to you, God DOES care! He is interested in every detail of your life! He knows every detail of your life, what you did and what you will do! He knows what you think and what's in your heart and mind at all times. God loves you and wants his best for you and He wants to bless you and work out his great plan for your life! God is always with you! Some people never realize this because their minds are earthbound and their hearts are closed to God. Others hear his voice once or twice in their lifetime, in rare moments of seeking Him above all else. His desire for His "sheep" is to hear His voice continually, for "I am the ever present Shepherd." Quietness is where you learn to hear His voice. Beginners need a quiet place in order to still their minds. As you advance in this discipline, you will gradually learn to carry the stillness with you wherever you go (Jeremiah 29:12-13; John 10:14, 27-28).

DEATH IS NOT THE END!

Many non-Christians do not believe in heaven or hell, God or a devil, or the hereafter. But yet they ask themselves the nagging question of "Why are we here? Why was I born? What is my purpose?" Because they do not understand or won't believe, their fear of death and the unknown only worsens and they will not know the answers to these questions. If they could only allow themselves to admit the possibility of the supernatural, and the unseen, and acknowledge the fact that the gospel, and a heaven and hell is true and Jesus is our Savior and then apply this truth to their life, they would come to know the fear of death is removed and the glorious peace of believing is now part of their life. There truly is a hereafter where we as believers will live eternally with Jesus in joy, peace, love and with no more pain, or hurt.

When you believe, you truly can have peace in your heart, and those nagging questions will be answered and you can have the assurance of salvation. If you will humbly acknowledge yourself as a sinner in God's sight, asking for His forgiveness and the cleansing by the blood of Christ shed on the cross, and trust in Jesus, God's Son, as your Savior and Lord He will forgive you and welcome you into the family of God. This can be your greatest experience today as you turn in faith to Christ and give your life to Him. God desires to bless you and give you the abundance of life. Read the Bible and learn of the God who loves you and died for YOU! Don't be an unbeliever anymore! Don't harbor the fear of death or the unknown anymore! Death only comes to those who do not believe and their spirit will go to a real HELL.

FASTING FOR CHANGE...

Shared from Bible study and Pastor Lou's Sunday Message

Breakthrough and change need prayer and fasting

(Matthew 17:21).

Breaking only happens through breaking and fasting brings

new opportunities, new seasons and anointing

(Dan. 10:1-4a; Acts 13:2; Neh. 1:4).

Fasting is going without voluntarily, generally for religious purposes. To fast "is to give up" for a period of time, such as food, or other items, such as TV, computer, Facebook, or anything that would take your time and attention from focusing completely on God. You want to feed your spirit, not your flesh! If you want breakthrough, or new opportunities, or break a habit, or going deeper with God it will take fasting and prayer together. Give to God, first your time, talent and your finances, give Him this year, you will never be disappointed when you give your all to God! Ask God to open your spiritual eyes so you can put yourself in position, change what has to be changed in your life. Don't stay stagnate, and don't give up, expand your souls growth, go deeper, get more of God! Allow God to flow and bring anointing. The flesh needs to be broken...break the fingerprint of the devil by invading the devil's territory of doubt and fear. He will give you opposition, so be ready for it. In the Bible, fasting could also mean a sign of distress, or repentance. Fasting is a spiritual discipline promoted in scripture. Jesus, Peter, the apostles, Moses, Elijah, Esther, Daniel, and many others fasted on a regular basis. Fasting is important for it is an expression of faith and spiritual diligence; it is to deny the flesh in order to emphasize building one's spirit and becoming more in tuned with the work of the Holy Spirit. Through fasting one can experience spiritual renewal, deliverance from sin, receive guidance from the Holy Spirit, receive answers to prayers, and develop greater spiritual discipline.

The law of Moses specifically required fasting for only one occasion...the DAY OF ATONEMENT (Jer. 36:6; Acts 27:9). Moses did not eat or drink water during the 40 days he was on Mount Sinai receiving the law (Ex. 34:28).

Jehoshaphat called a fast in all Israel when opposed by the Moabites and Ammonites (2Chr. 20:3). Reacting to Jonah's preaching, the men of Nineveh, at the king's order, fasted and put on sackcloth (John 3:5). Esther and the Jews of Shushan fasted when faced with the destruction planned by Haman (Esth. 4:3, 16; 9:31). In times of grief, people fasted. A seven-day fast was held when the bones of Saul and his sons were buried (1 Sam. 31:13; 1 Chr. 10:12). Fasting was also done by individuals in times of distress. David fasted after hearing that Saul and Jonathan were dead (2 Sam. 1:12). Nehemiah fasted and prayed upon learning that Jerusalem had remained in ruins since its destruction (Neh. 1:4). Darius, the king of Persia, fasted all night after placing Daniel in the lion's den (Dan. 6:18).

In the prophet Isaiah's time, people complained that they had fasted and that God had not responded favorably (Isa. 58:3-4). The prophet declared that the external show was futile. The fast that the Lord requires is to loose the bonds of wickedness, undo the wickedness, feed the hungry, shelter the poor, and clothe the naked (Isa. 58:5-7).

Fasting also occurs in the New Testament. Anna at the Temple "served God with fastings and praying night and day" (Luke 2:37). John the Baptist led his disciples to fast (Mark 2:18). Jesus fasted 40 days and 40 nights before His temptation (Matt. 4:2).

> "Then I proclaimed a fast...that we might humble ourselves before our God, to seek from Him the right way for us and our little ones and all our possessions. So we fasted and entreated our God for this, and He answered our prayer"
> (Ezra 8:21-23).

FISHING FOR SOULS

A fisherman once said, "No use fishing where they ain't," as he scanned the river for 15 minutes. That statement reminds us of a question: "Do I fish for souls where they ain't?" It was said of Jesus that he was a friend of tax collectors and sinners (Luke 7:34). As Christians, we are to be unlike the world in our behavior, but squarely in it as Jesus was. So we have to ask ourselves: "Do I, like Jesus, have friends who are sinners? I may be fishing for souls where they ain't." Being with nonbelievers is the first step in "fishing." Then comes love… a heart-kindness that sees beneath the surface of their offhand remarks and listens for the deeper cry of the soul. Such love is not natural instinct. It comes solely from God. So we pray: "Lord, when I am with nonbelievers today, may I become aware of the cheerless voice, the weary countenance, or the downcast eyes that I in my natural self-preoccupation, could easily overlook. May I have a love that springs from and is rooted in Your love. May I listen to others, show Your compassion, and speak Your truth today." Let us be as channels of God's truth that flows and as reservoirs that stay contained. Step out of your comfort zone and have a sensitive spirit to any unbeliever that the Lord sends your way. You may be the only Bible they will know or hear especially if their time has come. None of us know when our time is up so we have to be prepared and ready to share the Gospel in season and out, whether convenient or inconvenient. Also, be patient and instruct those who do not understand or accept it.

"Preach the Word! Be ready in season and out of season.
Convince, rebuke, exhort, with all longsuffering and teaching"
(2 Timothy 4:2).

"But you be watchful in all things, endure afflictions,
do the work of an evangelist, fulfil your ministry"
(2 Timothy 4:5).

FELLOWSHIP WITH THE FATHER AND SON

"That which we have seen and heard declare we unto you,

that ye also may have fellowship with us;

and truly our fellowship is with the Father,

and His Son Jesus Christ" (I John 1:3).

One of the greatest privileges of being saved is fellowship with the Father and Son. There is no greater joy than that of being in the presence of the Father and Jesus.

You have the blessing of fellowship with the Father and Son as a result of Jesus' suffering for your sins. There is no sin that the blood of Jesus cannot cover.

Strong faith is a product of close fellowship with the Father, Revelation knowledge flows out of intimate communion. As you come to know Him more personally, you come to know your victory in Him.

Walking in victory is not achieved simply by following a formula. Walking in victory is only a result of walking in fellowship with our Father and Jesus.

I encourage you to seek Jesus; don't just seek victory and success. "Seek ye first the kingdom of God…and all these things shall be added unto you" (Matthew 6:33).

The Father desires that we fellowship with Him. You need only acknowledge that your fellowship is with the Father and Son. Your fellowship is based upon promises in God's Word. Therefore, you stand in faith in this blessing.

Make this bold confession: My fellowship is with the Father and Son, Jesus Christ. I only hear the voice of the Shepherd. I will not hear the voice of any stranger. My fellowship is intimate and unbroken.

GOD WANTS US TO BE LIKE JESUS

Jesus talked about the Pharisees. These men had created long lists of dos and don'ts about behavior of every kind. They wanted to be pure. Many of them were very good. But in Matthew 5:20, Jesus made an incredible statement! "I warn you—unless your goodness is greater than the Pharisees and other Jewish leaders, you can't get into, the Kingdom of Heaven at all!" Wow! If the Pharisees couldn't make it, who can!

Those who make it into the Kingdom of Heaven are not just pure on the outside, like the Pharisees. Anyone can make sure their behavior is correct, at least for a while. Jesus was talking about being pure on the inside. This begins by accepting Christ's death on the cross as punishment for our sins. When we do this, we take on Christ's goodness, and, in God's eyes, we are pure and worthy of eternity in heaven.

It doesn't stop there, of course. God wants us to be like Jesus. This is a lifetime process of allowing God to mold us and change us. It happens by staying close to Christ and living like He wants us to. It's what keeps the Christian life fun, interesting and challenging.

A Christian who's really alive realizes that his or her eternity is settled. But they also genuinely want to be more like the one who paid such a high price for their soul: Jesus. His motivation is not to parade his goodness in front of others, but rather to please God.

Staying pure and growing as a Christian are "full-time jobs." But they are also natural byproducts of staying close to Christ and don't give up: "But as for you, brethren, do not grow weary in doing good" (2 Thessalonians 3:13). "Fight the good fight of faith, lay hold on eternal life, to which you were also called and have confessed the good confession in the presence of many witnesses" (1 Timothy 6:12).

GOD SO LOVED THE WORLD

"For God so loved the world that He gave
His only begotten Son, that whoever believes in Him
should not perish but have everlasting life"
(John 3:16).

God Is love! God wants us to know He loves us with agape love which is a freely unconditional and consistent and unfailing love. Agape is love that absolutely does not need any reciprocation, whatsoever. It is relentless, it is persistent, and it is aggressive. It will not take "no" for an answer. His love will never fail or fade away! This is God and He loves YOU! It is not like a worldly love which is phyllo; an earthly love of feelings and emotions; God's love is not like that. God's love is deep, spiritual, another dimension; a love by choice and by an act of the will. His love denotes unconquerable, aggressive, benevolence and undefeatable goodwill. It will never seek anything but the highest good for fellow mankind. His love does not need a chemistry, or feeling. God wants us to know, realize and understand He loves us with all His being! Let that sink in! When you realize His great love for you, your life is changed. He actually is obsessed with us! His love cannot be seen through the eyes of the world. He "treasures" us, which means, God has great value for us! He wants us! He didn't have to love us, but He did! We are His inheritance. We don't have to perform for Him to receive His love. God knew everyone of us while we were still in our mother's womb. He knew we would fall, He knew when and whether we would do bad or good things but He still wanted us! He knows things about us that no one knows and He still loves us! God won't force you to receive His love, or force you to return your love. It has to be our choice or it won't be love. He doesn't want robots. But God picked YOU...He chose YOU! You didn't pick Him. He wanted you and when you understood that, you wanted Him. The more you knew about God and His love for you the more you wanted an intimate relationship with Him. What moves God's heart for us is not our love for Him; it's His love for us! God moves God! It's His love for us that compels Him to move. God will move mountains for us. When God sent His Son to die for us, He gave; He gave his very best for us...His Son! He loved broken people and He was so obsessed with us that He gave His all! Remember, God knows who you are, who you were, and who you will be and He loves you. Because you are known by God, you don't have to pretend about anything. This alone allows a depth to your relationship with Him. Realize, we have value in His sight; we have worth! If we desire Him as much as He desires us, we will have a personal intimate relationship with Him. GOD IS LOVE AND HE LOVES YOU!

GIVE GOD YOUR BEST AND THEN EXPECT HIS BEST

Giving God our best, then asking Him for His best is God's way of doing things and our way of doing it with Him. This is how Jesus can keep His Word to us by telling us nothing shall be impossible unto you (Matthew 17:20). And it's how He will make a way for us where there is no way.

Once you have been converted and believed Christ to save your soul, and become your personal Savior, and understand the love of Christ and who you are in Jesus; turning your life over to Jesus, you become a disciple: "If any man will come after me, let him deny himself, and take up his cross daily, and follow me" (Luke 9:23). The key word is daily. It's not in one day or one act, but turning one's life over to Christ and being willing to daily follow Christ to become His disciple. It is a continuous daily action of becoming more than what you have been doing. It is going from your start as a baby Christian, born into the kingdom of God (John 3:1-21), growing into an adult in Christ, into Christian maturity in which the living Christ is being daily formed in you (Galatians 4:19). It means you take on Jesus' own life and lifestyle. You daily discover His way of doing things and do them joyfully and continuously. Every day you try to give God your best, and then ask Him for His best.

It is taking up your cross. The cross to Jesus was the giving of himself in sincere acts of love and concern, in doing good to people, giving of His time and talent (calling) and efforts, giving of His resources until one day it was all given. As Christians, seed-faith giving as a way of life is taking up our cross daily. Why is it a cross? Because you and I as human beings have been taught get—not give. And when we give we are taught not to expect anything back from God. But Jesus opened up the way of giving, cheerfully and finding God's love coming back (2 Corinthians 9:7). Discipleship as Jesus teaches us is to take up your cross daily and gladly follow Jesus. Learn of Him and His ways and follow Him.

GOD DEALS WITH SINFUL HUMANITY

Imagine you're out on an evening run when you happen upon your dream car. As you admire its beauty, you notice a key in the ignition...and unlocked doors. The car seems to say, "Take me out for a quick spin." You glance around. The street is deserted. "But that would be stealing!" your conscience protests. "No way!" another voice blurs in. "You're not going to keep it." For an agonizing long moment the inner voice battles—then adventure wins out. Your heart pounds as you slide into the driver's seat and the engine begins to hum to life. "This is awesome!" you say, slipping the car into gear. You intend to make one slow trip around the block but the speedometer goes up to 160 mph, and when will you ever get another chance like this? You head for the open road. What happens next is a blur. You remember the exhilaration of 143 mph, then flashing blue lights, cold steel handcuffs, being in court, and the judge's gavel pounding out a guilty verdict. The sentence: $10,000 and six months' incarceration. You deserve punishment, but that's a severe penalty! Then the judge does something curious. He removes his rope, whips out his checkbook, and pays for your fine! Next he announces he will serve your jail sentence. Then he looks you in the eyes and says, "I love you." This analogy isn't perfect, but it does help explain how God deals with sinful humanity who sincerely repents. The very penalty he demands (death for sin), he provided (the death of Christ on the cross). Sin, as you know, means refusing to do God's will and failing to do all that God wants. Since Adam rebelled against God, it has become our nature to disobey God: "...for all have sinned and fall short of the glory of God" (Romans 3:23). But when we do sin, it cuts us off from God. We want to live our own way rather than God's way. Because God is morally perfect, just, and fair, he is right to condemn. No matter what our background or how hard we try to live a good moral life, we cannot earn salvation or remove our sin. Only Christ can save us! Our sin points out our need to be forgiven and cleansed. Although we don't deserve it, God in his kindness reaches out to love and forgive us. He provides the way for us to be saved. Christ's death paid the penalty for our sin. God oversees and cares about his people—past, present, and future: "But God demonstrates His own love toward us, in that while we were still sinners, Christ died for us" (Romans 5:8). God's ways of dealing with people is always fair, Because God is in charge of all creation, he can save whomever he wills: "For by grace you have been saved through faith, and that not of yourselves; it is a gift of God, not of works, lest anyone should boast" (Ephesians 2:8-9).

If you'd like an even better explanation of God's perfect justice and intense love for you, read the Book of Romans!

GOD IS SOVEREIGN OVER ALL OF HUMAN HISTORY, PAST, PRESENT, AND FUTURE

We can learn much from the Book of Daniel. "Daniel" means "God is my judge." Daniel understood that God is Sovereign, refers to the unlimited power of God who has control over the affairs of nature and history (Is. 45:9-19; Rom. 8:18-39). The Bible declares that God is working out His sovereign plan of redemption for the world and that conclusion is certain! Daniel spoke with wise words and actions. He spoke the truth, at all cost and did the right thing even if it looked as though he was the only one doing it. He didn't give in to pressures. Daniel had strong trust and tenacious faith in God. Pleasing God was more important to Daniel than pleasing anyone else. He was a man of prayer and felt comfortable talking with God because he did it all the time. He knew prayer kept him in touch with God. Daniel and his three friends, Shadrach, Meshach and Abednego are examples of faith, dedication and commitment. They were determined to serve God regardless of the consequences. They did not give into pressures from an ungodly society because they had a clear purpose in life: to glorify God! They were determined never to worship another god, and they courageously took their stand. Are you ready to take a stand for God no matter what? When you stand for God, you will stand out. It may be painful, and it may not always have a happy ending. We should all be ready to say, "If he delivers me, or if he doesn't, I will serve only the Lord" (Daniel 3:16-18). Continue to practice righteousness even when it may be socially frowned upon or politically prohibited (6:10-16).

Nebuchadnezzar's pilgrimage with God is one of the themes of Daniel. In chapter 2 verse 47, he acknowledged that God revealed dreams to Daniel. He praised the God who delivered the three Hebrews. Despite Nebuchadnezzar's recognition that God exists and works great miracles, in 4:30 we see that he still did not acknowledge God as his own ruler. Many people today still do not recognize God as our creator and Sovereign God. Some may recognize that God exists and does wonderful miracles, but God will not shape their life until they acknowledge Him as Lord. God sends many messengers to speak to his people, through preachers, teachers and concerned friends but people are still ignoring them. We have to be open to instruction and have a teachable heart. Trying times are before us that remind us of our weaknesses and inability to cope. We reach out for answers, for leadership, for clear direction. God's Word begins to interest even those who, in better times, would never look at it. We who are believers should prepare ourselves for opportunities to share God's Word in needy and confusing times. We must also prepare ourselves for persecution and rejection as we teach God's Word. We are in the middle of many trials and persecutions that make little sense. But they can purify us if we are willing to learn from them.

God is all-knowing, and He is still in charge of world events. God overrules and removes rebellious leaders who defy Him. Yes, God will overcome evil; no one will escape. We must know that God will judge and that everyone will give an account to God for his/her conduct (5:22-24; 5:25-28). He will, however, deliver the faithful who follow. Although nations compete for world control now, one day Christ will rule! Our faith is sure because our future is secure in him. We must have courage as Daniel and put our faith in God who is Sovereign and controls everything, whether we see it now or not, or even if you don't believe, it won't stop the fact that God is in control and He Is a Sovereign God! Trusting and obeying God should be our true purpose in life. This will give us direction and peace in any situation. We can trust God to take us through any trial because He promises to be with us. He is always faithful, so we should remain faithful to Him! Believers, live in such a way that no charge (except your commitment to your faith) can be found (6:4-9). The individual devoted to God affirms that the Lord is Sovereign and seeks to glorify His name (2:20-23). When facing threatening circumstances, turn quickly to the Lord for help and believe that God is able to deliver you from the most difficult circumstances.

GOD LOVES YOU PERFECTLY

"Cease striving and know that I am God…" (Psalm 46:10).

God understands us perfectly and loves us eternally. But it is our soul He loves rather than our appearance or performance. Sometimes because we are dissatisfied with both of these, we tend to focus too much on them. We have to break free from this self-preoccupation and just relax in His Glorious Presence and let his love soak into our entire being. This will help us to change our focus from our self to God. We are to stop striving and enjoy the Lord who is the center of our life, and know that He is God! The world abounds with idols…things that we turn to feel better about ourselves, such as eating, entertainment, exercise or the mastery of something or someone. But none of these things can satisfy the thirst of our soul which truly yearns for the Lord our God! These idolatrous substitutes only suppress our appetite for the Lord but they don't provide satisfaction. When we get this gnawing sensation, we need to realize we must return to the Lord and focus on Him and the love He has for us!

"O God, you are my God, earnestly I seek you; My soul thirsts for you, my body longs for you, In a dry and weary land where there is no water. I have seen you in the sanctuary and beheld your power and your glory. Because your love is better than life, my lips will glorify you. I will praise you as long as I live, and in your Name I will lift my hands. My soul will be satisfied as with the riches of foods; With singing lips my mouth will praise you" (Psalm 63:1-5).

GOD WILL HAVE THE LAST WORD

"You are of purer eyes than to behold evil"

(Habakkuk 1:13).

We like to know what is going on in the world but to watch the news is like watching a scary movie so many times we just turn away to avoid watching. God reacts to evil in a similar way. He warned the Israelites that He would turn away from them if they turned toward evil (Deut. 31:18). They did and He did (Ezek. 39:24). The prophet Habakkuk had not forsaken God, but suffered along with those who had. "Why do You show me iniquity," he asked the Lord, "and cause me trouble?" (Hab. 1:3). God's response to His confused prophet indicates that even when evil obscures the face of God, our inability to see him does not mean He is uninvolved. God said, "Look among the nations and watch—be utterly astounded! For I will work a work in your days which you would not believe, though it were told you (v. 5). God would judge Judah, but He would also judge the invading Babylonians for their evil (see Hab. 2). And through it all, the just shall live by faith" (2:4).

When world events cause you to despair, turn off the news and turn to Scripture. The end of the story has been written by our holy God. Evil will not prevail for God will have the last word!

HEAVENLY HARVEST HOME

"You also be patient. Establish your hearts, for the coming of the Lord is at hand" (James 5:8).

The hymn "Come, Ye Thankful People, Come" is often sung at Christian services. It was written in 1844 by Henry Alford. It begins with thanks to God for crops safely gathered in before winter. But it is more than gratefulness for the bounty of the land. The hymn ends by focusing on God's harvest of His people when Christ returns: "Even so, Lord, quickly come to Thy final harvest-home: Gather Thou Thy people in, free from sorrow, free from sin; There, forever purified, come with all Thine angels, come—raise the glorious harvest-home."

As we give thanks for material needs supplied, it's essential to remember that our plans are uncertain and our lives are a vapor that quickly disappears (James 4:14). James encourages us to be like a farmer waiting for his crops to grow and mature. "You also be patient. Establish your hearts, for the coming of the Lord is at hand" (5:8).

As we thank God for His faithful provision for our needs, let's turn our thoughts to the promised return of Jesus Christ. In patient expectation, we live for Him and look for the day when He will come to gather His glorious harvest home.

Come now, you who say, "Today or tomorrow we will go to such and such a city, spend a year there, buy and sell, and make a profit, whereas you do not know what will happen tomorrow. For what is your life? It is even a vapor that appears for a little time and then vanishes away" (James 4:13-14).

GOD'S GOAL

God's goal is not to overwhelm us with our sin so that we should become discouraged. He knows when to point out sin in our lives.

Some people are basically pretty "good" people when they come to faith in Christ. They don't have many destructive habits to overcome, and their parents have tried to teach them right from wrong. Others come with a lot of sin and "baggage." God tells us to come as we are, Jesus will clean us white as snow! Don't be afraid to come, for God loves you and wants to give you value and purpose and blessings!

Although each person is unique, we're the same when it comes to our nature—we're sinners. In fact, we were born with a sinful nature. This is called "original sin." And throughout our lives, we do all sorts of things that are wrong.

When we accept Christ as Savior, God makes us "not guilty." But this doesn't mean that we're perfect and don't sin anymore. We must daily deal with sin while we're still on earth. It's part of being human. Christians, like everyone, have two types of sin to deal with; past sins and present sins.

When we become Christians, all of our past sins are wiped away: "He has removed our sins as far away from us as the east is from the west" (Psalm 103:12). That's a distance that can't be measured!

Ideally, having past sins removed should also take our guilty feelings. We can put the past behind us. We're forgiven!

But what about our present sin? One of the roles of the Holy Spirit is to remind us when we sin. He doesn't do it to condemn us, but to prompt us to confess it, forsake it, and move on. God has forgiven us for these present sins, too. We confess them to Him to keep the communication channels open and to keep the relationship close. So we should talk to God about our lives, and confess, whenever we need to. And remember, sins aren't limited to doing what is wrong. They also include not doing what is right.

The passage in James 4:17 is plain: "Remember, too that knowing what is right to do and then not doing it is sin."

Let God do the convicting in your life, not others, and you'll be glad to confess your sins to Him. He's eager to clear away the barriers between you and himself and start fresh.

GROWING IN GODLINESS

Understand that your conduct is the most effective sermon we will ever preach. Live a life that will give consistent, undeniable evidence of the truth of the gospel: "Therefore, the prisoner of the Lord, beseech you to walk worthy of the calling with which you were called" (Eph. 4:1). We are to model our life after Jesus, imitating Him rather than others. Jesus is the perfect example of the love God requires: "Therefore be imitators of God as dear children" (Eph. 5:1). We must realize that thinking as the world does will unavoidably lead to sensuality and impurity. "This I say, therefore, and testify in the Lord, that you should no longer walk as the rest of the Gentiles walk, in the futility of their mind" (Eph. 4:17).

Be careful how you speak and what you say. We are to reject evil attitudes; and develop compassionate, forgiving attitudes toward others. "Let no corrupt word proceed out of your mouth, but what is good for necessary edification, that it may impart grace to the hearers" (Eph. 4:29). Use time wisely, and do not squander it. Be certain that we will give an account of how we use God's gift of time. ("See then that you walk circumspectly, not as fools but as wise, redeeming the time, because the days are evil" (Eph. 5:15-16)).

GROWING IN GODLINESS

We need to know and understand that we will give an account to Jesus as Judge for every thought, word, and deed. Let this influence our conduct. "For we must all appear before the judgment seat of Christ, that each one may receive the things done in the body, according to what he has done, whether good or bad" (2 Corin. 5:10). Appropriate the fact that God has called us to live for Him. We are to avoid any selfishness or personal ambition. "…and He died for all, that those who live should live no longer for themselves, but for Him who died for them and rose again. Therefore, from now on, we regard no one according to the flesh. Even though we have known Christ according to the flesh, yet now we know Him thus no longer" (2 Corin. 5:15-16). Holiness requires that we live according to God's standard, not that of the world. We need to live according to the truth of God's Word and the testimony of His Spirit. "For we walk by faith, not by sight" (5:7). The Word tells us to allow Jesus' strength to be exhibited and exalted through our weakness. Know that his grace is large enough to meet our needs in all our problems. "And He said to me My grace is sufficient for you, for My strength is made perfect in weakness" (2 Corin. 12:9). We are to practice regular, diligent self-examination. "Examine yourselves as to whether you are in the faith. Test yourselves. Do you not know yourselves, that Jesus Christ is in you?…unless indeed you are disqualified" (2 Corin. 13:5).

GUARD YOUR THOUGHTS DILIGENTLY

"Therefore, holy brothers, who share in the heavenly calling, fix your thoughts on Jesus, the apostle and high priest whom we confess" (Hebrews 3:1).

Sometimes our thoughts seem disconnected from our will. They go in every direction at once. This makes it difficult to focus on one thing. Though we deeply want to fix our thoughts on Jesus, but it is a constant struggle...like swimming against the current!

But we shouldn't be surprised because we know the enemy and his evil army hate our close relationship with the, Lord, so they are constantly interfering. Other factors that can disturb our spiritual focus are poor sleep, nutrition, health, lack of exercise, busyness and of course, our fallen nature. But it is still possible to exert much control over our thinking. We can ask the Holy Spirit to help us in this endeavor. We cannot afford to let our thoughts run freely! We must set a guard over them; be self-controlled and alert! When you become aware of wrong, hurtful and unholy thoughts, bring them to Jesus. He understands the struggle we have. As we persevere in making good thought choices, we will enjoy the refreshing Presence of the Lord more and more.

"Repent, then, turn to God so that your sins may be wiped out, that times of refreshing may come from the Lord" (Acts 3:19).

GOD'S WORD IS LOVE

"...for God is love" (1 John 4:8).

"In the beginning was the Word,

and the Word was with God" (John 1:1).

There are some people who might find some of the articles uncomfortable or disagreeable with their way of thinking. But let us be reminded that each article was written as a reflection and inspiration of the Word and is followed by Scripture. One should look up the Scriptures that is found in the article and ask our Father God what He is saying to you; what He wants you to do, or understand, or learn in your journey. We all need to keep learning and growing. As I write these articles, I too take it to heart as a step of growth, I have not arrived either! I cannot just write articles that people only want to hear. It would be similar to some people who only read parts of the Bible they like. If we are to grow spiritually mature, we must accept all of God's Word.

Father God is so much greater in wisdom and love for us than any earthly father, and He is determined to strengthen our life with his love and wisdom, salvation, and keep us on our spiritual journey and to prepare us for Heaven and teach us the ways of the Kingdom. His Word is his love toward each of us. Jesus said, "If you abide in My word, you are My disciples indeed. And you shall know the truth, and the truth shall make you free" (John 8:31-32).

If you find yourself disagreeable or uncomfortable with a teaching, or an article based on the Word of God and given with Scripture, you might realize your faith is being tested and stretched, or God wants to talk with you about something in your life that He wants to change. Don't dismiss any genuine bible teaching from a Pastor, or a spiritual leader, or even an article that is written with Scripture. Also do not dismiss the written Word of God...the Bible, the whole Bible, not just parts just because you disagree, or feel uncomfortable. Examine it, and pray about it first, or go to your Pastor or Chaplin for advice and guidance. If you choose not to do this you might miss out on one of the Father God's blessings for you and be prevented from being transformed from glory to glory (2 Corth. 3:18).

"All Scripture is given by inspiration of God, and is profitable for doctrine, for reproof for correction, for instruction in righteousness"
(2 Timothy 3:15).

GOD LOVES YOU PERFECTLY

"Cease striving and know that I am God…" (Psalm 46:10).

God understands us perfectly and loves us eternally. But it is our soul He loves rather than our appearance or performance Sometimes because we are dissatisfied with both of these, we tend to focus too much on them. We have to break free from this self-preoccupation and just relax in His Glorious Presence and let his love soak into our entire being. This will help us to change our focus from our self to God. We are to stop striving and enjoy the Lord who is the center of our life, and know that He is God! The world abounds with idols…things that we turn to feel better about ourselves, such as eating, entertainment exercise or the mastery of something or someone. But none of these things can satisfy the thirst of our soul which truly yearns for the Lord our God! These idolatrous substitutes only suppress our appetite for the Lord but they don't provide satisfaction. When we get this gnawing sensation, we need to realize we must return to the Lord and focus on Him and the love He has for us!

"O God, you are my God, earnestly I seek you My soul thirsts for you, my body longs for you, In a dry and weary land where there is no water. I have seen you in the sanctuary and beheld your power and your glory. Because your love is better than life, my lips will glorify you. I will praise you as long as I live, and in your Name I will lift my hands, My soul will be satisfied as with the riches of foods; With singing lips my mouth will praise you." (Psalm 63:1-5).

GET READY FOR THE COMING OF THE LORD! REPENT! (JOHN 1:23)

Most of us have read these words in the Book of John. We know that John the Baptist was sent from God to be a witness of Christ. In John 1:30 John the Baptist says, "He is the one I was talking about when I said 'Soon a man far greater than I am is coming, who existed long before me!' For God had told him "When you see the Holy Spirit descending and resting upon someone... he is the one you are looking for. He is the one who baptizes with the Holy Spirit" (John 1:33).

Although John the Baptist would be called unique, he was a well-known preacher and attracted large crowds. But John was not interested in being unique; he just wanted to obey God and he was not afraid to ask others to do the same. He stood face to face with people and told them to repent! He knew his job was to tell the world that the Savior was about to arrive. John's message still applies today! It is more crucial now! But one cannot receive the Savior until one knows they need Him, and they won't know they need Jesus if they don't realize they are sinners.

Believers, today the world needs to hear John's favorite word...repent! We too are called and anointed to make way...make straight the way of the Lord! This is not a time to be timid or pass the buck to someone else to do. Someone could be going to hell because you didn't want to share Jesus and his love and forgiveness. Believers...this is what we do! We are God's message of salvation! As true Christians who love the Lord and want to be obedient, we show compassion for the lost and care about their life and destiny! We feel as God feels... we don't want anyone to perish. Each of us have our ways of sharing Christ Jesus such as the way we live, going out of our way to show kindness, giving a helping hand, sharing a gift with a neighbor, showing godly character on our job, or actually anywhere. These are all opportunities that open a door to share Jesus, because they know you are different and they want what you have. People have had enough of anger, hate, violence, etc. So when a believer comes along, it becomes a refreshing moment of peace and relief. People, we need to remember, we have the Holy Spirit to help us to witness and how and where. We just need to be in tune with the Spirit! He will guide us to those whose hearts are ready and will listen. Just pray and ask the Spirit to use you! He will, you just need to be willing and have compassion!

People need to know good works won't get them a ticket to heaven. They need to know without repentance they face judgment. They need to know without Jesus there is no hope of Heaven or forgiveness because He is the way the truth and the life! Jesus is the only way to heaven! Body of Christ, we need to wake up before it is too late! The fields are ripe for harvest! Don't let regrets for a lost soul you could have saved haunt you. Come on, Believers…be a John the Baptist! Be obedient and do what you were called to do in the way you were meant to, since each one of us is unique!

Repentance is motivated by the realization that you have taken the wrong way in life. Repentance is made complete when one admits their sin and makes a commitment, with God's help, to change your life. Tell people…just come as you are…Jesus will do the rest to help you live the life He has for you. "…and you will also perish unless you turn from your evil ways and turn to God" (Matthew 3:1-3).

Repentance leads to forgiveness of sin!

GIVE FOR YOUR SAKE

"Bring all the tithes into the storehouse so there will be enough food in my temple. If you do...I will open the windows of heaven for you. I will pour out a blessing so great you won't have enough room to take it in! Try it! Let me prove it to you" (Malachi 3:10).

You don't have to give for God's sake. You give for your sake. God already has given to us when He gave His Son who gives us...the gift of life, the gift of love, the gift of salvation, and forgiveness and the gift of eternity, all of these which is priceless. The purpose of tithing is to teach us to always put God first in our life (Deut. 14:23). Also God commands it. But we should never give just to get something in return (for that violates giving as an act of love), God does promise bountiful blessings for those who obey.

This is an example of how tithing can teach us. Consider the act of writing a check for the offering, First you enter the date. Already you are reminded that you are a time-bound creature and every possession you have will rust or burn. Best you give it away while you can.

Then you enter the name of the one to whom you are giving the money. If the bank would cash it, you'd write...God. But they won't, so you write the name of the church that has earned your trust.

Next comes the amount...ah, the moment of truth. You're more than a person with a checkbook. You're David, placing a stone in the sling. You're Peter, one foot on the boat, one foot on the lake. You're a little boy in a big crowd. A picnic lunch is all the Teacher needs, but it's all you have. What will you do? Sling a stone? Take the step? Give the meal?

Careful now, don't move too quickly. You aren't just entering an amount... you are making a confession. A confession that God owns it all anyway!

And then the line in the lower left-hand corner on which you write what the check is for. It's hard to know what to put. It's for the light bills and literature, a bit for outreach, a bit for salary. Better yet, it's partial payment for what the church has done to help you raise your family...keep your own priorities sorted out. Or perhaps, best of all, it's for you! It's a moment for you to clip yet another strand from the rope of earth so that when He returns, you won't be tied up.

You might ask, "I'm barely making it with my budget, how can I afford to tithe?" If we're not careful, we will never think we have enough. The secret of happiness is learning to be content with what we have, whether it is much or little, and learning to live abundantly even with little (Phil. 4:11-12). God will give generously and provide all you need. Then you will have everything and plenty left over to share with others (2 Corth. 9:8). Second Corinthians 8:12 tells us if we are really eager to give, it isn't important how much we are able to give. God wants us to give joyfully with what we have, not what we don't have. While the Old Testament specifically talks about giving one-tenth of what we make to God, the New Testament encourages us to give what we can, to give sacrificially, and to give out of a grateful heart. For many, this will mean giving far more than one-tenth!

"You must each make up your own mind as to how much you should give. Don't give reluctantly or in response to pressure" (2 Corinthians 9:7).

HOW IMPORTANT IS IT THAT YOU ARE AN EXAMPLE OF CHRIST JESUS?

This world is so upside down in morality that if a Christian started to really act like Jesus it would surely get their attention! Can you imagine yourself laying your hands on the sick and seeing them healed before your eyes, or sharing the Word of God to someone, and they fall to their knees, crying, repenting and accepting Jesus? Would you be surprised if your neighbors came over and said they wanted to go to church with you because they want to be like you… you are so different, we want what you have. Or how about this, you are driving down the highway and you see this terrible accident. You stop and run over there, you see the person is dead but you start praying and laying your hands on that person and you bring them back from the dead! Or, you encounter a person who needs deliverance from demons, you again pray the powerful Word of God and because you are so sure of who you are and the power you have in Jesus, you have set this person free from these demons! You might say, "This is great, but impossible."

Didn't Jesus do all this and then say, "Most assuredly, I say to you, he who believes in Me, the works that I do he will do also; and greater works than these he will do, because I go to My Father. And whatever you ask in My name, that I will do, that the Father may be glorified in the Son. If you ask anything in My name, I will do it" (John 14:12-14). He is talking to Spirit empowered believers. It doesn't mean we will do much greater works than Jesus, but rather in volume and numbers. This is the example of Jesus the world needs to know.

In our day-to-day routine we might forget that "I have been crucified with Christ; it is no longer I who live, but Christ lives in me, and the life which I now live in the flesh I live by faith in the Son of God, who loved me and gave Himself for me" (Galatians 2:20). You know what that means, WE ARE DEAD! We are dead to our old self; we are a new creation with Christ Jesus in us: "Greater is He that is in us than he that is in the world" (1 John 4:4). This means if you are filled with Jesus and the spirit of power, divine life flows through you. We were created to have dominion on earth. Jesus has given us grace and righteousness in order that we might reign on earth. But if you are just living your own life, the way you want day to day, you are doing NOTHING! You will show the world NOTHING! One has to live as Jesus and for Jesus, be obedient to the Word and give God glory by the works we do, pray every day, and worship the Lord each day. Jesus was obedient to the Father and did only what the Father said. Jesus got alone to pray to the Father often. Obedience always brings blessings.

If a Christian does not realize he or she is dead to their self and they belong to Jesus now and was bought by the blood of Jesus and sealed with the

Holy Spirit and their life is not their own, they will do NOTHING for the Lord and NOTHING for this world. If one does not go to church and hear the Word and fellowship with other Christians, or read and study their Bible, or pray and worship and fellowship with Jesus, they will not know Jesus, or will they know what He has promised to them as their inheritance and will have to deal with more than they need to. And how will they hear the voice of the Lord, or know the guidance of the Holy Spirit? They will never be the example the world needs to see! If this is you Christian, consider the difference you COULD make in the world, pray and let Jesus help you find your way. You are important and loved by God! Come on, Christian, you can do it!

HOW WILL YOUR SEARCH END?

How will your search end? You could reject Christianity, writing off Jesus as insane or a liar and then pursue some other faith. You could abandon your spiritual search altogether as a hopeless cause that can never lead to truth. Or you could become a Christian.

Let's say you have found in Christ what you were looking for. It's been an honest, sincere search neither impulsive nor superficial and you're ready to go forward, to follow through on what you have found. You are ready to enter into a relationship with God through Christ. What do you do next? The Bible points to four simple but very important steps.

Step one: You need to own up to the truth about yourself and own up to what God sees. He sees someone who is precious to him but in rebellion. You have to admit that you have rejected his leadership and are, quite frankly, a sinner in need of a Savior. The first step toward becoming a Christian involves total honesty and self-awareness that you are a sinner before a holy God. "If we say that we have no sin, we are only fooling ourselves, and refusing to accept the truth" (1 John 1:8).

Step two: You must be willing to repent. When you repent of your sins, you are going beyond just admitting them—you want to turn from them. You realize you have rebelled against a holy God, and you are sorry. You want to alter the course of your life and move away from your pattern of sin.

Step three: The third step involves believing the message God has given in the Bible. The message of the Bible is that Jesus was God in human form. As a man, Jesus lived a perfect, sinless life. He was kind, gentle, patient and sympathetic and He loved people. He worked miracles and taught people how to live lives that honored God. Then He died and was raised from the dead to take away the sins of the world and to become the Savior of all people. The Bible was written for this purpose; that we would believe. In fact, the Bible says that "if you confess with your mouth that Jesus is Lord and believe in your heart that God raised him from the dead, you will be saved" (Romans 10:9).

Step four: Now you are ready to just reach out and receive the free gift of what Christ did for you through his death on the cross. The Bible says, "For the wages of sin is death, but the gift of God is eternal life in Christ Jesus our Lord" (Romans 6:23). If you have taken the final step here is how you pray: "Jesus, forgive me. I am a sinner and I need You as my Lord and Savior. I want to live a life that honors God. I believe You are the Son of God who died for my sin. I thank you now I am saved! Amen."

If you now have given your life to Christ you need to tell someone, and then find a good Bible-teaching church that will help you grow in the knowledge of God's love and your purpose and plan God has for you. For those who are not ready to commit to Christianity, please keep seeking. It is the most important search of your life, one that hopefully will not end until you find a relationship with God!

HOW YOU SEE YOURSELF WILL DETERMINE YOUR VICTORY OR DEFEAT

"And we were in our own sight as grasshoppers,

and so we were in their sight"

(Numbers 13:33).

How well does the devil see you? Are you a threat to him or does he walk all over you? It's all up to you. The key to defeat or failure lies in the Scripture (Numbers 13; 33). It's what you are in your own sight that will make the difference between failure, defeat or victory. It was because the Israelites were so terrified, and saw themselves as grasshoppers and the enemy as giants they were a failure. They saw themselves so small. It was in their own sight that defeated them.

If we in our own sight see ourselves weak, a powerless Christian, we too will fail. For we cannot put the fear of God in the devil and put him on the run if we ourselves are not convinced in our faith or know who we are in Christ Jesus and the power that has been given to us through our Salvation, the Word and the Holy Spirit; how can we expect to have victory? But when we see ourselves as God sees us, a conquering son or daughter of the Almighty God, equipped with the very power of God Himself, the devil will want to steer clear away of us! The devil would rather do anything than come against someone who's bold and courageous because he's a coward himself. He shutters at the very Name of Jesus and the power it has!

If you want to put the devil on the run, be strong in the Lord and in your own sight! Be full of God's Word and the Holy Spirit and let the devil find out just what it feels like to be a grasshopper!

THANK THE LORD

"Enter into His gates with thanksgiving, and into His courts with praise. Be thankful to Him, and bless His name" (Psalm 100:4).

The heart of the Lord tells us to thank Him for the very thing that troubles us. If we don't, we find ourselves on the brink of rebellion, and anger, and tempted to indulge in complaining about His treatment of us. But once we step over this line, rage and self-pity can sweep us away. The best way to come against this indulgence is thanksgiving! It is impossible to thank the Lord and complain and get angry against him at the same time. Thanking the Lord for trials seems awkward at first, but when we persist, and understand why we need to go through them with our thankful words, prayed in faith, will eventually make a difference in our heart. Then His presence will overshadow our problems. A trusting response of including Him in our thoughts as we deal with the situations washes the fear and distrust away. The Lord's continual Presence is a promise, guaranteeing that we will never have to face anything alone. It grieves the Lord when we are not aware of His valued, powerful Presence (Ephesians 4:30). But when we walk through a day in trusting dependence on Him, the Lord's heart is soothed. When we find ourselves wandering away on our own, we need to gently bring our attention back to the One who loves us, longs to bless us and guide us and wants only the best for us. Jesus looks for persistence...rather than perfection in our walk with Him.

"When you are in distress, and all these things come upon you in the latter days, when you turn to the Lord your God and obey His voice for the Lord your God is a merciful God. He will not forsake you nor destroy you, nor forget the covenant of your fathers which He swore to them" (Deuteronomy 4:30-31).

HAVE YOU THOUGHT ABOUT YOUR FUTURE?

"I am the way, and the truth, and the life.

The only way to the Father is through Me"

(John 14:6).

We all at times think about our future. Many of us have longed to get just a peek at what lies ahead for us. Sometimes our motives are good...we want to make a wise decision about marriage, or a job, raising our children, or changing our home location. Sometimes our motives are not so good. But in either case God seldom reveals the future to us, probably because we would want to change it. Or maybe we just couldn't handle knowing what was going to happen to us. If we did know the future, we could be robbed of the freedom to choose and discern, and to grow in maturity as we learn to trust God to lead the way. God did pull aside the curtain for the apostle John and showed him the end times. But God had a good reason for giving John this glimpse of the future. It was so he could share it with us, God wanted to give us hope and assurance that He truly will conquer death and evil and that we truly will live with Jesus forever and in perfect peace.

God is in ultimate control of the world's outcome and his promises of eternal life to believers are reliable. Meantime, we must stay faithful to God through our trials, troubles, suffering or persecution. Only then will our faith prove itself genuine.

One cannot experience a fellowship with Christ when one is on the other side of the door unless it's open. Jesus stands at the door of your heart knocking and saying, "If you hear Me calling and open the door, I will come in and we will share a meal as friends" (Revelation 3:20). Jesus stands on the outside of your heart and knocks, wanting to come in. If you have not yet opened the door for Jesus, you might want to picture this.... Picture yourself on the other side of the door to heaven. You stand there knocking and it does not open! You are then excluded forever! Or, you could ask Jesus into your heart as you stand at the door of heaven knocking and it opens wide and Jesus welcomes you into his eternal home to live with Him forever. The first opening of the door is yours...the next one is his. If you want assurance of a heavenly future, ask Jesus into your heart NOW and pray this prayer: Jesus, I open the door of my heart and invite you in to live within me. I truly am sorry for my sins and I ask You to forgive me. I do believe You are the Son of God and I know You died on the cross for my sins and I thank You. Please come into my life and help me live the life You have for me. I now thank You for the assurance of the door of heaven to open for me when you call me home. If you have prayed this prayer, you are saved but continue on by going to a Bible-teaching church that teaches the Word and ways of God. Learn who God is through your Bible and through daily fellowship with Jesus in prayer.

HOW IMPORTANT IS FAMILY LIFE?

Family life today is failing drastically compared to God's plan for a family. The results speak for themselves; the crime, the run-a-ways, the suicides, the disrespectfulness toward parents and others, kids with guns, rapes, hit-and runs and the gangs. The facts indicate that many of the incarcerated in our prisons have come from broken and dysfunctional homes. Kids want to be loved, and belong and if they can't find it at home within the family, they will look for it wherever they are accepted. If there is no family love and guidance, acceptance or direction, your children will go astray. Also if either parent is on drugs or alcohol most likely the children or teens will follow in the same steps. We can't blame the children for our irresponsibility and neglect as parents. Many parents are too busy working their jobs and give there their children a key to the house. Parents don't have an idea what the kids are up to, or where they go or, who their friends are. I'm not saying all parents are irresponsible or not concerned for their children, but way too many are! Busy parents don't have time to even communicate with their children or, know what they are interested in or, what's on their mind. Children feel rejected when their parents aren't interested in them.

This is not God's plan for families. There is no greater institution, no better group of people to effect positive change in the world than the family who follows God's standard of a family. There is no better place to learn the essential principals of life than the family. Conversely, there is no group of people with more power and ability to destroy a person than a family. The failure of parents to teach spiritual truths to their children directly impacts their relationship with God and how they treat others. Family is the environment that shapes a child's lifetime direction! Proverbs 22:6 states, "Teach your children to choose the right path, and when they are older, they will remain upon it." Our responsibility as parents is to give our children spiritual training and explain the gospel of Jesus to them. Plus, we are to share spiritual experiences with them and remind them of their spiritual heritage (Ex. 10:2). Ephesians 6:1-4 tells us, "To love them and discipline them when necessary, and to teach them proper conduct; to be a good example," and Proverbs 29:15 states, "To discipline and reprimand a child will produce wisdom, but a mother is disgraced by an undisciplined child, and neglecting to teach your children spiritual truths and neglecting to discipline have tragic consequences."

I'm sure you now understand why families are important. As parents you have the choice of developing a strong godly, wise and loving family or a dysfunctional family! You are responsible for guiding your child's future and answering to God and bear the consequences if you choose the wrong choice and ignore God's plan for a loving family who loves one another, sympathizes with one another, and helps each other, being bonded together having tender hearts, and humble minds (1 Peter 3:8). As God abundantly cares for us, so we should joyfully care for our family, and pray for one another as well. How important is your family and does it follow God's standard of a family? Be careful parents that you are not raising your child to be incarcerated. You might want to make a few changes; ask God to help you bond your family together as He would have it.

HELL...THE PLACE OF ETERNAL PUNISHMENT

Hell is a word and a place not talked about, or preached about much. This is a vital mistake! For God's whole purpose is to save people from going to hell. God wants people to know hell is a real place! It's written in the Word, so one can count on it for being the absolute Truth because God can't lie, it's against his character. It's a real place that was really not meant for humans, but for evil angels and the devil. God sent Jesus into the world to save sinners through His death and resurrection. God does not want anyone to go to hell: "For God so loved the world that He gave His only begotten Son, that whoever believes in Him should have everlasting life" (John 3:16). God gave His best...His Son Jesus Christ. God gave His best for a reason, to get man back from Satan. God's deepest desire is to have everyone restored to Himself. But unfortunately, there are those who still choose to reject God.

Hell as a place of punishment translates Gehenna, the Greek form of the Hebrew word that means "the valley of Hinnom"—a valley just south of Jerusalem. In this valley the Canaanites worshiped Baal and the fire-god Molech by sacrificing their children in a fire that burned continuously. King Josiah put an end to this worship.

In the time of Jesus the Valley of Hinnom was used as the garbage dump of Jerusalem. Into it were thrown all the filth and garbage of the city, including the dead bodies of animals and executed criminals. To consume all this, fires burned constantly. Jesus used this awful scene as a symbol of hell. The word Gehenna occurs 12 times in the New Testament. It is used by Jesus in Matt. 5:22, 29-30; 10:28; 23:15, 33; Mark 9:43, 45, Luke 12:5. Jesus said hell was a place of worms, maggots, fire, and trouble. The evil ones there are full of remorse and torment (Mark 9:43-48). Jesus also said that hell would be "outer darkness...weeping and gnashing of teeth" (Matt. 8:12). Here the image is one of terrible loneliness: separation from God and man. Those who are consigned to hell will be put out into the inky blackness of eternity, with nobody to turn to or talk to constantly alone. They will suffer the remorse of knowing they had the opportunity to come into heaven with God but turned it down.

The Book of Revelation describes hell as a lake of fire burning with brimstone (Rev. 19:20; 20:10 14-15; 21:8). Into hell will be thrown the beast and the false prophet (Rev. 19:20). At the end of the age the devil himself will be thrown into it, along with death and hades and all whose names are not in the Book of Life. And they will be tormented day and night forever and ever (Rev. 20:10b).

The Bible speaks of a lake of fire reserved for the Devil and his angels (Matt. 25:41). As said before, human beings were never intended to go to hell, but those who reject God will one day follow Satan right into this eternal torment. There will be no exit from hell, no way out, and no second chance. That is why it is so vital that you know about hell and believe it's a real place of torture for all of eternity and for all those who don't choose to receive the pardon that God extends to all people through the Cross of Jesus Christ (Rev. 20:11).

Whether or not you believe in hell, or heaven, it is a fact that they are real places, and your spirit will most definitely go to one of these places at the end of your life on earth, depending on your choice. So choose carefully…choose Jesus as your Lord and Savior! "I am the way, the truth, and the life. No one comes to the Father (in heaven) except through Me" (John 14:6).

HITTING THE WALL

"I can do all things through Christ which strengtheneth me"

(Philippians 4:13).

As Christian believers, we are all running a race, a race of spiritual growth. As we are moving ahead with confidence with God's blessings, suddenly, wham! We hit the wall. When ongoing problems require us to stick it out over the long haul, our faith sometimes falters. Something unexpected shows up. It could be a financial problem, a problem on the job, a family problem or a spiritual problem. It could be a roadblock from the enemy, or a stepping stone forward that God wants us to overcome. Regardless of the form it takes the effect of "the wall" is the same. It stops us cold. That's when we need to make a choice. The question is, once we hit the wall, what do we do? We may be tempted to be discouraged and quit, to turn back in defeat. But if we do, it will stop the spiritual growth, a victory, or a blessing. Plus, we will have to face a similar problem until we learn to overcome and take charge and face this problem for what it is...a breakthrough for a blessed spiritual step forward, or a victory over the enemy. We must keep in mind God is sovereign over the circumstances in our life so there are always opportunities to be found in them. God will gladly give us Glory-strength; it is limitless and it is exceedingly potent because the Spirit Himself empowers us. The truth is, the more difficult our situation, the more treasure there is for us to discover in it. Ask any athlete. He will tell you because he too has been there. The truth is, it's tough. But if you want to be a winner you have to push through the wall! An athlete has to push his body to what seems the maximum even though his body is hurting and he feels he can't go on. Athletes call that "hitting the wall." The body says, that's all I can do, I can't do any more, I quit. But the seasoned athlete knows that "the wall" isn't the end. It's a signal that he's on the verge of a breakthrough. If he will just toughen up and push himself a little more, he'll reach a level of excellence he couldn't reach any other way. When we feel like the problem is too big and failure is breathing down our neck, that's when we have to press in. For we have to remember, the only Christian that fails is one who quits. When it gets tough...the tough get going! That's when our faith should tell us, God will enable us to break through that wall and keep on going! This is the time to press into the Word as never before. We can mediate on a scripture concerning our problem, and pray even if it takes days or weeks. Whatever it takes to break through to obtain our victory that belongs to us! We WILL get the victory that is ours, if we don't quit. All we have to do is punch one little hole in that wall of problems with our faith and the Word of God! Each time we do something that is hard that we need to do, even though we don't want to do it, our problem becomes easier to face and overcome, and it will strengthen our faith walk. It only takes one breakthrough like that to make a never-dying, never-quitting champion believer out of us!

Do you not know that those who run a race all run, but only one receives? Run in such a way that you may obtain it. And everyone who competes for the prize is temperate in all things.

Athletes who break the rules become disqualified: Paul's illustration stresses the necessity of self-discipline and the danger of flaunting one's liberties. Believers must practice self-denial and self-control even in matters that are morally indifferent. We cannot be like the lazy, irresponsible servant who hid his master's talent in the ground because he was disgruntled with his circumstances. He gave up and took the easy way out: blaming his hard situation rather than making the most of his opportunity (Matthew 25:14-30). The wise use of gifts and abilities entrusted to us results in greater opportunities, while their neglect results not only in the loss of more opportunities, but that which was entrusted to us. The truth is, the more difficult our situation, the more treasure there is for us to discover in it.

"We pray that you'll have the strength to stick it out over the long haul... not the grim strength of gritting your teeth but the glory-strength God gives. It is strength that endures the unendurable and spills over into joy" (Col. 1:1).

HOLINESS IS NORMAL

"But now you must be holy in everything you do,

just as God—who chose you to be his children—is holy"

(1 Peter 1:15).

Faith people know that they are not to conform to this world because the world is headed for hell. People who don't know God are putting so much trash in front of their eyes and in their ears. They watch so many ungodly programs and movies and think this is normal life. Their conscience is seared to a point where they don't know what is right or wrong. They hardly remember the Ten Commandments.

For us believers sin is not normal and all who believe in Jesus Christ are made holy. We are brought into a state of holiness not by what we do, but by what Jesus did for us. We also have the Holy Spirit to guide us and keep us on the right path. Obeying God and living in faith in Him is normal and our way of life. We need to spend time with Him in the Word and fellowshipping, worshipping and praying, feeding our hearts and minds teaches us how to live a godly and holy life. The Word teaches us God's exceeding great and precious promises. Our Bible is the last will and testament of Jesus Christ. It is a record of our inheritance. Everything that belongs to a believer has been written down in that Book and the smartest thing we can do is to find out what is in it! We base our prayers on it. The Word provides and makes us, stronger in our faith and our spiritual walk as we feed on the Word and meditate on the Word. Faith is what God needs from us to bring us to the place He has called us to be and to bring our dreams to come to pass. The word is a daily guide and has answer for anything we have to accomplish or overcome. Faith simply believes, and saying and obeying God's Word. As we open our Bibles, the Spirit of God will direct us to the words we need to empower us. God doesn't make us read the Bible, it's our choice. It depends on each person how much or how little attention we give. But to have strong faith for the reality of dreams to come true, it will take more time than just skipping lightly through the Word.

Holiness is simply being wholly dedicated and devoted to God and separated from the world's way of living and committed to right living and purity. Holiness is the absence of sin and evil, and wrongdoing. Holiness is much more than the absence of sin. It is the presence of righteousness, purity, and godliness. When we became Christians God makes us holy by forgiving our sins.

He looks at us as though we had never sinned. But while He sees us holy, we have not perfected holiness. We must still strive each day to be more like Jesus, more holy. Only when we get to heaven will we be completely holy. Meanwhile we must strive to be holy while we live in this world because.... "You must be holy because, I the LORD your GOD, am holy" (Leviticus 19:2). So each believer has a choice. God has given us His Word and through it He has set before us life and good, blessing and cursing. Now it's up to us to decide what we're going to do about it. What will you choose?

HOW DOES ONE KNOW IF THEY ARE A TRUE CHRISTIAN?

"He that believeth on Him is not condemned; but he that believeth not is condemned already, because he hath not believeth in the name of the only begotten Son of God" (John 3:18).

If we were to conduct a man-on-the-street interview, asking people what it means to be a Christian, we would probably receive several different answers. There are so many opinions what a Christian is. The basic definition is one who believes in the Lord Jesus Christ as Savior and Lord in their life. The one who does not believe is not a Christian. Jesus stated that definition in John 3:18.

Many who confess to believe in Christ may act like Christians to a certain degree, but they turn out to be imposters or simply misinformed about the nature of salvation. For example, 1 John 2:19 identifies some people who claimed to be Christians but eventually left the fellowship. One way you can identify false Christians is that they will abandon Christianity. But when they are interacting with true believers, it is some time difficult to tell them apart. Another example of a Christian is by their fruit: "You will know them by their fruits. Do men gather grapes from thornbushes or figs from thistles? Even so, every good tree bears good fruit, but a bad tree bears bad fruit" (Matthew 7:17-18).

Many people have doubts and wonder if they are saved. In 2 Peter 1:9-10 Peter explains how a believer can be assured of their salvation: "He that lacketh (the qualities of spiritual maturity) is blind and cannot see afar off, and hath forgotten that they were purged from their old sin. Therefore, brethren, give diligence to make your calling and election sure; for if ye do these things, ye shall never fall." There are certain Christians who can't remember that they have been saved. They lack the confidence of knowing they're saved. The manifestation of godly works in our lives assures us that something has transformed us. If we don't see those things, we may question whether any change took place. Therefore, Peter encourages us to make sure those qualities (faith, virtue, knowledge, self-control, patience, godliness, brotherly kindness, and love) are in our lives so we can have the security of knowing we're saved. So if you see these things in your life, you can have the assurance and it will confirm your salvation.

The visible proof to the individual, church and the world that you are a Christian is the attitudes and actions that are produced by the Holy Spirit in your life.

A tests by which you can prove to be a Christian is to ask yourself: (1) Do I confess Christ? Being truly saved is a matter of confessing, or agreeing that Jesus is the Christ (1 John 5:1). (2) Do I confess sin? If someone tells you he's a Christian but doesn't acknowledge his sin, don't believe him (1 John 1:6, 8). (3) Do you obey God's Word (1 John 2:3)? (4) Do you love others (1 John 2:10)? The issue in 1 John 2:3-11 is the objective moral test of a true Christian: obedience and love. If a person claims to be a Christian but is disobedient to God throughout his or her life, the apostle John says they "are a liar and the truth is not in him" and "He that saith, I know Christ, and keepeth not his commandments, is a liar, and the truth is not in him" (verse 4). We can identify a Christian because he keeps the precepts of Christ. ARE YOU A TRUE CHRISTIAN?

IT'S ALL ABOUT...JESUS

Let's face it, believers, at times the Christian walk can be difficult. The growing and stretching process can be painful. No matter how long you have been walking with the Lord, or who you are, we all fall short of the glory and need to continue to grow spiritually if we are to mature in our walk. If we are to reap those rewards in heaven, there is no short cut, we have to learn to walk upright, without spot or wrinkle.... so we have to continue on. As long as we stay focused on the Lord, He will be there to pick us up when we fall, help us wipe the dust off ourselves and start on our way again. When we do fall, and we will, we must not run from God, but to Him! He knows we fail at times, and He is not going to stop loving us, but He does expect us to come to Him when we do. Just as any loving father wants to help his child when they fail or fall, so it is with our heavenly Father. Our earthly fathers don't stop loving us because we do something wrong, but they do hope we will learn from our mistakes.

The important thing to remember is what we are going through at the moment is really NOT the issue! What is important is how we handle the issue. The devil would like you to think, the people involved in this circumstance are your enemies, but believers, we know that is a lie from the pit of hell! Anyway, we have to remind ourselves, no matter what the issue is, it's NOT about us...it's all about Jesus. We are NOT the important factor here... Jesus is! We seem to fail to realize as we are battling through these circumstances, that it is not us that should be lifted up, but Christ Jesus! At this time and moment we are thinking about...self. How can God open the windows of blessings to pour down on us if we have put Him below us through our worldly and carnal ways and we have exalted ourselves above Him? God has to be lifted up through our love, worship and by walking and talking His Word! We tend to think we have been unjustly treated and need to defend ourselves, but doesn't God say, judge not, for "vengeance is Mine says the Lord." Also His Word tells us in Psalm 103, verse 6, "The Lord executes righteousness and justice for all who are oppressed." So even when life is not fair, God will handle it, if we let it go and give it to Him. Plus there are benefits, blessings and rewards for handling these unfair issues in a godly way, here on earth and waiting for us in heaven. Yes, our hearts can deceive us, and the Word tells us it would, "Those things which proceed out of your mouth come from the heart, and they defile a man" (Matt. 15:18). We should always guard our hearts and let God rule in our hearts. God is always concerned with what is in our hearts, and that's why He reveals and tests what is in our hearts so we too can see if there is sin or evil hiding within it (Psm. 7:9). If we are to see God, our hearts need to be pure.... "Blessed are the pure in heart, for they shall see God" (Matt. 5:8). If we keep our hearts full of God's Word, we won't sin against Him: "Your Word I have hidden in my heart that I might not sin against You, O Lord" (Psm. 119:11).

These uncomfortable and hurtful issues we come up against actually help us to die to self, put the flesh down and the spirit in control! When we get deceived and caught up in petty sins, and spiritual compromises, it casts a shadow over our Christ-like example for others, leaving us to shame, guilt, bitterness and a pity party. Growing spiritually mature is a slow, dying to self process, and at times a painful experience. The apostle Paul tells us in Romans 12:17 "to live above reproach in the sight of men," and 1 Timothy 4:12 tells us, "Be thou an example of the believers in word, in conversation, in spirit, in faith, in purity." Our example will go a lot further than words, but we are to conduct ourselves in a way that will put to rest any question about whether we are a Christian believer. People around us need to see our love, faith and purity in every situation. Our home, our children, the neighborhood and place of work will learn from being the example God is calling us to be.

It surely is not easy walking the spiritual path, but the rewards are great, and we never walk alone! The Lord is right by our side to carry your burden! He said, "Cast your cares upon Me, for I care for you" (1 Peter 5:7); "Fear not, for I am with you; Be not dismayed, for I am your God, I will strengthen you, yes, I will help you, I will uphold you with My righteous right hand" (Isa. 41:10).

God reminds us to stir ourselves up, even when we don't feel we have the inner resources we need to do it. Everything IS within us: "He who is in you is greater than he who is in the world" (1 John 4:4). There IS faith, there IS power and there IS love.

So keep your focus, for we are all called to be conquerors. Don't lose sight of who you are in Christ Jesus, or your purpose on earth! Don't let the Devil steal your joy or your heavenly rewards that you could have by rising above those situations and issues of rejection and persecutions!

IS THERE MEANING TO LIFE?

We have gotten pretty "shockproof" about what we hear and read in the news nowadays. It is sad to hear about so many teens have committed suicide. Why…? Some have said, "They are just bored with life." What a statement to make about our world. The sad fact is that suicide is the second leading cause of death among American teenagers today. Many people, including young people, struggle to find meaning and purpose in life.

The message of Ecclesiastes is brutally straightforward. The writer, Solomon, tells us that he tried everything life has to offer (wine, women, and sex, drugs, and rock-'n-roll for those of today). His conclusion was to fear and obey God.

God is the only one who gives meaning to our lives. No God…no meaning! Think of it this way: without God, you are just a bunch of molecules thrown together by chance. If there is no God, you came from—and are headed toward—impersonal nothingness. Any attempt at finding purpose is utterly ridiculous, and doomed to failure. You might just as well be a lizard, or a rock, or nothing at all…if there is no God. Sounds pretty bleak, doesn't it? It absolutely is if we subtract God from the equation. This belief that there is no God and therefore no meaning is what has driven many, including some of the greatest minds in history, to despair, alcoholism, and even suicide. The noted historian Will Durant puts it this way: "The greatest question of our time is not communism verses individualism, not Europe verses America, not even the East verses the West; it is whether men can live without God."

The good news is: there is something more to life! We don't have to run pointlessly after illusions like a slightly more sophisticated version of a hamster on a treadmill. There truly is a personal God who created you, knows you by name, loves you, and wants you to know him intimately. He gives purpose and meaning to life as he calls us to follow him in his adventurous journey. If you're searching for meaning follow the writer of Ecclesiastes to its source: a lifelong personal encounter with God. Don't waste time by searching endlessly in despair for the meaning of your life, only to find God is truly the answer to your fulfillment, purpose, value. After finding the truth, that there is a real God who loves you, don't wait to join God's family by putting it off for another day, for you do not know what lies ahead tomorrow.

Amy, age 17, shares what she learned from reading Ecclesiastes and 1 Peter:

My best friend and I weren't speaking. We had had an argument, and I still stewed over some of the things she had said to me. I wasn't going to let her get away with treating me like she did. Then I came cross 2 verses: Ecc. 10:2: "A wise man's heart leads him to do the right, and a fool's heart leads him to do evil," and 1 Peter 4:8, "Most important of all, continue to show deep love for each other, for love makes up for many of your faults." As I read these verses over and over, whatever we had argued about became less and less important, and maintaining a friendship with someone who also knew God's love became very important. I also realized that there were some faults in me that needed forgiveness. I didn't waste any time. I called my friend on the phone, read her the passages, and told her I was sorry for letting something petty come between us. She was so glad I called and said she didn't feel right about us fighting. These verses clearly showed me how precious Christian friendship is; it's something to be guarded and treasured. I thank God for not letting me throw away the gift He had given to me in my friend, and for giving me a "wise man's heart," and helping me to work things out with my friend.

IS THERE A GOD?

Many people are still asking, "Is there a God? Is there a Supreme Being or Ruler of the universe? How can I be certain?" The answer to that question is of the utmost importance because, if there is a God and I ignore Him, what will the consequence be?

Throughout the ages of time people have felt compelled to worship something or someone greater than themselves. It is apparent that inside every person is something that longs to relate to a higher power.

One must ask themselves, "How can there be the harmony and balance of nature? Who put the calendar in the heads of the wild birds so they know when to migrate to a warmer climate? How do they know when to return? Who placed this instinct within them? Who put the map in the brain of the salmon that tells it how to leave its ocean home and find a river and the very stream where its life began?" Do you think it just happened by chance? I don't believe so!

We know the universe is so well ordered that clocks are set by the rotation of the earth and the various stars and planets. Who or what set this precise rhythm of the universe in motion? Is it only by chance that among the hostile environments of the heavenly bodies this earth has the right mixture of those elements necessary for plant and animal life?

The plan for the universe, for nature, for our bodies and our inner personal needs has been set in order by the GREAT GOD OF HEAVEN! No mortal man, past or present, begins to have such power! We cannot see God but we can see indications all around us that point to His existence. God reveals Himself to us as we accept His existence. One of the most convincing evidence that there is a God is the change that takes place in a person's life as he becomes intimately acquainted with Him. Where there was turmoil within, there is now a quiet peace. Where there are endless questions, there is now confidence. God changes the selfish person into one who cares for others, God reveals Himself through His Word, the Bible. The Bible is history; it is prophecy; it is instruction for life. But it is also God's love story to us which guides us and gives us direction for the inner needs of the soul. God takes great interest in man and his happiness.

It is going to take faith which means believing in something and someone we cannot see. God has intended that we could not see Him but rather that we could accept His existence by the obvious evidences which testify of Him.

Do you feel restlessness inside or a longing for something, but you are not sure what it is? Do you fill a need to fill a void in your life? Do not stifle that feeling or try to cover it up. It is your soul reaching out to God. If you believe and have faith in the God of heaven, your life can be changed. Instead of resenting the trying circumstances of life, you can rest in the knowledge that God sees and hears and cares for you! God is a God of compassion and a holy, righteous God who cannot tolerate sin. That is why He sent His Son Jesus to die on the cross and take our punishment for sins we have committed. But God also raised Jesus and Jesus lives and He is here to forgive you as you repent to Him and accept Him as your Lord and Savior and to receive the promise of eternal life in heaven. "Jesus is the only way, the truth, and the life; No man cometh unto the Father, but by Me" (John 14:6). Don't wait any longer, come to Jesus now. "If we confess our sins, he is faithful and just to forgive us of our sins, and to cleanse us from all unrighteousness" (1 John 1:9). Come, have faith and ask Jesus into your life and to be your Savior. You will have new life: "Therefore if any man (or woman) be in Christ, he is a new creature: old things are passed away; behold, all things become new" (2 Corinthians 5:17, and Galatians 5:19-23).

HOW IMPORTANT IS FORGIVENESS?

"But if you will not forgive, neither will your Father in heaven forgive your trespasses" (Mark 11:26).

The lack of forgiveness blocks access to the kingdom and to its marvelous power. We must understand that God forgives us of our sins as we forgive others (Luke 11:4) who has sinned against us. Forgiveness should be adopted into our daily prayer life as a discipline (Matt. 6:14, Mark 11:25). Jesus showed us how unforgiveness can restrict what God would do for us and others. He also teaches how the spirit of unforgiveness exacts its toll on our bodies, minds, and emotions. Every "kingdom" person is advised to sustain a forgiving heart toward all other persons. Kingdom privileges and power must not be mishandled (Matt. 18:18-35). This is not legalism nor is it a scare tactic. Rather, it states the seriousness of responsible forgiving and demonstrates how unforgiveness clogs the channel of communication and sanctification between God and His people.

The first person you probably have not forgiven is yourself. We have to remember God has forgiven us when we repented and made Jesus our Lord and Savior. He no longer remembers our past sin. He has already cleansed our conscience from dead works so we might serve God (Heb. 9:14). God cleanses us for service in order not to leave us with the guilt of past sin. We have to be free from ongoing conscious sin and rebellion against God! Obviously, we cannot have continuing sin in our lives and expect forgiveness. So, "If our heart does not condemn us, we have confidence toward God" (1 John 3:21).

The second person we have to forgive is God Himself. There are people who blame God because they are sick, or a child died, or a husband left, or they don't have enough money, Consciously or unconsciously they think all of these things are God's fault. You have to rid yourself of any bitterness toward God! God is love and He is not capable of doing wrong! He cannot sin or lie! But He is a holy, righteous, and just God! He tells us to be holy, because He is holy ("just as He chose us in Him before the foundation of the world, that we should be holy and without blame before Him in love…") (Ephesians 1:4).

The third thing you have to forgive is any member of the family. All must be forgiven! All lack of forgiveness has to be eliminated, especially toward every family member.

Finally, there has to be forgiveness for anybody else who has ever done anything against you. It may be that your resentment is justified. But if you want to see kingdom life and power flow in your life, it is absolutely imperative that you forgive! Forgive them to the point where you actually feel yourself cleansed of resentment and bitterness and are actually praying for them. If you do not, the lack of forgiveness will make it impossible for God's power to be released to and in you. The miracle life depends 100 percent on your relationship to God the Father. That relationship is built strictly on strength of His forgiveness of your sin.

FORGIVENESS IS THE KEY! Other sins can be present, and if your heart condemns you for something else, then of course you do not have confidence before God. But it is lack of forgiveness that most often comes between people and God.

HOW THE OLD AND NEW TESTAMENTS RELATE TO EACH OTHER

The Old Testament was given to us for several reasons. After explaining Creation, its main purpose was to point out the way to God's solution for the problem of mankind's sin. In Matthew 5:21-46, we see Jesus contrasting the Old Testament and the New Testament. Romans 7:7 tells us that the Old Testament Law was good because it showed us what sin was, and thus, showed us our need for a Savior. The Old Testament points directly to Christ as the Savior that we needed. There are dozens of verses that tell the exact place of Jesus' birth, his sinless life, his death on a cross, his resurrection, and his return. Though the Old Testament was written from about 1450-430 B.C., it predicted minute details about the life of Jesus! This also serves to prove the authority of the Scriptures. Also, the Old Testament is what helps the New Testament make sense. In Matthew 5, the beginning of the Sermon on the Mount, Jesus points to something that people had never heard before. The Old Testament speaks of sacrifices (picturing Jesus as the ultimate sacrifice) and having faith in God's promise. This was how God prepared the way for Christ.

"But now you need no longer worry about the Jewish laws and customs. Now you can really serve God; not in the old way, mechanically obeying a set of rules (the Old Testament) but in the new way, with all of your hearts and minds (the New Testament). Well then, am I suggesting that these laws of God are evil? Of course not! No, the law is not sinful, but it was the law that showed me my sin. I would never have known the sin in my heart-the evil desires that are hidden there—if the law had not said, 'You must not have evil desires in your heart.' But sin used this law against evil desires by reminding me that such desires are wrong, and arousing all kinds of forbidden desires within me!" (Romans 7:8).

If people feel fine without the law, why did God give it?... Because sin is real and dangerous. Imagine a sunny day at the beach. You have just plunged into the surf and you've never felt better. Suddenly you noticed a sign on the pier: "No swimming: sharks in water." Your day is ruined. Is it the sign's fault? Are you angry with people who put it up? Of course not. The law is like a sign. It is essential, and we are grateful for it—but it doesn't get rid of the sharks. And that's why we needed a Savior, Jesus and the teaching of the New Testament. The Old Testament showed us our sin but did not have the power to save us from our sin. The New Testament shows us we are forgiven of our sin by repenting and through the blood that Jesus shed for us, and accepting Jesus Christ as our Lord and Savior and how to live for Him.

Some people try hard to get right with God by keeping his laws. They may think church attendance, church work, tithing and being nice will be enough. This approach never succeeds. We can never earn God's favor by being good enough, for we can never be good enough! We all have to depend on Christ. Only by putting our faith in what Jesus has done will we be saved: "But the Jews, who tried so hard to get right with God by keeping his laws, never succeeded. They were trying to be saved by keeping the law and being good instead of depending on faith" (Romans 9:31-32).

HOW TO RECEIVE THE BAPTISM IN THE HOLY SPIRIT

The baptism of the Holy Spirit is not the same as when you received the Holy Spirit when you were born-again. You need to do a number of things in order to receive this blessing. First, you need to be born-again. The person who is going to be filled with the Spirit must have the indwelling Spirit and belong to Jesus (Rom. 8:9), describes two basic functions.

The second thing you have to do is ask. The Bible says, if we ask for the Holy Spirit, that prayer will be answered (Luke 11:8).

The third thing you have to do is surrender. The apostle Paul made this need clear in the Book of Romans when he said, "Present your bodies a living sacrifice" (Rom. 12:1).

Fourth, you must be willing to obey the Spirit. God does not give this power to someone and then say, "You can take the part you like and leave the part you do not like." If you want to be immersed in the Holy Spirit, you need to be prepared to obey the Spirit (Acts 5:32).

Fifth, you need to believe. The apostle Paul said, "Did you receive the Spirit by works of the law, or by hearing of faith?" You have to believe that if you ask, you will receive.

Finally, you have to exercise what God has given you. Having asked, having received, having been willing to obey, and having believed, you need to respond in a biblical fashion.

The Bible says those baptized with the Holy Spirit on the Day of Pentecost "began to speak with other tongues, as the Spirit gave them utterance" (Acts 2:4). This means they spoke the words that the Spirit gave them. There was action based on faith, not merely passive acceptance of the blessing. That is the way it is with God. God is offering the baptism in the Holy Spirit to people who need only to reach out and take it and enjoy the blessing.

In regards to those who "received" the Holy Spirit, and now speaks in "tongues" the Bible describes as two basic functions of speaking in tongues: it is for personal edification and for public exhortation. Speaking in tongues (or a language you do not understand) functions as a sign of the Holy Spirit's presence. Thus, speaking with tongues is a properly expected sign, affirming the Holy Spirit's abiding presence and assuring the believer of an invigorated living witness. Speaking in tongues is practiced devotionally by the believer in his most intimate and intercessory moments of communication with God as he is moved upon by the Holy Spirit.

The Spirit-filled experience is more than speaking in tongues. In reality it is coming into the fullness of the gifts and fruits of the Spirit as outlined in the New Testament (Cor. 12:7-11; Gal.5): Speaking in tongues is a means by which the Holy Spirit intercedes through us in prayer, it also can be a spiritual means for rejoicing (1 Cor. 14:15). Speaking or singing in tongues is a spiritual gift for communicating with God in private worship. It is also a spiritual gift for the edification of the church when accompanied by interpretation.

Remember…ask…believe you received…. Then speak out whatever comes from your mouth. You will not understand it, just keep doing it with confidence!

IN REMEMBRANCE OF ME

Some Christians like to take communion at home as well as church for many different reasons. Taking communion is a faith confession. It is declaring and confessing before all heaven that not only do you believe, but you have not forgotten. "In remembrance" involves more than just memory; the word suggests an "active calling to mind." It is an acted sermon, for it "proclaims" the Lord's death. The outward act of faith, as the bread and cup is taken, is explicitly said to be an ongoing, active confession...literally "you are proclaiming." Each occasion of partaking is an opportunity to say, proclaim, or confess again: "I lay hold of all the benefits of Jesus Christ's full redemption for my life...forgiveness, wholeness, strength, health, and sufficiency." The Lord's Supper is not to be simply a ritual remembrance, but an active confession, by which you actively call to memory and appropriate today all that Jesus has provided and promised through His Cross (1 Corth. 11:23-26). To partake in a "worthy" manner is to attribute the full worth of Christ's redeeming work to this action—to partake with faith in His full forgiveness, full acceptance, and full power to restore, strengthen, and heal.

As you partake in the Lord's Supper, see the Lord carrying all your sins and diseases. He took your sins in his body on the cross. See Him taking on his body all your physical conditions too. Whatever sickness you might have, see it on his body. It is no longer on you. See his health come on you. As you partake, release your faith in the bread and wine.

After partaking, thank Jesus for your healing, for by the stripes and beatings He bore and the lashes He felt on his back, brought our healing. Now believe and receive! Thank Jesus for the blood He shed which made you righteous which is preservation, healing, wholeness and prosperity.

THANK YOU, JESUS, I LOVE YOU BECAUSE YOU FIRST LOVED ME.

JESUS STILL ROCKS THE PLANET!

Jesus was the Messiah, the One for whom the Jews had waited, who was to deliver them from Roman oppression. Yet, tragically, they didn't recognize him when he came. They were not ready to accept his kingship because it was not what they expected. They didn't understand that the true purpose of God's anointed deliverer was to die for all people, to free them from sin.

Because Jesus was sent by God, we can trust him with our life. It is worth everything we have to accept Christ and give ourselves to him because he came to be our Messiah, and Savior.

Jesus is revealed as the King of kings. His miraculous birth, his life and teaching, his miracles, and his triumph over death show us who he really is.

Jesus cannot be compared with any other person or power. He is the supreme ruler of time and eternity, heaven and earth, men and angels. We should give him his rightful place as King and Lord in our life.

Jesus came to earth to begin his Kingdom. His full Kingdom will be realized at his return and will be made up of all those who have faithfully followed him. The way to enter God's Kingdom is by faith—by believing in Christ to save us from sin and change our lives. Then we must do the work of his Kingdom, helping prepare it for his return. Jesus taught the people using sermons, illustrations, and parables. He showed the true ingredients of faith and how to guard against an ineffective and hypocritical life. Jesus' teachings show us how to prepare for his life in his Kingdom by living proper right now. His life was an example of his teachings, as our lives should be. Matthew 5-7, known as the "Sermon on the Mount," introduces the values of Christ's Kingdom. Jesus gave showing how he wants those who belong to the Kingdom to live.

Two thousand years ago Jesus of Nazareth launched a spiritual revolution that is still going on today. He has been the motivation behind more songs and sermons, the inspiration underlying more works of charity, and the object of more affection than all the other figures of history combined. And don't forget the millions of lives that have been transformed by his timeless touch. Jesus is the King, Messiah and Lord God for eternity. Jesus still rocks the planet! You might say, "We know who Jesus is and what He has done for us," but with this knowledge, as a Christian, does your life line up with what he has taught and expects of you?

MARRIAGE IS A SACRED RELATIONSHIP, ONE NOT TO BE ENTERED INTO LIGHTLY

Marriage is a two-way street and it is all about love and respect, commitment and devotion. It's a lifetime of working, worshipping playing, loving, raising children, solving problems TOGETHER! God's loving relationship with his people is so similar to the marriage relationship that he uses human marriage to illustrate his covenant with people in the Old Testament and Christ's love for the church in the New Testament. Marriage was designed to help children learn about love by being born into a loving relationship. The keys to a happy marriage is a united purpose to serve the Lord, give honor to marriage and remain faithful, working out each and every problem with love, understanding each other's differences. It's a mutual submission. Also pray together and for each other. Learn to forgive and say "I am sorry." Keeping the romance steady and always communicate, don't hold things inside, it's not healthy. Marriage should unite each other as one, and a oneness with God. Here is a list of some things that destroys a marriage:

1. Living beyond your means, and arguing over money, having separate accounts for selfish reasons
2. Bad management of what you have
3. Lack of affection and not understanding each other's needs
4. Being negative and having criticism; walking in the flesh instead of the spirit
5. Contempt and insults, cutting remarks
6. Putting other things before your spouse (except God) like children, job, hobby, friends, or sports
7. Lack of communication and not taking time to listen
8. Giving the silent treatment
9. Withholding encouragement, compliments, or praise
10. No security through honesty, trust and integrity, being unfaithful or on drugs or alcohol
11. Selfishness and wanting your own way, and wanting to be right at all times, win all the time
12. Having no patience, or having anger problems and not wanting correction or guidance
13. Not having God in your life and putting Him first and not growing spiritually

LAST WORDS

He told his disciples, "I have been given all authority in heaven and earth. Therefore go and make disciples in all the nations, baptizing them into name of the Father and Son and of the Holy Spirit, and teach these new disciples to obey all commands I have given you; and be sure of this that I am with you even to the end of the world" (Matthew 28:18).

When someone is dying or leaving us, their last words are very important. Jesus left the disciples with these last words of instruction: they were under his authority; they were to make more disciples; they were to baptize and teach them to obey him; he would be with them always. Whereas in previous missions Jesus had sent his disciples only to the Jews (10:5-6), their mission from now on would be worldwide. Jesus is Lord of the earth, and he died for the sins of all those who would trust him, everywhere.

We are to go—whether it is next door or to another country—and make disciples. It is not an option, but a command to all who call Jesus Lord. All of us are not evangelists, but we have all received gifts that we can use in helping to fulfill the Great Commission (Mark 16:15). As we obey, we have comfort in the knowledge that Jesus is always with us.

When Jesus rose from the dead, he rose in power as the true King. In his victory over death, he established his credentials as King and his power and authority over evil.

The Resurrection shows that Jesus is all-powerful—that not even death could stop his plan of offering eternal life. People who believe in Jesus can hope for a resurrection like his. Our role is to live in that victory and share the message of his victory with those who do not yet know that "Jesus is alive!"

Today there is still a great stir over the Resurrection, and there are still only two choices—to believe that Jesus rose from the dead, or to be closed to the truth, denying it, or rationalizing it away.

LET DOWN YOUR NETS

Pastor Pippin, my former Pastor, is considered a very good fisherman, for fish and for souls. He knows how to catch any type of fish. He knows where the fish lurk, their feeding habits and the best time to go fishing. He has his own lures and successful strategies. So I'm pretty sure he is a bit reluctant to take advice of someone who rows over and tells him how to catch fish.

Just as Peter in Luke 5, he too knew how to catch fish in the Sea of Galilee. It was his "lake," but he had been out all night and hadn't caught a thing.

Then Jesus told him, "Let down your nets for a catch." Peter said, "Master, we have toiled all night and caught nothing; nevertheless at Your word I will let down the net." He caught so many fish, he needed help to bring them to shore! Jesus then told Peter, "From now on you will catch men." Jesus was more concerned that Peter learn to fish for souls. When you give something to God, He will give it back in a way that is even better...plus He will be in it with all His grace and power!

When it comes to fishing for souls, the issue is not how good we are at persuading people. It's whether we are obeying the Master whenever His Spirit directs us to share the gospel story. Today "let down your nets for a catch." You never know, the next person you meet may need to meet Jesus!

THE MOUNTAIN OF WILDERNESS

Have you been battling with the same problem, day after day or even year after year? Have you been going around the mountain more times than you can count? You say you have prayed and prayed and did not get results. You are getting discouraged and ask why God? Don't blame God. He heard your very first prayer but wants to reveal the root of the problem before giving you victory over this problem. We can make the same mistake over and over if we don't have the wisdom and understanding to handle it and learn the root of it. Sometimes deliverance is delayed because you need to pray for wisdom instead of results. The Lord will not take us up the ladder of glory until we have understanding. We grow from glory to glory, one step at a time. Until we grow or be chastised in our weaknesses we will not move pass them. But you can be sure God will perfect what concerns you. God wants us to have His complete joy and fullness.

If you are tired of dragging yourself around the mountain of wilderness, pray and ask God to reveal where you are missing it and to open your eyes to understanding and give you a teachable heart. Consider also there might be something you need to repent about or you might have some unforgiveness. This is why you must spend time in prayer and share your heart with the Lord, but also take the time to listen, then obey.

LETTERS TO GOD

The headline read: UNANSWERED PRAYERS: LETTERS TO GOD FOUND DUMPED IN THE OCEAN. The letters, 300 in all, were sent to a minister in New Jersey. They had been tossed in the ocean and how they came to be floating in the surf off the Jersey shore is a mystery. The letters were addressed to the minister because he had promised to pray, but he had died a long while ago. Some of the letters asked for frivolous things; others were written by anguished spouses, children or widows. They poured out their hearts to God, asking for help, some asked for help with relatives who were abusing drugs and alcohol, or spouses who were cheating on them. One of the letters asked for a husband and a father to love her and her child. The reporter concluded that all were "unanswered prayers."

Not so! If those letter-writers cried out to God, He heard each and every one of them. Not one honest prayer is lost to His ears! "All my desire is before You," David wrote in the midst of a deep personal crisis, "and my sighing is not hidden from You" (Psm. 38:9). David understood that we can cast all our cares on the Lord, even if no one else prays for us (1 Peter 5:7). He confidently concluded, "In my day of trouble I will call upon You, for You will answer me" (Psm. 86:7). The Lord hears our faintest cry! One who entrusts cares to Christ instead of fretting over them will experience the peace of God to guard him from nagging anxiety.

BE ANXIOUS FOR NOTHING, BUT IN EVERYTHING
BY PRAYER AND SUPPLICATION, WITH THANKSGIVING,
LET YOUR REQUESTS BE KNOWN TO GOD;
AND THE PEACE OF GOD WHICH SURPASSES ALL
UNDERSTANDING WILL GUARD YOUR HEARTS AND
MINDS THROUGH CHRIST JESUS.
(Philippians 4:6-7)

LIVING A GOOD LIFE DOES NOT MEAN HEAVEN AWAITS

Teachers have developed two systems for grading their students' performance. First there is the "curve" system and then there is the "set" system. Most people would like to believe that God grades on a curve; 50 percent of people will be above average and 50 percent will be below average. With this system, a certain percentage determines your grade. If you get below a 75 percent grade, for example, you fail. In other words, if some are better than others, it will be all right with God. All they have to do is not steal or kill anyone, mind their own business, and wait for heaven. Unfortunately, God doesn't grade that way.

In God's eyes, there isn't any one who is good; Psalm 14:2-3 states it clearly: "The Lord looks down from heaven on all man-kind to see if there are any who are wise, who want to please God. But no, all have strayed away; all are rotten with sin. Not one is good, not one!" All of us have strayed away. This doesn't mean we're all murders, it means our hearts are stained with the sin of Adam...the desire to be god of our life and run it ourselves. No one has a pure heart (see Luke 18:18-26 for a great illustration).

God has one method of salvation. In His wisdom, He gave everyone the opportunity to go to heaven by faith, not works. All a person has to do to be saved is believe that Christ paid the penalty for sin and rose again from the dead: "Because of His kindness you have been saved through trusting Christ. And even trusting is not of yourselves; it too is a gift from God. Salvation is not a reward for the good we have done, so none of us can take any credit for it" (Ephesians 2:8-9).

Most people say this is too simple. But that's the whole idea! God isn't trying to make it tough on us. He wants us to be with Him forever!

Throughout your life you will run into people who believe that simple living a good life means heaven awaits. A good life is important to a holy God, but it will not buy you a ticket to heaven! That ticket has already been paid for by Jesus Christ! But you must come to Him to get it.

GOD HAS TOLD YOU
WHAT HE WANTS,
AND THIS IS ALL IT IS: TO BE FAIR AND JUST
AND MERCIFUL, AND TO WALK HUMBLY
WITH YOUR GOD.
From Micah 6:8

LIVING TO MAKE A DIFFERENCE

Our minds and attitudes have a profound effect in shaping the way we live. If we are to know the joy of the Christlike difference, the results will be seen in a way that reflects His character.

The church at Philippi was characterized by division and selfishness. If they were to put Christlike difference into practice, they had to do what Paul urged: "Let nothing be done through selfish ambition or conceit, but in lowliness of mind let each esteem others better than himself" (Phil. 2:3). This can be done by putting into practice the "one another statements of the New Testament that put others first." For example:

- Love one another (John 13:35)
- Admonish one another (Rom. 15:14)
- Serve one another (Gal. 5:13)
- Bear one another's burdens (Gal. 6:2)
- Be kind to one another (Eph. 4:32)

- Comfort one another (1 Thess. 4:18)
- Live in peace with one another (1 Thess. 5:13)
- Confess sin to one another (James 5:16)
- Be hospitable to one another (1 Peter 4:9)
- Be subject to one another (Eph. 5:21)

Jesus was obedient to die for us out of love. Now we are to be obedient to live for Him out of love. It demands that we truly allow His mind…with all its selflessness, sacrifice humility, and patience to shape our lives. May we move toward a life rooted in the difference Christ makes by allowing His mind to govern our hearts.

GOSSIP IS DAMAGING!

"Where there is no wood, the fire goes out;

and where there is no talebearer, strife ceases"

(Proverbs 26:20).

The Proverbs have a lot to say about gossip: Those who gossip are untrustworthy (11:13) and should be avoided (20:19). Gossip separates the closest of friends (16:28) and keeps relational strife boiling (18:8). It pours fuel on the coals of conflict, feeding the flames of hurt and misunderstanding (26:21, 22). The Hebrew word for "gossip" or "talebearing" actually means "whispering that is damaging." We fool ourselves into thinking that those juicy, whispering comments here and there are not harmless. But gossip leaves behind a wide destruction and is never a victimless crime. Someone is always hurt. So here's a word to the wise: "Where there is no talebearer, strife ceases" (Prov. 26:20). Let's leave the dirt-moving to big machines. Put the shovels away and revel in the joy of gossip-free relationships!

Many things that other say
Are not for us to tell;
Help us, Lord, to watch our tongue—
We need to guard it well.
—Branon

JESUS BREAKS THE POWER OF SIN

The flesh as we know is anything in us which gives sin its chance; it is human nature without God. To live according to the dictates of the flesh is simply to live in such a way that our lower nature, the worst part of us, dominates our lives. All people have sinned by nature, or by choice, or by practice, and having casual attitudes and blinded minds have lured people to overlook the desperate state of being lost. Romans 3:23 says: "…for all have sinned and fall short of the glory of God." It is this lifestyle which is deserving only of the wrath of God, and Romans 6:23 warns us that "The wages of sin is death." There are many people whose life is embittered because they feel that in this life they have never had what talents and gifts and work they deserved; that may be so; but in the sight of God there is no one who deserves anything but condemnation (Romans 3:10-18). It is only God's love in Christ which has forgiven us who have grieved His love and broken His law. It is through faith in the blood of Christ that mankind is justified in God's eyes. The blood of Christ is what bonds people to God's covenant provisions. The blood is forever the only means of right relationship with the holy God (Romans 3:25 and Ephesians 2:13).

Paul tells us, we are dead in sins and trespasses; but God in His love and mercy has made us alive in Jesus Christ (Ephesians 2:1). What exactly did he mean? Through what Jesus did for us on the Cross something happened to reverse the process of life. There are three things involved in being dead in sins and trespasses. Jesus has something to do about each of these things. (1) Sin kills innocence. No one is precisely the same after one has sinned. (2) Sin kills ideals. In the lives of so many there is a kind of tragic process. The fatal power of sin is that each sin makes the next sin easier; each indulgence makes the next indulgence easier. (3) Sin kills the will. Once one engages in some forbidden pleasure because they want to do so; in the end, one can no longer help doing so, and then it is allowed to become a habit and one is then mastered by this forbidden practice and becomes a slave to it.

Sin does kill innocence and even Jesus cannot give one's innocence back, or turn the clock back. But what Jesus can do is take away the sense of guilt which the lost innocence necessarily brings with it. When one realizes they have sinned, guilt and oppression separates us from God. Instead of running to God because they sinned, one runs away from God because of guilt. Jesus begins by taking that sense of estrangement away. He came to tell us no matter what we are like; the door is open to us to the presence of God. Jesus came to take the sense of guilt away by telling us that God wants us just as we are. Sin killed the ideas by which people live. Jesus reawakens the ideal in our hearts. He gives us glory. The grace of Jesus Christ rekindles the ideals which repeated falling to sin had extinguished. And by that very rekindling, life is set climbing again. But greater than anything else, Jesus Christ revives and restores and recreates the lost will! The fatal and deadly thing about sin was that it slowly but surely destroyed a person's will that the indulgence which had become as a pleasure became necessary, that one's sins sapped his strength of will and forged chains by which they became helplessly bound. Jesus recreates the will. That is what love does. The effect of great love is always a cleansing thing. The new love then compels us to goodness. The love of sin is defeated and broken. That is what Christ does for us! When we love Him, that very love recreates and restores our will toward goodness.

But God, who is rich in mercy, because of His great love with which He loved us, even when we were dead in trespasses, made us alive together with Christ (by grace you have been saved), and raised us up together, and made us sit together in heavenly places in Christ Jesus, that in the ages to come He might show the exceeding riches of His grace in His kindness toward us in Christ Jesus.
(Ephesians 2:4-7)

JUDAS ISCARIOT

Jesus chose Judas to be one of his disciples. Judas was also chosen to keep the money bag for the expenses of the group. We may miss the point that while Judas betrayed Jesus, all the disciples abandoned him at times. The disciples, including Judas, all had the wrong idea of Jesus' mission on earth. They expected Jesus to become a political leader. But when He kept talking about dying, they all felt a mixture of anger, fear, and disappointment. They couldn't understand why Jesus had asked them to follow him if his mission was going to fail.

We don't know exactly why Judas betrayed Jesus. But we can see that Judas let his own desires become so important that Satan was able to control him. He got paid to set up Jesus for the religious leaders.

He tried to undo the evil he had done by giving the money back to the priests, but it was too late. How sad that Judas ended his life in despair without ever experiencing the gift of forgiveness God could give even to him through Jesus Christ.

In betraying Jesus, Judas made the greatest mistake in history. But just the fact that Jesus knew Judas would betray him doesn't mean that Judas was a puppet of God's will. Judas made the choice. God knew the choice Judas would make, and made it part of the plan. Judas didn't lose his relationship with Jesus; rather he had never found Jesus. Judas is called the "son of hell" (John 17:12) because he was never saved.

Judas' life can help us if he makes us think about our commitment to God. Is God's Spirit in us? Are we true disciples and followers, or uncommitted pretenders? We can choose repentance, forgiveness, hope, and eternal life. Will YOU accept Christ's free gift, or like Judas…betray him?

Evil plans and motives leave us open to being used by Satan for even greater evil. The consequences of evil are so devastating that even small lies and little wrongdoings have serious results. When Judas first betrayed Jesus, perhaps he was trying to force Jesus' hand to get him to lead a revolt against Rome. This did not work, of course. Whatever the reason, Judas changed his mind, but it was too late. Many of the plans we set into motion cannot be reversed. It is best to think of the potential consequences before we launch into an action we may later regret.

PROVERBS

The wisdom contained in the Book of Proverbs is as meaningful today as when it was written. Yet it is neither a prosperity pamphlet nor a "how to succeed" handbook in the worldly sense. It tells rather how to order one's values, which leads to character, which leads to wholeness, which leads to satisfaction. It warns of the pitfalls along the way, and declares the folly of not developing the fear of the Lord.

Since the Book of Proverbs is a compilation, its writing was spread over a period of years, with the main work probably centered about 950 B.C. Chapters 25 through 29 are identified as copied by "Hezekiah's men," which places the copy at about 720 B.C., though the material itself was by Solomon, perhaps in a separate document found in Hezekiah's time. Solomon's reputation of wisdom springs not only from its practical results, but also from the direct statements of Scripture.

Solomon, king of Israel, was the son of David and Bathsheba. He reigned for 40 years, from 970 to 930 B.C., taking the throne at about twenty years of age. No doubt influenced by the psalm-writing of his father, Solomon has left us more books than any other Old Testament writer except Moses. Solomon's strengths were not on the battlefield, but in the realm of the mind: meditation, planning, negotiation, and organization.

Proverbs is about wise living and it often focuses on a person's response and attitude toward God, who is the source of wisdom. A number of proverbs point out aspects of God's character. Knowing God helps us on the way to wisdom, "Wisdom is the principal thing; Therefore get wisdom. And in all your getting, get understanding" (Pro. 4:7).

God wants his people to be wise. Two kinds of people portray two contrasting paths of life: The fool is the wicked, stubborn person who hates or ignores God; the wise person seeks to know and love God. When we choose God's way, He grants us wisdom. His Word, the Bible leads us to live right, have right relationships, and make right decisions.

Proverbs gives us advice for developing our personal relationships with others, including friends, family members, and coworkers. In every relationship, we must show love, dedication, and high moral standards. To relate to people, we need consistency, sensitivity, and discipline to use the wisdom God gives us. If we don't treat others according to the wisdom God gives, our relationships will suffer.

What we say shows our real attitude toward others. How we talk reveals what we're really like. Our speech is a test of how wise we've become. To be wise we need self-control. Our words should be honest and well chosen. What we say affects people!

God considers a good reputation, moral character, and spiritual devotion to obey Him to be the true measure of success. A successful relationship with God counts for eternity. Everything else is only temporary. All our resources, time, and talents come from God. We need to do our best to use them wisely.

Read and meditate on the book of Proverbs and let it help you mold a wise character that will please God and build strong relationships and help you live a satisfactory, wholesome life.

OPPORTUNTIES TO SHARE THE MESSAGE ABOUT CHRIST

"Be wise in the way you act with people who are not believers, making the most of every opportunity" (Colossians 4:5-6).

In these evil last days we as Christians need to be praying, staying alert and always thanking God. It is very important that we pray to God to give us an opportunity to tell people about his message and praying that we can reach the secret that God has made known about Christ (Col. 4:3). We are to be wise in the way we act with people who are not believers, making the most of every opportunity. When we talk, we should always be kind and pleasant so we will be able to answer everyone in the way we should. Pray that you can speak in a way that will make it clear for people to understand.

Whether you are with someone you know well or with someone you've met for the first time, the best way to turn the conversation toward a spiritual direction is to ask the person if you may pray for them. Although it is routine to the Christian, most non-Christians don't know of anyone who is praying for them, and so most people become deeply moved by this unusual request of concern.

But the point in all these possibilities is that you will have to discipline yourself to bring people about by praying for opportunities. They don't usually just happen. Discipline yourself to ask your neighbor how you may pray for them. Or you might have to discipline yourself to get your coworker during off-hours. Many opportunities for evangelism will not take place if you just sit around and wait for them to occur spontaneously! Plus the world, the flesh and the devil will do their best to see that these opportunities do not come your way, so it's important that you pray about them to come about. You are backed by the power of the Holy Spirit who can make sure the enemies of the gospel do not win.

So Christians, followers of Jesus, pray and ask God to give you the opportunities to tell others about Jesus, especially those you encounter every day regularly. Also be sure nothing in your daily conversation contradicts the message you proclaim. Don't just have good intentions which will get you nowhere, be bold and follow through, for time is short and important! It may be the only opportunity that person will ever hear about the gospel. Be set apart from non-Christians by what you say.

"While it is daytime, we must continue doing the work of the One who sent me" (John 9:4).

OUR UNION WITH CHRIST MAKES US SAINTS

"To the saints and faithful brethren in Christ

who are in Colossae..." (Colossians 1:2).

It's probably not a name we would use for ourselves, but the apostle Paul often called believers "saints" in the New Testament (Eph. 1:1; Col. 1:2). Did he call them saints because they were perfect? No. These people were human and therefore sinful. What then did he have in mind? The word saint in the New Testament means that one is set apart for God. It describes people who have a spiritual union with Christ (Eph. 1:3-6). The word is synonymous with individual believers in Jesus (Rom. 8:27) and those who make up the church (Acts 9:32).

Saints have a responsibility through the power of the Spirit to live lives worthy of their calling. This includes, but is not limited to, no longer being sexually immoral and using improper speech (Rom. 16:2). We are to put on the new character traits of service to one another (Rom. 16:2), humility, gentleness, patience, love unity of the Spirit in the bond of peace (Eph. 4:1-3), obedience, and perseverance during hardship and suffering (Rev. 13:10; 14:12). In the Old Testament, the psalmist called saints "the excellent ones, in whom is all my delight" (Ps. 16:3).

Our union with Christ makes us saints, but our obedience to God's Word through the power of the Holy Spirit makes us saintly.

Saints are people whom God's light shines through!

MERCY

"You cannot stay angry with your people forever,

because you delight in showing mercy"

(Micah 7:18).

God delights in showing mercy. He does not forgive grudgingly but is glad when you repent. He offers forgiveness to all who come back to Him.

God delights in faith that produces fairness, love to others, and obedience to Him. True faith in God generates kindness, compassion, justice, mercy, and humility. We can please God by seeking these results in our schools, family, church, job, and neighborhood.

Godliness and mercy or fair-minded people are hard to find. Society rationalizes sin; Christians sometimes compromise what is right in order to do what they want. Too often we convince ourselves it's okay, especially when "everyone else is doing it." But our standards for behavior come from God, not society! God is truth, and we are to be like Him.

Today, pray and confess your sins and receive God's loving forgiveness. Don't be too proud to accept God's mercy. Receive your salvation and make Jesus your Lord and Savior. Step up to being a fair-minded person with mercy, who cares about the lost, needy and oppressed. Share God's love and neglect society's standards.

"As for me, I look to the Lord for his help. I wait confidently for
God to save me, and my God will certainly hear me"
(Micah 7:7).

"The Lord will bring me out of my darkness into the light,
and I will see his righteousness"
(Micah 7:9).

MARRIAGE SEEN FROM GOD'S PERSPECTIVE

Why is it that two people who are "made for each other" so often end up looking for the escape hatch labeled "divorce"? Maybe a better question is: What does it take a marriage from becoming a casualty? If marriage were just another human institution—like a corporation or a university—then getting out of it would be no more significant or painful than changing jobs or switching schools. Indeed, many people have tried to treat marriage that way, as something to enjoy when it's good or helpful and to terminate when it isn't. But those who have experienced a divorce will explain that a failed marriage is infinitely more painful. There's more to marriage than the human dimension. Marriage was God's holy and sacred idea. He performed "THE FIRST WEDDING" in the Garden of Eden (Genesis 2:18-25), thus setting up guidelines for all people to follow: marriage is for one man and one woman for life. There are valid reasons for sometimes breaking this pattern (for example, death or adultery). But the intended pattern is ONE MAN, ONE WOMAN, FOR LIFE. Unfortunately, in a fallen world it often is difficult to submit to God's standards, especially since his standards do not change. Marriage is a covenant between a husband and a wife. A covenant is an agreement between two people (or groups) that has benefits for keeping the arrangement and penalties for breaking it. Our relationship to God is described in covenant language throughout Scripture. The marriage relationship is described as a covenant (Malachi 2:14-15), and is used as an illustration of our relationship with God (Hosea 1:2; Ephesians 5:22-23). Just as our relationship with God is built on his steadfast, unchanging love commitment toward us, so a marriage relationship is designed to be solid, faithful, and committed. Therein lies another extremely important—but often overlooked—principal for a successful marriage: commitment. Marriage is based on commitment, not emotions. The EMOTIONAL RUSH two people experience when they "fall in love" and when they decided to marry is wonderful but it is a terrible inadequate basis for marriage. That "rush," as powerful and enjoyable as it may be, will undoubtedly wear off at some point. If that's what the relationship is based on—physical attraction, romantic ideals, or passion—the flame may burn brightly, but it will not burn for long. Romance, sexual attraction, and passion are tremendous God-given elements of a love relationship. But do not mistake them for the foundation of a lifelong commitment. They are like icing on a cake, icing makes the cake sweeter, but a diet of 100-percent refined sugar doesn't make for good health. To survive the pressure and temptations that attack a marriage, both husband and wife have to be totally committed to make it work. Even when the romance is gone (as it sometimes will), when the money is tight, or the urge to run out is overwhelming, Christians must stand strong on the commitment they have made. Instead of allowing the stresses to divide them, they must cling that much tighter together. "What God has joined together, let no one"—and no thing separate. Marriage when seen from God's perspective can be one of his greatest gifts to his children!

MISUSING WORDS

"A man of knowledge uses words with restraint, and a man of understanding is even-tempered" (Proverbs 17:27).

We all need to use our words with restraint. Misusing words is one of the easiest ways to sin, and one of the deadliest ("Death and life are in the power of the tongue, and those who love it will eat its fruit" (Proverbs 18:21)). The Word tells us, "But the tongue of the wise promotes health" (Proverbs 12:18); "Lying lips are an abomination to the Lord, but those who deal truthfully are His delight" (Proverbs 12:22). In fact, the tongue is a fire that corrupts the whole person, sets the whole course of their life on fire, and is itself set on fire by hell. David prayed: Set a guard, O Lord, over my mouth; keep watch over the door of my lips. Controlling our tongue is so difficult that one cannot do it without help. The Holy Spirit is always willing and able to help us; all we have to do is ask.

Not only do we have to guard our words, but we also must guard our thoughts. The contents of our thoughts have an enormous influence on our health and wellbeing. We can set our attitude to be distorted; anxious, depressed, and unbiblical thoughts will cause action to the thought. Thinking wrong, negative or unbiblical thoughts not corrected will cause a problem; it can lead to breakdown to our health. However, Scripture provides correction: Pleasant words are sweet to the soul and healing to the bones. When the Holy Spirit is controlling your thoughts and words, your soul and your body will flourish. When your mind and spirit are as one the body (flesh) will follow. Flesh will always be the follower to whatever is first. Ask the Holy Spirit to think and speak through you. He lives in your innermost being so He can easily influence you, but He is a gentleman and likes to be invited. The more you invite the Holy Spirit into your life, the healthier and happier you will be! Your words will be pleasant blessings not only for you but also those around you.

Keep in mind we will one day have to account for our useless words ("But I say to you for every idle word men speak, they will give account of it in the day of judgment" (Matthew 12:36)).

Get in the habit of paying attention to the words you say. The Bible tells us we should listen more and speak less. What we say is what is what we will get. If you speak negative, you will get negative. If you speak positive, godly, words that is what you will receive. You always reap what you sow ("For he who sows to his flesh will of the flesh reap corruption, but he who sows to the Spirit will of the Spirit reap everlasting life" (Galatians 6:8)). Remember also, wrong actions and words start with a wrong thought!

PRIORITIES

"Thus says the Lord of hosts: 'Consider your ways!'"

(Haggai 1:5, 7)

One might consider rereading the Book of Haggai as it very much relates to today's world. The Book of Haggai addresses the problems common to all people of all times. One of the problems was disinterest, another was discouragement and dissatisfaction.

People then had become more concerned with their own interests and building beautiful homes. All their efforts and ours at building and wanting our own selfish desires can never produce lasting results. The older people became discouraged because any temple could no longer compare with their former temple. The discouragement of the older people had quickly influenced the younger ones. Haggai issues a clear call to his own people and to us that we should set ourselves to the task assigned to us by God. We should not allow difficulties, enemies, or selfish pursuits to turn us aside from our divinely given responsibilities.

God had given the Jews the assignment to finish the Temple in Jerusalem when they returned from captivity. But after fifteen years, they had not completed it. They were more concerned about building their own homes than about finishing God's work. Haggai told them to get their priorities straight. It may be easy to make other activities more important than doing God's work. But God wants us to build his Kingdom and our temple within us. We need to set our heart on what is right and do it! We need to be centering our priorities on Christ; putting Him first in our lives!

It is a fact that holiness won't rub off on others, but contamination will. If we insist on harboring wrong or toxic attitudes and sins, or maintaining close relationships with sinful people, we will be contaminated. Holy living will only come when we are empowered by God's Holy Spirit. Have you become toxic? Have you let God slip from your life? God refuses to be forgotten! He demanded priority in the Jew's life and He demands priority in our life!

As you read the Book of Haggai, notice how God blesses those who make Him number One and makes Him first place in their life.

The challenge to faith is the same in every generation; seek first the things of God and trust Him to provide the daily necessities of life. God calls us to commit what we are, what we have, and all that we do to Him! When we repent, and turn from selfish ambitions and personal agenda to focus on advancing God's kingdom God will bless us also. We do not need to become discouraged, or lose interest or be dissatisfied as the Jews were if we keep our heart and mind on God's work and the advancement of the Kingdom. Also, knowing we will be blessed! The nature of our calling and the promised presence of God and His Holy Spirit encourages us to fulfill our commission.

PRAY THE PERFECT PRAYER

Have you ever prayed, "Lord, save so-and-so that it might be a glory to Your name"; "Lord, so-and so is sick; heal him for Your glory"; or "Lord, so-and-so is so sick and might die. Do whatever gives You the most glory"? That's the way to pray. When we pray for our sake, we reverse the priorities. If you always pray for what you want, you'll never be able to pray according to the will of God because you won't be interested in it. But when you pray, "Do whatever gives You glory, God," you are really praying the right way. You've got to care about the glory of God first. Sometimes that isn't easy because we want so many other things. If you pray just for yourself, you are being selfish and don't understand the importance of God's glory. Jesus said, "If ye shall ask anything in my name, I will do it" (John 14:14). In other words, "If you ask anything for the sake of My name—anything that will give Me glory—I'll do it." So your prayers should be, "Father, do this because I believe it will be for the glory of Christ." A person who consistently prays that way reveals his spiritual maturity. Sometimes it's difficult not to pray for ourselves, surely God understands that. But in the back of our minds we must remember that everything is for His glory. If you're having trouble accepting that, then you'll have trouble attaining spiritual maturity.

HOW DO YOU KNOW WHEN YOU ARE SPIRITUAL?

You know you've arrived at that level of maturity when false doctrine doesn't interest you but gets you angry. If someone asks, "What do you believe?" you are able to tell them and support your answer with Scripture. A person has outgrown their emotions and feelings and looks to the Word for guidance. A spiritual person no longer functions on their emotions because they know where they stand doctrinally. Also if you are spiritual, you have overcome Satan. If you are going to overcome Satan, you are going to have to be strong; by letting the Word of God abide in you. Whereas spiritual babies are primarily concerned about their own needs, the mature is not. Did you ever know of a baby that cried because his little brother or sister had a problem? No, because children are naturally self-centered. However, the concern of a spiritual person is to learn the Word to become well established in sound doctrine. A spiritual baby is ignorant, but the mature person has understanding. But when you get to the place where you know a lot, you need to watch for the stumbling block of spiritual pride! Spiritual babies delight in their experiences, and the mature delight in their understanding. There are different levels of maturity within God's family. Some are little children, some are mature men, and some are spiritual fathers. The spiritual father has plumbed the depths of the knowledge of God. He doesn't just know doctrine; he knows the God who revealed it. A spiritual father has a personal, experiential, in-depth knowledge of God. Regardless of the level you are at, there is probably nothing more important than growing spiritually. Spiritual growth isn't a mystical or a psychological process. It is simply the result of two things: the Word of God and holiness. As you study the Word and walk in obedience to it in holy living, maturity takes place. Spiritual growth is not an instantaneous gimmick. God wants us to grow. If we are spiritual babies, let's grow up and be mature Christians! The mature Christian does not love the world because of what it is...the enemy of God and because of who we are... "The Family of God!"

PRAYING IN JESUS' NAME

"If you ask anything in My name, I will do it"

(John 14:14).

In Bible times a person's name signified or represented the person who bore the name. Even today, when we think of someone's name, we automatically think of the person who bears the name. We think of the individual's personality, nature, authority, character, reputation, abilities, integrity, etc. The name represents the total sum of the person. To do something in someone's name is to do it as his representative with his authority, his character, and his purposes and intent in mind. It is to do as if the other person was doing it.

To pray in Jesus' name relates to our lives, not our lips. We must humble ourselves before God and walk in humility and integrity. We must not waver between serving God and our own selfish interest. We must commit ourselves to the plan and purposes of God and pray for His glory in our lives. Then, and only then, can we pray in Jesus' name.

So you see, Jesus really meant it when He said we could ask anything in His name. But He knew he could only ask in His name only by living in His name. As we live in His name, our prayers will be the kind that He can answer. They will be consistent with His name and character.

Jesus has given us His name. We are called Christians. We are His name bearers, His representatives on earth. When we live like Christ, we will pray like Christ. When we pray like Christ, we can ask anything and God will answer our prayers.

Prayer is a way of life. It flows out of our relationship to God and our concern for His will to be accomplished on the earth. God will answer our prayers when we are in right relationship to Him and when our prayers are an expression of His desires for humanity in general and for our lives specifically. Psalms 37:4 tells us: "Delight yourself also in the Lord, and He shall give you the desires of your heart." When we delight ourselves in the Lord, He puts His own desires into our heart and we simply pray them back to Him.

We must also always pray in faith, for without faith we cannot please God. The prayer of faith is not some vain repetition or confession of a supposed formula for getting things from God. Neither is it to be confused with our feelings and emotions. The prayer of faith is simply an inward assurance and confidence that God has already made provision for our need and will supply the provision when required. Our believing must come from our heart, not just our head, otherwise prayers might not get answered. If we just believe a promise in our mind and it don't get into our heart we may act on presumption rather than from real Bible faith, or we might blame God for not answering our prayer. God is always working on our behalf. He always makes a provision for us before He makes a promise to us. So live a godly life, pray in faith and in the Name of Jesus, then be confident and expectant.

PLAYING THE GAME IS A LOT BETTER THAN PRACTICE!

"For I know the plans I have for you," says the Lord. "They are plans for good and not for disaster, to give you a future and a hope..." (Jeremiah 29:11).

Some people are afraid to give their whole life to God. They are afraid He might ask them to do something they don't want to do. So what happens when one holds back part of their life? Imagine...going out for basketball and telling the coach that you only want to practice, not play in the games. Or that you only want to play in the first half of each game. How would the coach react? What would your teammates say?

Undoubtedly they would be a little put off by your selfish attitude. After all, if you are going to be on the team, you should play all the games. And if you play, you shouldn't avoid the last half when the team needs you the most. Playing the game is a lot better than practice and the second half is when the game is on the line!

Unfortunately, many Christians, by their attitudes and their actions, tell the coach (God) two things: they don't really want the benefits and the fun of playing on the team (except heaven, of course); and they don't want to contribute during the times when other people might need them the most!

God wants our whole life, so He can make something extraordinary out of it. Jesus told his followers, "The thief's purpose is to steal and kill and destroy. My purpose is to give life in its fullness" (John 10:10).

The Christian life was never meant to be done halfway. You are either sold out for God or sold out to the world. For God to give you "abundant life," you must give your life in full to God. Jesus said, "If you cling to your life, you will lose it; but, if you give it up for me, you will find it" (Matthew 10:39).

Don't worry about what God will ask you. If He asks you to be a missionary, or do something else, in effect He is saying: "I know you better than anyone else does. I made you, and I love you more than you know. Because I put you together, I know what it takes to make you the happiest and most fulfilled in life. If you choose any other direction, you will be settling for second best."

God's goal isn't to make his kids miserable. God wants to lead us in a direction that will cause us to say, "The game isn't easy, God, especially the last quarter. But thanks for believing in me enough to put me in."

OVERSTEPPING YOUR BOUNDS

God created man and woman to glorify and enjoy God. But many people are too busy living life, life without purpose. Their soul is not awakened to the joy of the Presence of the Lord. They are overly focused on negative things, buying into the world's version of the good life. They do not realize they have treated the Lord with much less reverence than He deserves! When they hurt, they blame someone or they blame God.

God with his tender mercies has given us, as his children, the privilege of intimacy with Him, not as an invitation to act as if we are his equal, but the blessing of sharing our heart of joy or sorrow with Him, to ask for wisdom and direction.

God took a huge risk when He created mankind in his image. He created us with the potential to reverence and love Him freely. God wants us to worship Him as King of kings while walking hand in hand down the path of life. What the Lord searches for in his children is the awakening of their soul that thrills to the joy of His Presence!

Many believers view devotion and worship as a duty. Actually, the more fully we enjoy the Lord, the more capacity we have to appreciate the blessings He showers upon us. When we make Him our Ultimate Pleasure, we glorify Him by desiring closeness with Him. As we delight ourselves in Him, He is free to bless us with many things that pleases us.

The Lord should always be first place in our life; our treasure, our delight, our love! The Lord wants us to share all of our life with Him with trust and a teachable and humble heart. Some believers are selective about which parts of themselves they will share. Some hesitate to bring Him the traits they consider shameful. Others are used to living with painful feelings, loneliness, fear, guilt that it never occurs to them to ask the Lord for help in dealing with these things. Still others get so preoccupied with their struggles that they forget the Lord is even there. Then there are those who think they can handle everything themselves. God wants us to share everything...every part of our life for He has the victory, joy, peace, blessings and all the answers we will ever need. He can help us break free from these worldly weights. He will help us reach our potential and desired goal in life. But without the Lord, we can do nothing!

We can never ever take the Lord for granted, or see Him as anything but holy, righteous, powerful, just, merciful and gracious! He deserves our love, worship and all the praise, glory, devotion and honor reflecting and radiating through a life that is laid down for Christ Jesus! Anything less than that is disobedience and overstepping our bounds! Our lives are to be an example of who Jesus is. We are not here on this earth just to work to buy material things, or have big houses, new cars, not that they are bad, but if Jesus is not first and when it's not all about Jesus, then it's wrong. We are to take back what the devil stole from us, help the poor and the widows and the needy and set the captives free. God has equipped us to do this! That is what it means to live our life for Jesus! Don't allow regrets about the things you could of, should of, or would have done, or say, weigh you down. Always be ready and obedient to the leading of the Holy Spirit. As God leads you to the opportunity He has given you, be a blessing to someone.

"For the eyes of the Lord range throughout the earth to strengthen those whose hearts are fully committed to him"
(2 Chronicles 16:9).

"Do what is right and good in the Lord's sight,
so all will go well with you..."
(Deut. 6:1-25; 11:26-28; 28:1-68).

PRAYER IS ESSENTIAL AND VITAL FOR THE LIFE OF A CHRISTIAN

"Be still and know that I am God" (Psalm 46:10).

If you say you are a Christian, you know how important a good prayer life is. If a Christian neglects their prayers, they lose sight of the Lord and become proud and arrogant people who think they don't need God. A lifestyle of prayer leads us to the truth that without God, we can do nothing of lasting value. We also know when we neglect our daily prayer; things seem to go wrong throughout the day. With daily prayer our life becomes richer and more peaceful and makes our purpose in life stronger. A successful day is staying in touch with Jesus! A spirit of prayer is one of the most important things in our spiritual walk with Christ Jesus. Jesus taught his disciples that prayer is an intimate relationship with the Father that includes a dependency for daily needs, commitment to obedience, and forgiveness of sin (Matt. 6:5-13). Prayer helps us to know the heart of our Lord.

By seeking and focusing on our Lord in prayer, we can align ourselves with His desires. Prayer should honor God. The Scriptures are filled with verses that show us how to honor, worship and praise God. We should always enter His Presence with an attitude of gratitude and praise. Also all our communication with God should begin with confession.

Before we pray we must cleanse any worldly thoughts and its busy agendas so our minds can be focused on God. If we allow these to clutter our minds, we will not be able to seek His will or listen to His guidance: "...Fix your thought on what is true and good and lovely, and dwell on fine, and good things in others. Think about all you can praise God for and be glad about" (Phil. 4:8).

Our motive for prayer is important and should not be what we can get for ourselves, but about surrendering ourselves to God and His will. James 4:3 states: "You ask, you do not receive, because you ask with wrong motives that you spend what you get on your pleasures." Keeping our proper focus on Jesus will keep those wrong requests from consuming us, otherwise we end up telling God what we need done; we attempt to control Him. We then make God to be something He is not. Remember, the reason for our salvation is not to be saved from our problems, but to be saved from our selfishness. If God answered our selfish prayers, we would continue to ask Him for all the material we could get and we would not know we are to surrender our will to Him. When we pray in His Name, we ask for His will to be done (John 16:23-24). When we pray like that, we hand Him our selfishness.

Besides having clean thoughts, we must also have a clean heart when we pray. If we have known sin and we try to hide it, the sin will create a wall that prayer cannot overcome. Always be honest with God, for He already knows of our sin (Psm. 66:18-19). Also as God forgives us, we must forgive others (Mark 11:25). Unless we forgive, we can never be in a true relationship with the Lord.

To prepare for prayer we need to be ready to listen to God, which means take the time, and the effort, of putting all distractions of our job, our families, and the world on hold and have an open, honest, and joyous intimate relationship with God in prayer, making sure our motives are aligned with God's Word and will. When we pray for that which we know pleases God, we can pray in confidence (1 John 5:14-15). Our prayers must also be accompanied by a willingness to obey with our actions.

PREPARING FOR ETERNITY

"If I go and prepare a place for you, I will come back and take you to be with me that you also may be where I am" (John 14:3).

Most people are too busy each day and don't take time to think about eternity. They don't realize what they do today makes a huge difference in the tomorrow. Living and doing good or sinful will determine one's destiny. We never know when our time is up. We think we have a real long life, but that isn't always the case.

Living for Jesus and learning to trust Him takes time, it doesn't come overnight, and it's a process. Planning for the life to come can't come at the time of our death. The goodness we do now is like depositing money into our bank account. Pleasing the Lord in obedience, and showing love to others and sharing the Gospel all accounts for our rewards in heaven. We will be judged for what we have done or not done.

If the nonbeliever does not accept Christ in their life, and does not believe there is a real heaven or hell, their destiny does not have rewards, only empty darkness and the agony of regrets, and the continuance of battling with evil. Then it's too late, one is stuck with the choice they made for eternity.

For the Christian it is important they are constantly growing in their spiritual life; continuing to keep their focus on the Lord if they hold their life important and rewarding in the life to come. We as Christians must slowdown in living the life we have now and keep in mind to be constantly preparing for eternity, keeping oil in our lamps, remember the Parable of the wise and foolish virgins (Matt. 25:1-13): "Watch therefore, for you know neither the day nor the hour in which the Son of Man is coming" (Matt. 25-13). Don't be foolish and be too busy for Jesus. Don't be left behind!

I speak to the one who thinks they have a time and wants to wait to come to Jesus... You are being like the foolish virgin and may never get the chance to come to Jesus. You do NOT know your time on this earth! Be wise and except Jesus NOW and prepare your heart by accepting the gift of salvation which Jesus made possible for all mankind by his sacrifice on the cross.

For those unbelievers, you will be doomed to hell forever! You still have time...right now to change your heart and mind...don't wait until it is too late! Don't be foolish, my friend! Eternity in hell would be disastrous! No one deserves to go there when Jesus has given them the choice of a wonderful life in heaven. Won't you make this choice and pray this prayer? Heavenly Father, I confess I am a sinner, and I need Jesus to forgive me and come into my heart and life and help me live as I should. I now make this commitment to turn away from sin and desire a new life of love and obedience with the Help of the Holy Spirit. I do believe Jesus is the Son of God and died on the cross for my sins. So Jesus come into my life and help me be all you desire me to be. I can now be assured of eternity in heaven with You one day. Thank you Jesus…I am now saved. Amen.

ROYAL PRIESTHOOD

"And have made us kings and priests to our God;

and we shall reign on earth" (Revelation 5:10).

As a royal priesthood the saints (Rev. 17:14 the "called, chosen, and faithful") reign now with Christ on earth by their worship, their prayers, and their witness in word and deed. The sacrifice of Jesus has given to all believers the privileges that had belonged to ancient Israel (Ex. 19:6; 29:1, 9; Pet. 2:9, 10). He has made us kings and priests, is clearly a present tense reference to the believer's function now in witness and in worship. We, through His glorious dominion, have been designated "kings and priests" to... a present calling. Thus, these dual offices give perspective on our authority and duty and how we most effectively may advance the kingdom of God.

First, we are said to be kings in the sense that under the King of kings we are the new breed...the reborn, to whom God has delegated authority to extend and administrate the powers of His rule. This involves faithful witness to the gospel in the power of the Spirit and loving service to humanity in the love of God. It also involves confrontation with dark powers of hell, assertive prayer warfare, and an expectation of miraculous works of God (2 Cor. 10:3-5, Eph. 6:10-20; 1 Cor. 2:4). However, this authority is only fully accomplished in the spirit of praiseful worship, as we exercise the office of "priests."

Worship is foundational to kingdom advance. The power of the believer before God's throne, worshiping the Lamb and exalting in the Holy Spirit of praise, is mightily confounding to the adversary (Ex. 19:5-7 and Ps. 22:3). "But you are a chosen generation, a royal priesthood, a holy nation, His own special people, that you may proclaim the praises of Him who called you out of darkness into His marvelous light; who once were not a people of God, who had not obtained mercy but now obtained mercy."

RESPECT THE ELDERLY

It is so sad to see how disrespectful people of all ages treat the elderly! In many nursing homes, young adults, and even some of the family members and children of the elderly have no compassion and treat them as if they are no longer useful or have importance. People don't realize the older people have led a full life of problems to overcome, and victories they won and experienced life as it came day after day. Some of these older people have made way for people of today to live successful lives, some have fought for our freedom, and some have made discoveries that made our life today better. Instead of disrespecting them, they should be treated with honor. Many elderly people have such interesting stories to tell, if only people would really take time to listen to them. They helped to make history come alive!

In the Eastern countries, the elderly are treated with great respect and are asked to make the important decisions. All family members also obeyed their decisions. They have lived a life of experience and learned how to correct their mistakes and how to handle circumstances they had to endure in life. If people would take the time to share with them, they would find the elderly have much wisdom and much needed advice for today's life.

They should not be discarded like an old shoe, but treated as vital loving family members not to be taken lightly. Someday all of us will enter our "golden age" and depending how we have treated the elderly during our younger years will be how we will be treated, for the Bible tells us we will reap what we have sown!

So the next time you have an opportunity to do something kind and caring and show compassion for an elderly person, remember they are precious people who aren't meant to be forgotten, or discarded, on the contrary, they deserve to be remembered and shown value, honor, care, love and respect for their hard lived life and who they still are! When you have an opportunity, stop at a nursing home, or visit someone you know is alone with no family and do something kind and let them know they are important too and not forgotten!

Remember God loves them and they too are part of the body of Christ which makes them even more precious. God knows and sees how each of us treat the elderly, and we will one day have to give an account of what we did or didn't do.

REMEMBERING THE DECADE OF THE 1950s

The decade of the 1950s was probably the apex of America's greatness. Enough time had passed to erase much of the sorrows of World War II. Back then, Christianity was far less complex than it is today. It was an imperfect time, and men and women did not always do what was right, but they knew the right thing to do. Morality had a standard that was accepted that generally formed to God's principals. There was more fear of God and his Word…a reverent respect. Families and businesses honored Sunday as God's day. Families went to church and businesses were closed.

Then marriage was sacred and was considered a lifetime commitment, not like today, "I'll try but I can always get a divorce." Also then children were considered a heritage and blessing from God and brought up with love and discipline. Today, both parents are working; don't have much time for their children, and really don't know what their children are doing, where they go, who they hang out with, or even what is on their minds, or in their hearts. Families today are far from the way they were in the past. Families then would eat together, pray together, do things together as a family, go to church as a family, and was taught about Jesus and His ways. The parents knew their kids friends and what they were up to. Families had time for love! Parents today don't realize how important they are in their children's future life! How they grow up in their childhood will determine the child's future! In the past parents cared about their child's education and guided them toward their goals.

Premarital sex was wrong and considered a sin. Not today, premarital sex is considered a normal activity. And an unwed or pregnant woman brought shame to the family. Drugs or dope was for those who were considered dumb. Homosexuality was sinful, an abomination to God and a perversion of humankind. Instead of helping these people find the truth, the world now accepts them, only because they don't know the Word of God. We are to love the people but hate the sin.

Pornographic materials were outside the parameters of the moral…off limits. Now porno material runs rapid on the internet, TV, movies, magazines and is just overlooked as a problem and there is nothing wrong with it they feel. The problem is, it leads to the addiction of pornography which is very hard to overcome. It also is the cause of trafficking men and women and children. It is also a sin and not accepted by God, if anyone is concerned, and if one can believe, it will lead to the destiny of hell! Tragically, men's minds can become so seared by sin that they cannot discern between good and evil.

America would now be seen for the "Sodom and Gomorrah" of today. We have to realize, one day we all have to give an account to God, whether you believe it or not, it is a fact! It seems that those days of morality, integrity, honest, committed marriages, the love of family life and much spirituality are faded away. Lies are natural in a normal conversation without a conscience. Lies are a sin!

WHERE IS THE FEAR OF GOD! Don't people care about their destiny...heaven or hell? Don't people care about the pride, honor, respect and love of America? Don't people want to care more about their family life? Don't people care if they sin? It is a sad situation, and an embarrassment to our country and to the world! People, we can turn it around! One man turned the world upside down, who was Jesus. Just think what all of us Christians can do! Stand up for RIGHTEOUSNESS!

"Most assuredly, I say to you, he who believes in Me,
the works that I do he will do also; and greater works than these
he will do, because I go to My Father"
(John 14:13).

"Therefore, whatever you want men to do you, do also to them,
for this is the law and the Prophets" ("The Golden Rule!"
(Matthew 7:12).

SEEKING GOD

"When Thou didst say, 'Seek My face,' my heart said to Thee, 'Thy face, O Lord, I shall seek" (Psalm 27:8).

Maturity starts as we break the cycle of seeking God only during hardships; holiness begins the moment we seek God for Himself. A touch from God is wonderful, but we are in pursuit of more than just experiences. We are seeking to abide with Christ, where we are continually aware of His fullness within us, where His Presence dwells in us in glory.

How do we enter this place? If we study the life of Moses, we will see how he sought God and lived in fellowship with Him. "Now Moses used to take the tent and pitch it outside the camp, a good distance from the camp, and he called it the tent of meeting. And it came about, that everyone who sought the Lord would go out to the tent of meeting which was outside the camp" (Ex. 33:7).

Notice that "everyone who sought the Lord would go out." If we are going to truly seek the Lord, we must "go out" as Moses did and those who sought the Lord. We must pitch our tent "a good distance from camp." What camp is that? For Moses, as well as for us, it is the "camp of familiarity." There is nothing wrong or sinful with things that are familiar, but remember when Jesus told His disciples to follow Him, He called them to leave the familiar pattern of their lives for extended periods and be alone with Him (Matt. 19:27, Lk. 14:33). Jesus knew that men, by nature, are unconsciously governed by the familiar. If He would expand us to receive the eternal, He must rescue us from the limitations of the temporal.

This does not mean we neglect our families or become irresponsible as we seek God. God gives everyone time to seek Him. We must redeem the time put away the hobbies for a while, turn the TV off, and put away the newspaper and magazines. Those who want to find God will find the time.

Sadly, many Christians have no higher goal, no greater aspiration, than to become "normal." Their desires are limited to measuring up to others. Paul rebuked the church at Corinth because they walked "...like mere men" (1 Cor. 3:3). God has more for us than merely becoming better people; He wants to flood our lives with the same power that raised Christ from the dead! We must understand: God does not merely want us "normal," He wants us Christlike! Christlikeness must become our singular goal.

For most people, our sense of reality and our security is oftentimes rooted in the familiar. How difficult it is to grow spiritually if our security is based upon the stability of outward things! Our security must come from God, not circumstances, nor even relationships.

When we work all day only to come home, watch TV, then collapse in bed, our lifestyle becomes a chain of bondage. These things may not trap us in sin, as much as they keep us from God. Every minute you seek God is a minute enriched with new life, new power from God. If we are going to become holy, we must sever the chains and restraints, the bondage of desiring just an average life. We will choose to leave the camp of familiarly and place our tent in the Presence of God. Christ desires us to leave the familiar, distracting world of our senses and abide in the world of our hearts, bearing in mind that the highest goal of prayer is to find God.

SATAN IS AFTER YOUR MIND FOR A REASON!

"Be sober, be vigilant, because your adversary the devil walks about like a roaring lion, seeking whom he may devour" (1 Peter 5:8).

Satan is after your will. In order to get to your will, he has to get to your mind. In your mind there is the will, the emotions, and the intellect. These three are in the soulish area. A person has a mind, and a will and an intellect. Of course man is more than a soulish man…man is a spirit, soul and body, Satan is after your mind for one reason. He knows that if he can get to your mind, and get you to thinking like everybody else does, then you have given him the legal right to enter your mind and dominate your will.

If you are doing something wrong and you say you can't help it, you have to recognize that this is the area that has weakened, and there is someone controlling or influencing your will. Then you must call upon the Name of the Lord. He will answer you and help you get your will back from the one who stole it from you, or whom you gave.

Your mind, your will, your intellect, and your emotions are in the soulish realm. Your soul does not have direct fellowship with the Father. That is to say, your spirit has direct fellowship with the Father. Your spirit receives the revelation from the Father by the Holy Spirit. It is the spirit of the man within you that is "born again" and not your soul. Therefore, the object is to cause our soul (the unrenewed mind) to be subject to our spirit. For in our spirit, by the power of the Holy Spirit comes the influence to our soul to do good. And then of course, the body has no choice but to line up with the Word of God. There are certain things we can do with our intellect. But the spiritual things come from God the Father. They come into our spirit.

As an individual, and a Christian, we have to recognize where our thoughts are coming from. If you are a Christian and you are having trouble in this area, you must renew your mind with the Word of God, and use the spiritual authority and weapons that God has given you and pull down the strong hold that is attacking you.

These strongholds occur in our mind when the mind begins to think and imagine things contrary to God's Word. You then take your will and emotions, or intellect and confess the Word of God to help you expel the negative imaginations which are happening in the mind. You must cast them out!

Satan is after one thing, and that is to destroy your spiritual relationship with the Father. However, in order for him to get to your spirit, he will have to go through your mind first. Having gone into your mind, he will now try to take over your will and destroy your spirit. That is how the enemy tries to come in and dominate person's lives.

Be alert what you put into your mind and watch your negative confessions, because "Thou art snared and taken captive with the words of thy mouth." Any time that your soul is in control instead of your spirit confusion occurs. The spirit is supposed to be in charge at all times. The soul helps the spirit fight fleshly desires and to live victoriously. Do not let the devil get a foot hold in your mind, keep it renewed with the Word of God. When your mind and heart are full of the Word, no demon or devil can have foot hold on you.

John 8:31-32 reads: "If ye continue in My Word then ye are my disciples indeed. And ye shall know the truth and the truth shall set you free."

SPIRITUAL ENTHUSIASM

Enthusiasm is a quality of buoyancy, exhilaration, joy, liveliness, or ecstasy that fills the air. And with enthusiasm, comes hope. Newlyweds, new parents, or people on vacations are enjoying life, bubbling with life! Do you lack enthusiasm? This may mean you have lost your sense of purpose; that you don't know what you are living for. It may also mean that you've become bogged down by the details of life; too busy to stop and enjoy the wonder all around you. The new Christian, especially, should indeed be enthusiastic, for something special has happened with eternal substance. Then there are those new Christians who seem naturally bubbly...enthusiastic, about the Lord and they want to yell it from the rooftops! So many older Christians have become complacent about their first love. It's essential that we all return to our first love... Jesus, with enthusiasm!

The Christian life is not always serious. Although, there are areas of Christian life that are...sin and its consequences, church discipline, or fighting the present of evil. But there should be a great delight in knowing God of the universe loves US, and He has a plan for US! God tells us to serve Him enthusiastically...joyfully and with a great sense of delight. God understands that enthusiasm lights the fire of service.

Christians who have lost spiritual enthusiasm are called dropouts; having no depth, and no place for the seeds of God to grow, and without that depth, the hot sun of persecution, or adversity causes enthusiasm to wither. The sense of purpose fades and along with it, one's valuable, precious and intimate relationship with God (Matthew 13:20-21).

The sin of the church at Laodicea was the sin of being lukewarm or indifferent about the Lord and spiritual things. Being lukewarm or indifferent, lacking enthusiasm is a sin, for it treats God as someone of little worth. When we value something or someone greatly, we are naturally enthusiastic!

"I am the one who corrects and disciplines everyone I love. Be diligent and turn from your indifference" (Revelation 3:19).

"Love the Lord your God, walk in all his ways, obey his commands, be faithful to him, and serve him with all your heart and soul" (Joshua 22:5).

"Nevertheless I have this against you, that you have left your first love" (Revelation 2:4).

Jesus requires absolute devotion and rejects lackadaisical, halfhearted followers. Zeal for the Lord is not optional! We must give love for Jesus first place in our life: "I know your works, that you are neither cold nor hot. I could wish you were cold or hot. So then, because you are lukewarm, and neither cold nor hot, I will vomit you out of my mouth" (Revelation 3:15-16).

If you find in your heart that's you, return to your first love, stir up enthusiasm and commit yourself both emotionally and intellectually to Christ, and avoid lukewarmness. Stir up zeal for the Lord! Do not allow yourself to be lulled to sleep; keep on pressing into Jesus, and obey God's Word to you.

SPIRITUAL KNOWLEDGE AND UNDERSTANDING

This is the time of moment to moment decisions and changes that we now live in. This is a vital time to know what God's will and purpose for our lives are. God is changing and rearranging things, lining them up for the end-time move of the Spirit. If we are to keep up, we must know God's perfect plan for our life, and how to carry it out in power. We do this through prayer. God has already provided us with a prayer that we can use to receive the wisdom and understanding we need for this critical time. It is Colossians 1:9-11:

"For this cause we…do not cease to pray for you, and to desire that ye might be filled with the knowledge of (God's) will in all wisdom and spiritual understanding; that ye might walk worthy of the Lord unto all pleasing, being fruitful in every good work, and increasing in the knowledge of God; strengthened with all might according to his glorious power, unto all patience and longsuffering with joyfulness."

It is a powerful Holy Ghost-inspired prayer that will not only enable you to know what God's will is, but to have the wisdom and understanding to carry it out. Put your name in it. It's a prayer you can be sure God will answer. Put it to work in your daily life and God will fill you with His knowledge and understanding. Read Colossians 1:9-11.

SIN IS A DISEASE OF THE SOUL

One does not need to be a rocket scientist to know what sin is. The Bible teaches that God is concerned about sin; not to limit our freedom and enjoyment of life, but because sin is a disease of the soul that destroys our lives and leads to spiritual death. Sin is falling short of the standards of a holy God. Sin is violating God's moral law. To sin is to disregard God and ignore his teachings, and deny his blessings. Sin is a power that seeks to influence, enslave, and destroy us. Sin, in its most basic element is obedience to Satan! Also there is no such thing as a private sin. Sin always hurts someone. The Ten Commandments were given as God's absolute moral and ethical standard. We will always struggle with sin, but in Christ we are guaranteed the victory! Sin loses its influence over us as we increasingly yield our lives to the control of the Holy Spirit. First John chapter one, verses five to nine tells us, "...But if we confess our sins to him, he is faithful and just to forgive us...." The greatest sin is pride which has no use for God. It is opposite of humility. It's all about... "Me and what I can do, or have done"...selfishness, it's the attitude of the devil.

Many people feel that they have sinned too much, or too bad to be forgiven. They think a person can request forgiveness only so many times. But that is the way humans think. That is exactly how the Devil wants us to think and believe! It is a lie from the pit of hell! God on the other hand says, "For My thoughts are not your thoughts, Nor are your ways My ways says the Lord" (Isaiah 55:8). You have to know in your heart, and not in your head that God says, He will always forgive you. One does not need to hide from God because of sin, on the contrary, run to Him knowing you are loved, and will be forgiven of your sin. Jesus already knows when we fail or fall. But He expects us to immediately repent so we don't open the door for the devil to get a foot hold on us. Plus unconfessed sin can hinder our prayers and blessings! Jesus says His "perfect love expels all fear" (1 John 4:18). If God loved with an imperfect love, we would have high cause to worry, for imperfect love keeps a list of sins and consults it often. When God forgives, He no longer remembers your heartfelt, sincere, confessed sin, Mark 3:28-29 says, "I assure you that any sin can be forgiven...." Forgiveness is not based on magnitude of the sin, but the magnitude of the forgiver's love. No sin is too great for God's complete and his unconditional love. There is one unforgivable sin which is an attitude of defiant hostility toward God that prevents us from accepting his forgiveness. Those who don't want his forgiveness are out of his reach. When God forgives us, He looks at us though we have never sinned. We are blameless before Him. If God has forgiven us, we also must forgive ourselves! Don't hold on to past sin; it will cause many problems. Also by not forgiving yourself, you are telling Jesus, "I don't believe You." You cannot please God without faith. By not forgiving yourself you are still holding on to the harmful guilt, shame and anxiety which causes physically and spiritual problems. Carrying past unforgiven sin that has not been confessed is like dragging a corps around or a heavy bag of rocks. Why would anyone want to do that? Forgiveness frees us from the slavery to sin! If we do sin, it's best to confess right away, don't let it linger. Confess your sin to Jesus and be free from the harmful heaviness and damage to your soul. Forgiveness brings joy.... "Oh, what joy for those whose disobedience is forgiven, whose sins are put out of sight" (Romans 4:7). God has promised to forgive sins, no matter how big...(Isaiah 1:18); God is always willing to forgive us...Jeremiah 3:22. There is no limit to God's love or his forgiveness! God is a loving, kind, good, and caring Father!

Don't doubt God's forgiveness when you have repented. Emotions might try to tell you that you are not forgiven, but emotions don't count. Listen to your spirit man and not flesh. It's faith in God and HIS LOVE AND WORD. So when feelings of doubt and fear, or dread creep in, send them back to Satan, for they are not of God! God said, "There is therefore now no condemnation to them which are in Christ Jesus, who walk not after the flesh, but after the Spirit" (Romans 8:1). So you as a believer must refuse all guilt, fear or shame over past sins and failures. You are free in Jesus for you have received God's forgiveness and grace. All judgment for our sin has passed upon Jesus. So put your faith in the blood of Jesus, there is a perfect cleansing from all sin. God offers reconciliation (forgiveness and pardon) to the ungodly; to all who will accept His Son. Since you as a believer, are no longer condemned, you have no need to condemn others. What a freedom to see others reconciled to God and tell them of the Good News!

SEND THE RIGHT MESSAGE

When you are tempted do you remind yourself that God is with you? It's not easy when the tempter is attacking, but if you remember to keep your eyes on God, you will be able to overcome it all. The point is: never lose sight of God, lest you dishonor Him and disrespect yourself. Don't deceive yourself into thinking that it's okay to dwell on thoughts that, if acted out, would dishonor God. Don't think you are going to get away with disrespecting yourself by sinning. Sin always catches up with you. It's just a lie to think otherwise. Let's face it; we have enough people in this world lying to us! Why would you want to lie to yourself? Instead, challenge yourself with the questions "What message am I sending?" and "Is God glorified in me?" I'm sure you don't want to dishonor God or disrespect yourself. Thank God for His grace and mercy! Place your standards high, higher than the worlds. You can't be an example to the world if you are acting exactly like them. You want to bring the destiny that God has for you. When temptation comes, and it will, you don't have to dishonor God or disrespect yourself by falling for it. You can live a higher life and show others how to do the same. If you are struggling, look at God and all that He has done for you. Remember where you were before you knew Him and ask yourself, "Do I really want to sin and bring reproach on the Gospel?" And "Do I really want to send the wrong message to the world?"

God wants to let His glory shine through you. He trusts you with His glory because He has resolved NOT to be a loser. God knows what you're capable of and He believes in the power of His Son's redemptive blood. Your price for sin has been paid, but that is not an excuse to continue in sin. If you are a believer, it's time to take up your cross and follow Jesus. You see, your life is a hymn to God and your calling is to promote His interest in the world. God is interested in reaching people and changing lives. He wants everyone to have the opportunity to accept eternal life through Jesus Christ and to learn to live well. When all Christians start living in peace, joy, and love we will be sending the right message to the world.

Don't settle for less than God's best for your life. Don't let the devil lie to you and cause you to sin. What God has for your future is so much better than what the devil may be dangling in front of your eyes today. Choose to resist that idiot and press on with Jesus....the Author and Finisher of your faith!

If we lead a Christian's life, it glorifies His cross, if we have Christian hope, it glorifies His name. If we perform a Christian duty, it glorifies His grace, and when we make it through a trial, a sinful habit, or the lust that led to it, it glorifies His working power and support in our life. And this is how we do it:

"I am crucified with Christ: nevertheless I live; yet not I but Christ liveth in me: and the life I now live in the flesh I live by faith of the Son of God, who loved me, and gave Himself for me" (Galatians 2:20).

SAILING THROUGH STORMY SEAS

Life can be unfair at times. When we are in the depths of despair, some feel as though they can't go on. There are those who feel Christians should be immune to depression. They feel Christians should not have anything to be depressed about because they have a relationship with God, a family of brothers and sisters who love them, and a guaranteed ticket to heaven. But when the person who is carrying the weight of gloom hears this, he not only feels depressed but now feels guilty as well because it's "unspiritual" to be down in the dumps. It is a fact of life that such feelings as depression happen in this broken world. Humanity's fall into sin in the Garden of Eden affected every area of our existence. Yes, God's chosen people also experience anxiety, despair, and darkness in their soul. Jesus experienced grief and despair to the point of death, in Gethsemane (Matt. 26). Obviously, depression that is too deep, or lasts too long indicates a need for counseling; but there is nothing unusual or unspiritual about "walking through the dark valley" from time to time. So when you are caught in one of those unpleasant times, don't add guilt to your load. There is nothing wrong with you. When sailing through stormy seas, expect a little motion discomfort. And know for certain, THE CAPTAIN IS NOT ASLEEP ON THE BRIDGE. Turn your trouble to Him and He will guide you safely through the stormy sea. He is well aware of your trouble and is waiting for you to come to Him for rest.

"We are hard pressed on every side, but not crushed; perplexed, but not in despair, persecuted, but not abandoned; struck down, but not destroyed" (2 Corinthians 4:8).

"When you pass through the waters, I will be with you, and through the rivers, they will not overflow you...Since you are precious in My sight.... and I love you..." (Isaiah 43:2-4).

"So do not fear, for I am with you; do not be dismayed, for I am your God. I will strengthen you and help you; I will up hold you with my righteous right hand" (Isaiah 41:10).

"Come to Me, all you who labor and are heavy laden, and I will give you rest. Take My yoke upon you and learn from Me, for I am gentle and lowly in heart, and you will find rest for your souls" (Matthew 11:28-2).

SAVING THE LOST

As believers we know these are the end times, and as we watch and pray for the return of Jesus we also need to pray for compassion for the lost. This is our calling, to share the Gospel of Jesus (Mark 16:15)! The Bible tells us, "The harvest truly is plenteous, but the labourers are few; Pray ye therefore the Lord of the harvest, that he will send labourers into his harvest" (Matthew 9:36-38). Why do you think the labourers are few? Could it be because they do not have compassion in their hearts and do not see out of the eyes of Jesus? When Jesus saw the multitudes, He was moved with compassion. Jesus saw them as sheep without a shepherd. He looked into the spirit realm and really saw them. He saw people who were hurting, people who were being attacked and destroyed by the enemy. When Jesus saw them He was moved with compassion. Have you ever looked that way at the unsaved? All Christians know of someone who is not saved, maybe in their family, or at work, or a neighbor and those we see who are homeless. There are millions of unbelievers who are ready to be saved. So many times we are inclined to look at the harvest and say, "It's too difficult. That person does not want to know the Lord." God won't override their will. But have you ever had an unbeliever tell you they wanted to be an awful person? Most unbelievers want to do right, have a good life, and go to heaven, but they say they can't, for the Gospel is hidden to the lost (2 Corth. 4:3).

When you see the unbeliever as Jesus does, you too will be filled with compassion and want to pray for them. You wouldn't want to see anyone go to hell where they will suffer forever, crying out and regretting they never accepted Jesus. The unbeliever is ignorant of what the true hell is like! Most don't know there is a real hell, or heaven. We as believers need to cause their blind minds to see the light to shine which will cause them to be born-again. We can pray that their eyes of understanding be enlightened (Eph. 1:15-19). Then pray the Lord of the harvest to send forth laborers filled with the Holy Spirit, and also for those to be prosperous and healthy. It is also helpful to have a godly partner who will pray the prayer of agreement with you for the unbeliever such as: "Father, we pray (name or names) they are sanctified, separated from the world, and are being set apart unto God. We are agreeing that while that process is happening, the eyes of their (name or names) understanding will be enlightened and they (name or names) will understand the Gospel of Jesus Christ. And as we pray, the Lord of the harvest will send forth laborers who know the Word and know how to lead people to the Lord Jesus. Send those that are full of faith in God's Word. We thank you Father and declare that blind eyes and minds are being opened to spiritual things. Their (name or names) hearts are being prepared by the Holy Ghost for the moment the laborers arrive. (Name or names) will be saved, for it is done in Jesus' Name.

"Satan, we take authority over you, in the Name of Jesus your work is done and over, for you will no longer have control over (name or names). Even as one shall put a thousand to flight, two shall put ten thousand to flight, we have now prayed in agreement. In the Name of Jesus we pray…AMEN." Now that you have done all, just stand… (Eph. 6:13).

If you have not been praying for the lost, you might want to pray and ask the Lord for true compassion, so you can look upon the lost and feel and see as Jesus did, for the time is short and you could be saving souls now from hell! You will surely be blessed to see all the people in heaven that you had prayed to be saved!

Remember, Christian, YOU have a calling and a commission to bring glory to God.

TWO BLIND MICE AND ONE "COOL CAT"

The worldly person, also known as the natural man (also meaning women too) are body beautiful conscience. Their main objective in life is outward beauty. They are blind to the truth that Man is a spirit. He was made in the likeness of God. Man is NOT just a body; he has a soul but lives in a physical body. When the physical body of man is dead in the grave, the spirit lives on into eternity. The beauty of the body is temporary but the part of man that is born-again is his spirit which is the real beauty that lasts forever! It is our spirit that is made a new creature in Christ; it is the life of God, and the nature of God within us (2 Corth. 5:17). When one becomes born again (spiritually) and becomes a new creature, you do not get a new body. The outward man is just like it was before. God does something with the inward man…your spirit is no longer dead but alive to God. God makes the man on the inside a new man in Christ.

There are three types of "man.": (1) The natural man (1 Corth. 2:14), who has never yet passed out of death into life, which means his spirit has not been born again. He's never been recreated. He's never become a new creature in Christ. He is motivated by demons and ruled by Satan. They are in the kingdom of darkness and so the natural, worldly man is a Satan-ruled man. He is motivated by the flesh, the physical and not a spiritual man. So the natural man cannot know the things of the spirit. He cannot understand the Bible because it is of the Spirit of God.

(2) The carnal man (1Corth. 3:1) is a new creature, a babe in Christ, and has been born-again (1 Corth.3:1-3). But he's never developed or grown spiritually. It is sad but true that the carnal man may remain in this condition all his life long. He may never develop beyond the babyhood state of his new creation. He is governed by his body; by his physical senses, rather than by his spirit. Backbiting, bitterness, strife and jealousy are signs of underdevelopment on the part of the believer. These things are caused by being selfish. As long as one is selfish, sensitive, and can be hurt, you are a babe in Christ and are not growing. God wants us to grow and there is no other way to get out of the carnal state except to grow out of it. It doesn't happen overnight any more than you grew up mentally or physically overnight. But there's one thing about it…there's no need of you not growing.

(3) The Spiritual man is one who has developed in divine things. His spirit has gained the lead over his intellectual processes, his physical senses. God now governs him through the Word. This is a man who has come to know the Father in reality. The believer now knows who and what he is in Christ. He also has come to know the intimacy of the Holy Spirit and is God conscience and knows the presence of the Holy Spirit's indwelling. He has learned to walk

in the light of the Word and remains calm and collected in time of crisis. He walks in love in all situations and with others. He values the unity of the church family. The spiritual man understands and knows his inheritance and gives thanks as he has the ability now to enjoy it. The spiritual man is the one whom the Word has gained complete control over his mind and body but still desires to continue to grow spiritually. The Word has brought him into harmony with the will of God, for the Word of God is the will of God.

Which are you...one of the blind mice or the...cool cat"?

TRUST GOD WITH YOUR FEARS

"...If God is for us, who can be against us?"

(Romans 8:31, 33)

How did Jesus endure the terror of the crucifixion? He went first to the Father with his fears. He modeled the words of Psalm 56:3: "When I am afraid, I will trust you." We are to say the same when we are afraid. Don't avoid life's Gardens of Gethsemane. Enter them. Just don't enter them alone. And while you are there, be honest. Pounding the ground is permitted, tears are allowed, and if you sweat blood, you won't be the first. Do what Jesus did; open your heart, and be specific, Jesus was. "Take this cup," He prayed. Tell God everything, all the details, He has plenty of time and is willing to listen. He also has plenty of compassion.

He doesn't think your fears are foolish or silly. He won't tell you to "buck up" or "get tough." He's been where you are. He knows how you feel. And He knows what you need. Is God willing? Yes and no. He didn't take away the cross, but He took the fear. God didn't still the storm, but He calmed the sailor. Who's to say He won't do the same for you and I? "Do not worry about anything, but pray and ask God for everything you need, always giving thanks" (Philippians 4:6).

Don't measure the size of the mountain; talk to the One who can move it. Instead of carrying the world on your shoulders, talk to the one who holds the universe on his.

INSPIRATION...

Many years ago, Fredrick Nolan was fleeing from his enemies during the North African persecution. Hounded by his pursuers over hill and valley with no place to hide, he fell exhausted into a wayside cave where he fully expected to be found. Awaiting his death, he saw a spider weaving a web. Within minutes, the little bug had woven a beautiful web across the mouth of the cave. The pursuers arrived and wondered if Nolan was hiding in there, but they thought it impossible for him to have entered the cave without dismantling the web. So they went on. Having escaped, Nolan emerged from his hiding place and proclaimed, "Where God is, a spider's web is like a wall. Where God is not, a wall is like a spider's web." God is our wall of defense. He is the one who delivers us from our hurts and fears. He is the One who gives us comfort and strength we need to be courageous and endure the trials and troubles that enter our lives.

Remember, God is for us. God dominates the enemy through you. Jesus is living big in you. You are never alone. Fear is a thing of the past. There is no force that can stand against you when your heart trusts God! Winning is now your way!

TRIALS WRAPPED IN BLESSINGS

"And we know that all things work together for good to those who love God, to those who are called according to His purpose" (Romans 8:28).

How many times do we get frustrated when things go wrong, and we do not have control, and we wonder why is this happening? Especially for husbands because they feel they are the head of the household and they are to take care of the family, so they feel they failed, or they don't know how or they just can't handle the situation that just came upon them unexpectedly. This is where the devil trips us up if we don't recognize what has just happened!

We have to learn to trust GOD with our whole being, knowing and remembering what His Word said: "But as for you, you meant evil against me, but God meant it for good, in order to bring it about as it is this day, to save many people alive" (Genesis 50:20), and "Grow in the grace and knowledge of our Lord and Savior Jesus Christ. To him be glory both now and forever! Amen" (2 Peter 3:18), and "Give thanks in all circumstances, for this is God's will for you in Christ Jesus" (Thessalonians 5:18).

God understands our frustration and He warned us that we would have tribulation in this world, but God can make good from what the devil meant for evil! God will use these circumstances, trials and troubles for our good! But God expects our response to maintain thanking Him, because when we do, we are acknowledging God for being greater than ourselves and our problem. This also requires the help of the Holy Spirit. When we give thanks, even when we don't feel like it, our feelings of frustration diminish. Instead of trying it our way to solve the situations, we need to release them to the Lord, depending on Him and His mighty Word! We have to keep our eyes and mind open to look for the blessings within these trials and troubles. God tells us: "Forget the former things, do not dwell on the past. See I am doing a new thing! Now it springs up; do you not perceive it? I am making a way in the desert and streams in the wasteland" (Isaiah 43:18-19). If we seek to see the things from God's perspective, we will discover treasures in our trials.

So don't resist or run from difficulties in life. These problems are not random mistakes; they are hand-tailored blessings designed for our benefit and growth. We are to embrace all the circumstances that God allows in our life, trusting Him to bring good out of them! So when you start to feel stressed, let those feelings alert you to your need for God. The more we need and trust and depend on God, the more our intimacy with Him increases!

The world teaches us to depend on ourselves, be self-reliant, but that is idolatry. We are to depend on God, thanking and praising Him for all things which provide protection and deliverance and it will also make the devil flee! Reliance on God produces abundant living in His kingdom!

"I am the vine, you are the branches. He who abides in Me, and I in him, bear much fruit: for without Me you can do nothing"
(John 15-5).

TREASURES IN YOUR TRIALS

"But as for you, you meant evil against me;

but God meant it for good, in order to bring it about

as it is this day, to save many people alive"

(Genesis 50:20).

Many of us have a hard time thanking God when we are going through hard times. Sometimes we just want some relief from troubles. We know our problems are to trust in God, and we desire to trust God with our whole being, but at times, trusting doesn't come easily.

Because God loves us so much He wants us to stay openminded to his perspective so we can understand why we have trials. He is not punishing us; but preparing us; making us stronger. Remember, our lifespan on earth is miniscule, compared with the glory that awaits us in heaven. We have to view our life through God's perspective. By being open to accepting adversity as a blessing shows God we are indeed learning to trust Him more. Remember, the evil one attacks us continually with arrows of accusation. When we use our faith skillfully we can stop these missiles. Even when some of these arrows find their mark and wound us, we don't despair. We know our God is the Great Physician. His loving Presence can strengthen our wounds and train us to trust Him more. God tells us to come close to Him when we are wounded, and pay attention to his teaching as we do, our faith becomes stronger, enabling us to grow in grace and in knowledge of Him, the Lord of Peace.

But grow in the grace and knowledge of our Lord and Savior Jesus Christ.
To him be glory both now and forever! Amen
(2 Peter 3:18).

TOTAL AUTHORITY

"I will give unto thee the keys of the kingdom of heaven; and whatsoever thou shalt bind on earth shall be bound in heaven; and whatsoever thou shalt loose on earth shall be loosed heaven"

(Matthew 16:19).

The word keys in the scripture denote authority. Jesus is passing on to his church His authority or control to bind and to loose on earth. Jesus activated this provision through His Cross, the church (Christian believers) is then charged with implementation of what He released through His life, death, and resurrection. In other words, Jesus is stating that the church will be empowered to continue in the privileged responsibility of leavening the earth with His kingdom power and provision. Jesus alone made this provision possible (Matt. 12:29).

As believers, we have total authority over the powers of Satan. We can take authority over all the powers of Satan. We have the Name of Jesus: Philippians 2:9-10 says, "Wherefore God also hath highly exalted him, and given him a name which is above every name: That at the name of Jesus every knee should bow, of things in heaven, and things in earth, and things under the earth." We can take authority over them in the Name of Jesus and pull down their strongholds. Jesus has told us in Luke 10:19-20, "Behold, I give you the authority to trample on serpents and scorpions, and over all the power of the enemy, and nothing shall by any means hurt you." Serpents and scorpions are symbols of spiritual enemies and demonic power. Remember, it's the spiritual enemies and not flesh and blood we war against: "For we do not wrestle against flesh and blood, but against principalities, against power, against the rulers of the darkness of this age, against spiritual hosts of wickedness in the heavenly places" (Eph. 6:12). The heaven Jesus was talking about is not where God resides but the battle zone where Satan's forces are operating.

Believers, it's time we began to realize how important we are to world affairs. Since the day Jesus gave us the Great Commission, the life or death of the world has been in the hands of the church. We are the ones who have the mighty Name of Jesus and the awesome strength of the gospel. We are the ones whose prayers can change every office of authority in this land. It's up to us to begin to intercede right NOW and use the power God has given us. We can alter the spiritual complexion of this earth. One day Jesus will ask us, "What did you do with the authority I gave you?" What will you answer, for there will be no excuse unacceptable? Believers, we have Divine life that flows through us, we have Jesus in us and He is greater than he that is in the world and we have the promise: "No weapon formed against me prospers" (Isaiah 54:17). Since God never changes we don't change our position of victory, for we always triumph in Christ! We have to stay consistent, constant, and steadfast! We are NOT to worry about troubles or tribulations, regardless of the circumstances because God always puts us over. So we are free to fulfill our purpose as a church and that means putting our given total authority to work for the glory of God and the blessing of others and to witness to the lost and hurting! We have the keys, we have the authority and we have the powerful Name of Jesus.... So church, let's get busy about our Father's business!

TO BE A CHRISTIAN IS TO BE GRACIOUSLY OBEDIENT

"He that hath my commandments,

and keepeth them, he it is that loveth me....

If a man love me, he will keep my words"

(John 14:21, 23).

Obedience is one way to know you are a Christian. If a person claims to be a Christian but is disobedient to God throughout his or her life, the apostle John says they are liars and the truth is not in them (1 John 2:4-5). The way to be assured that we truly know Him as a child knows his father is by keeping His commandments. Obedience results in assurance. Christians who have doubts usually are involved in sin, because sin breeds doubt.

The Greek word translated "keep" conveys the ides of a watchful, observant obedience. It is not an obedience that is the result of external pressure, which might cause someone to say, "I have to do this, because I'm afraid that if I don't I'll get whacked by the divine hammer!" The term is more than just the act of obeying the commands. It is a holy desire to obey God because you love Him. Rather than being a negative fear, obedience is inspired by love to become your heart's greatest desire. We are to keep Christ's commands in the spirit of obedience. Henry Alford's Greek Testament defines "keep" as "guarding, as some precious thing." The Christian can know that he knows God when the great desire of his heart is to obey Him. When people claim to be Christians and then live any way they please, in complete disregard of God's command, they under-mine their claim. We can identify a Christian because he keeps the precepts of Christ, not because he subscribes to the law of Moses. John did not say, "By this do we know that we know him, if we keep the law of Moses." But if we desire to obey and honor the precepts of Christ, we prove that we have come to a saving knowledge of God and the Lord Jesus Christ.

There is a distinction one must understand between legal obedience and gracious obedience. Gracious obedience pertains to God's desire for us to exhibit a loving and sincere spirit of obedience. Although it is marked by defects, it is still accepted by God, and its blemishes are blotted out by the blood of Jesus Christ. The obedience that our Lord is after is not legal obedience qualified by the law but gracious obedience qualified by love. It's not based on fear;

it's based on friendship. God is not expecting absolute perfection. As a Christian, you don't need to live under the fear that if you ever do something wrong, you're going to be severely punished and lose your salvation. True Christians have a desire to submit to Jesus Christ. Nonbelievers do not submit to the lordship of Christ; they fulfill their own desires at their own pace. Titus 1:16 states, "They profess that they know God, but in works they deny him, being abominable, and disobedient." False believers fail the moral test.

Our love for God is made visible by our obedience. Love is made manifest in our obedience and is evidence that we are saved. There is no such thing as Christianity without obedience! In Matthew 22:37-40 when Jesus says, "Thou shalt love the Lord, thy God, with all thy heart, and with all thy soul, and with all thy mind. This is the first and great commandment. And the second is like it, Thou shalt love thy neighbor as thyself. On these two commandments hang all the law and the prophets." If you keep the commandments of loving God and others, you don't have to worry about the rest. That is the essence of the Christian life.

THROUGH THE EYES OF GRACE

As Christian believers, we know and understand we are to walk in unity with our brothers and sisters in the Lord. God wants the Body of Christ in unity; walking in love and in the Spirit with one mind and heart, "a oneness with" God. But many Christians are looking through the eyes of judgment and legalism. Seeing one's faults and weakness and how we perform is totally wrong because performance will always be insufficient to meet holy standards. We will never be perfect until we are in heaven with the Lord.

We as believers have to learn to look at one another as the Body of Christ, with value, for we need each other. No one is more important than the other. As a born-again Christian we are all clothed in the Lord's royal righteousness. To Jesus we are radiant, especially when we gaze at Him. And we are lovely when we reflect His Glory back at Him. He rejoices over us with shouts of joy, "The Lord your God is in your midst… He will exult over you with joy… He will rejoice over you with shouts of joy" (Zephaniah 3:17).

The best way to see through eyes of grace is to look through the lens of the Lord's unfailing love. But one needs to practice this daily, and gradually you will find it easier to extend grace both to yourself and others. We need to be kind to ourselves and not be troubled by fear of failure, for the Lord views us through the eyes of Grace. Although because God is infinite, He can see us simultaneously as we are now, as well as how we will be in heaven. When He sees us as we are now helps Him work on the things we need to change. The heavenly vision enables Him to love us with His perfect, everlasting love: "I sought the Lord, and He answered me; He delivered me from all my fears. Those who look to Him are radiant; their faces are never covered with shame" (Psalm 34:4-5).

THIS NATION UNDER GOD

What happened to "This Nation under God"? Has the meaning of these words been long forgotten and no longer valued that God is the ruler of the nations, and King of kings? God has said, "I am the Lord, and there is no other, besides Me there is no God." If there is no other God, there is no person or power greater than He. In his hands is the destiny of nations. To make or acknowledge a state or nation as a god is a direct violation of the first Commandment: "You should have no other gods before Me." Indeed, God is superior and sovereign to the state and nations because He is the creator of the universe! God is over all and controls everything. Not only is God over the state and nations but God is the absolute and final authority on earth as well as in heaven. Whether one believes it or not it is a fact! The authorities are given by God for his purposes. They are accountable to God for governing the nation, State officials must not only answer to the people at election time but to God also! Many who have abused their position and power will one day stand before God's Supreme Court! God is the ruler of a nation but it does not mean the church or religious leaders are to govern. Their job is to teach people God's morals and standard and their spiritual character. To have God above the state and nation simply means that citizens are responsible to govern themselves by properly electing leaders to fulfill God's demands of liberty and justice for all. To do this, a nation needs a people committed to God, a nation that knows God's laws, and a people who fear (deep respect) God enough to obey Him.

Because God is over a nation, He chooses a nation at various times to carry out a mission for him. Are we a nation God has chosen? Undoubtedly America at the present is the strongest, wealthiest, and most highly educated and advanced nation in science and technology. America has been chosen, apparently, to be the stronghold of democracy and supreme champion of human rights in the world. Throughout the world, America stands for liberty and a good life. God chooses a nation not only for power but for righteousness. When it comes to godly living, democracy, and righteousness, can we really be God's chosen vessel in the world? Where is the honesty, integrity and where is the godliness? Have we forgotten that we will be judged for not carrying out our responsibility to God and respect, love and honor for God? God has not stopped being God; He has not changed. His Word says, "He is the same yesterday, today and forever" (Hebrews 13:8). One sure thing…sin always brings judgment. It may come through another nation or it may come in other ways within a nation. People, we as Americans and Christians have to ask ourselves, have we thrown away traditional values and morals that made America great? Have we stood by and allowed God's righteousness of standards, values, and Commandments defiled our homes, communities, schools, jobs and government? Why did we stand by and let prayer be taken out of the schools and government? The success and wellbeing of America or any nation depend upon saying, and practicing "This Nation under God," and the Bible says, "Blessed is the Nation whose God is the Lord." May we as a nation pay heed to the words of President Reagan uttered in a 1983 address in Orlando, Florida: "While America's military strength is important, let me add here that I have always maintained that the struggle now going on for the world will never be decided by bombs or rockets, by armies or military might. The real crisis we face today is a spiritual one; at root, it is a test of moral will and faith." Today this statement by President Reagan still holds weight and truth!

If we are to honor God, and be people chosen by God to carry out his will in this world, and stand for liberty and good life, we need to go back to the Cross and remember the sacrifice the Lord made for us, pray for our nation and leaders, and stand up for righteousness; be a living example of God's love, and honor his Name and godly standards, not only for our well-being but for the generations to come! Let us restore the respect and honor of this nation and be responsible to uphold righteousness and receive the blessings God promised! Let the world know we are people of God! We will not have victory without God! Let God live big, starting first in our own families.

THE WORLD'S SYSTEM

"Love not the world, neither the things that are in the world.

If any man love the things in the world,

the love of the Father is not in him"

(James 4:15).

Satan has developed a system in which he can captivate men. It is anti-God and anti-Christ. It is in rebellion against the truth and contradicts the divine perspective. Behind that system is Satan. He isn't directly responsible for everything that the world does, but he's behind it. Satan is behind what's happening today in opposition to God's kingdom.

First John 2:15 tells us to stop loving the worldly system and the things that are in it; for if anyone is in love with it, his claim to love God is invalid. The system that Satan has developed is in total opposition to God. A person cannot love both. James 4:4 makes a similar exhortation: "Adulterers and adulteresses! Do you not know that friendship with the world is enmity with God? Whoever therefore wants to be a friend of the world makes himself an enemy of God." A person cannot love both at the same time. A true Christian does not love the world! Christians do not love the world because of what the world is and because of who Christians are. The world's system is designed to tempt a person to sin. God wants to generate holiness in our lives as we become more like Jesus Christ. Satan uses the world to tempt us. Some are able to resist the temptation because of our maturity in Christ. But that does not change the evil intentions of the world, which opposes the holiness that God desires in every Christian's life. We should live in such a way that the watching world cannot accuse our lifestyle: "For God hath not called us unto uncleanness, but unto holiness" (1 Thessalonians 3:12-13). The distinguishing mark of a Christian is that he does not want to sin; we desire to be holy. We cry out, "Create in me a clean heart, O God, and renew a right spirit within me" (Psalms 51:10).

One may not love the world's system but are attracted to the things that are in it. As an example: this world has godless religion, materialistic economics, and self-centered morality. These things are inconsistent with who we are and how we live. Some people say it's hard to live a pure life today. It is and always has been hard, but the media today has probably made it more difficult to maintain a pure life. The TV has much profanity, violence, and sexual immorality. When you watch it, you are sold the world's standards in a very slick way. Movies are presented the same way. The ideas that are conveyed through music of the world rarely square up with what the Word of God says. The world's system is geared to generate sin, and if you want to play with it, it will generate sin in your life. If you want to put yourself in the world's mold-its materialism, humanism—you are going against the very nature of your identity in Christ. "Since we are called to shine as lights in the world" (Phil. 2:15), we had better make sure people can see that there's something different about us. We need to disconnect ourselves from the system by saturating our minds with the Word of God to establish the right thought patterns.

> "In everything you do, stay away from complaining and arguing so that no one can speak a word of blame against you. You are to live clean, innocent lives as children of God in a dark world full of people who are crooked and stubborn. Shine out among them like beacon lights, holding out to them the Word of Life" (Philippians 2:14-16).

THE WAGES OF SIN IS DEATH

"The wages of sin is death, but the gift of God is eternal life in Christ Jesus our Lord" (Romans 6:23).

The following story was often told by Charles Haddon Spurgeon: A cruel king called one of his subjects into his presence and asked him his occupation. The man responded, "I'm a blacksmith." The ruler then ordered him to go and make a chain of a certain length.

The man obeyed, returning after several months to show it to the monarch. Instead of receiving praise for what he had done, however, he was instructed to make the chain twice as long.

When the assignment was completed, the blacksmith presented his work to the king, but again was commanded, "Go back and double its length!" This procedure was repeated several times. At last the wicked tyrant directed the man to be bound in the chains of his own making and cast into the fiery furnace.

Like that cruel king, sin exacts from its servants a dreadful price: "The wages of sin is death" (Rom. 6:23). But the good news is the last part of that verse: "The gift of God is eternal life through Jesus Christ our Lord." If you are not a Christian and have not made Jesus Christ your Lord and Savior, you may want to consider the consequence of your sin. If you want your sin to be forgiven, and your life changed and look forward to eternal life with Christ Jesus, you must believe on the Lord Jesus Christ, then repent of your sin and ask Jesus to come into your life and help you live the life He has for you and you will be saved: "Believe on the Lord Jesus Christ, and you will be saved, you and your household" (Acts 16:31). Then find a Bible-teaching church and learn of the Lord and His ways, pray and fellowship with your spiritual family. Then share the love of God and the gospel with those who are lost in their sin and don't know the way.

Lord, give me courage to confess,
To bare my sinful heart to Thee;
Forgiving love You long to show
And from my sin to set me free.

THE UNRENEWED MIND

Uncontrollable thoughts, vile imaginations, impure pictures, wandering thoughts, confused ideas, and double-mindedness are symptoms of the unrenewed mind.

How many times have you gone to bed and couldn't sleep? How many times have you had problems with thoughts that you couldn't control? You say to yourself, "I don't want to think about them anymore," and yet you keep thinking the disturbing or bad thoughts. Who is giving them to you? If someone else is giving them to you and God does not control the mind of His people, then who would it be? If you are saved and Spirit filled, but you have these thoughts that you cannot control, it is evident that you are not in charge of your mind. If you are a Christian you should realize that you are in Christ Jesus. You should take authority and take the thought back, and take back your will from whomever has stolen it from you, or to whom you have surrendered your mind, will, and personality. Who is putting those thoughts in your mind? If they are not coming from God, and they are not coming from you, then they are coming from the devil himself.

Even a Christian can be tormented by demons just as Jesus was. Peter, Paul, and others were also tormented by them. That's why the Bible says, "For though we walk in the flesh, we do not war after the flesh for weapons of our warfare are not carnal, but mighty through God to the pulling down of strongholds. Casting down imaginations and every high thing that exalteth itself against the knowledge of God, and bringing into captivity every thought to the obedience of Christ" (Il Corinthians 10:3-5). Where are the strongholds? They are in your mind. It's time that Christians realize how the enemy will come to attack and rob them if their mind is not renewed in God's Word. Whoever keeps his mind upon the Lord, He will keep them in perfect peace: "Thou wilt keep him in perfect peace, whose mind is stayed on thee: because he trusteth in thee" (Isaiah 26:3). The next time the devil starts bombarding you with thoughts that you know are from him, begin to think about the Lord, speak the Word of Scripture, and sing praise to the Lord. Don't ever think you cannot control thoughts that are not from God! Make it a practice to be aware of your thoughts and take control of your mind!

THE TRUE DEVOTIONAL LIFE

As Christians, we have truly missed the mark of a real devotional life. Many Christians take God too lightly, seeing Him as a spiritual Santa Claus...give me, give me, give me. There is no heartfelt, deep reverence of who God actually is. Then there are the microwave Christians who have no time or very little time for a valued, quality time for God. Their focus is on what they feel is more important, their self and their personal busy life. Some folks are calling themselves Christians who don't know they have to be born-again to be a Christian, or they are pretending to be Christians by word only and showing up at church so they will make a good impression. We are no better in public life than what we are in private life with our God.

A survey conducted by Christianity Today revealed that the average person prays only three minutes a day! That's hard to believe, but the facts are there. Another survey showed that 93% of students preparing for ministry in a well-known theological college confessed that they had no devotional life. If Jesus as God-man knew how much He needed a regular prayer time, how much more you and I are in need of a quality devotional life. Jesus, Himself is our example in Mark 1:35 as He arose long before daylight and prayed, after a full day and a much needed night's rest. So none of us can excuse our devotional life on the grounds of a busy program, and certainly none of us can afford to forego our daily Quiet Time. Our time with God and our prayer is both an attitude and an activity of the soul. All great men of God have been those who rose up early in the morning to worship, Abraham (Gen. 22:3), Jacob (Gen. 28:18, Joshua (Josh. 3:1), Gideon (Judg. 6:38), and Samuel (1Sam. 9:26), and David (1Sam. 17:20). These great men knew the most important thing they had to do was to give themselves to God in prayer and meditation in order that they might be comforted, encouraged, warned, reproved and instructed in the day that they were about to start. We all need the nourishment from God each and every day. We need the wisdom and insight, guidance and direction to successfully fulfill the day to God's will and for our blessing. Our spiritual life is determined by one supreme word in the Christian vocabulary, and that is obedience. All the sacrifice of our ministry, witnessing, preaching, our giving, or laying down our life, means nothing, if it isn't backed up by total obedience to God's Word. If we are walking in love and the Word our natural overflow of a devotional life has the ability to speak a word in season to a needy man or woman around us. The Bible reminds us that "out of the abundance of the heart the mouth speaks" (Matt. 12:34). The reason why our lives are often so stale is because we haven't spent time alone with God. It doesn't take long to detect whether or not a fellow Christian is walking with God. What overflows is obviously what is occupying his or her heart and mind. Our prayer time should always reflect the reverent respect, honor, pure of heart, an attitude of gratitude and an openness and willingness to fulfill the desires of God's heart and the willingness to be corrected and forgiveness when you know it's needed, and the love and devotion for our God, praises and sharing everything with God and then…to listen! For prayer is a two way conversation with the sharing of hearts! Remember this time is a holy time with your Heavenly Holy Father and it is not to be taken lightly! Our God does not want, except, or tolerate a rushed, empty, disrespectful effort of prayer and rushed time that is not sincere or heartfelt. If you want the light of Jesus to shine and radiate from you, make your worship time worthy of the Lord! Don't settle for anything less than a true devotional life!

THE TRUE CHRISTIAN THINKER

True Christian thinkers begin from the principle that Jesus Christ has given the full revelation of God. Their thinking is based on faith. Faith means taking God at His Word; it means believing that we are as Jesus proclaimed us to be.

Their thinking is motivated by love. To think in love will always save us from certain things. It will save us from arrogant thinking and contemptuous thinking. It will save us from condemning either that with which we do not agree or that which we do not understand. It will also save us from expressing our views in such a way that we hurt other people. Love saves us from destructive thinking and destructing speaking. To think in love is always to think in sympathy.

A true Christian thinker thinks from a pure heart. A pure heart originally means clean as opposed to soiled or dirty. A pure heart is a heart whose motives are absolutely pure and absolutely unmixed. In the hearts of true Christian thinkers, there is no desire to show how clever they are, no desire to win a purely debating victory, no desire to show up the ignorance of opponents. Their only desire is to help and shed light to lead others nearer to God. Christian thinkers are moved only by love of truth and the love for others.

Their thinking comes from a good conscience. The real meaning of conscience is a knowing oneself. To have a good conscience is to be able to look in the face the knowledge which one shares with no one but oneself and not to be ashamed. Christian thinkers are men and women whose thoughts and whose actions give them the right to say what they do.

The true Christian thinkers are men and women of undissembling faith. The phrase literally means the faith in which there is no hypocrisy. That simply means that the great characteristic of true Christian thinkers is sincerity. They are sincere both in their desire to find the truth and in their desire to communicate it. They know the purpose of the commandment to love does not lead to strife and debate but rather to love God and man.

"Now the purpose of the commandment is love from a pure heart, from a good conscience, and from sincere faith, from which some, having strayed, have turned aside to idle talk, desiring to be teachers of the law, understanding neither what they say nor the things which they affirm" (1 Timothy 1:5-7).

THE SUPERNATURAL POWER OF GOD

We as believers say, "Oh, I want to see Him." "I can't wait for the return of the Lord." If, we really want to hasten the coming of the Lord Jesus Christ, we will forget the diversities of the past, unite together around the Word of God, and deliver the world from the chains that bind it. That is where we are today. For the salvation and deliverance of this world, it will take all of us... and more, bound together in unity, letting the mind of Christ dwell in us. Jesus was not double-minded. He had one purpose: to set the world free. That IS OUR purpose. Our formula for success is found in Philippians chapter 2: PHILIPPIANS 2:1-5:

1. If there be therefore any consolation in Christ, if any comfort of love, if any fellowship of the Spirit, if any bowels and mercies,
2. Fulfil ye joy, that ye be likeminded, having the same love, being of ONE ACCORD, of ONE MIND.
3. Let nothing be done through strife or vain glory, but in lowliness of mind let each esteem other better than themselves.
4. Look not every man on his own things, but every man also on things of others.
5. Let this mind be in you, which was also in Christ Jesus.

This is the message of the hour: Unite! Unite in God's Word to see the power of God prevail. Forget the incidentals and unite ourselves on the Word of God to fight this last day onslaught of the enemy.

Satan is going to bring every power from the depths of hell against God's people and all humanity in these last days. The Word of God says he has come "to steal, and to kill, and to destroy" (John 10:10). Satan knows his time is short, and he's going to give it everything he's got. As we band together, however, in the unity of the Word of God, the Body of Christ will rise in triumphant power over Satan...because he already has been defeated! We have yet to see all these greater works be accomplished (John 14:12) because the church of the Lord Jesus Christ has failed to unite, and therefore the power of God has been unable to move. Where there is unity, every gift of the Spirit and every fruit of the spirit will be in operation. Then and only then can the supernatural power of God move. Do you know why most people are not in unity and harmony? Because they don't have enough of the Word of God...enough power in them. How can the gifts of the Spirit or fruit of the spirit operate in them? Too many Christians have forgotten Galatians 5:22-23, where the fruit is listed. We need to put away our strife, criticizing other churches, judging and be about our

Father's business...building the Kingdom of God in unity, love, harmony and the Word of God. Remember, where there is no unity, strife comes in. Then division, then faith quits working, and when faith quits working, sickness comes in, financial disaster appears, spiritual stagnation sets in, and everything becomes a mess, simply because somebody thought more highly of himself than he should have. We must unite, put on the whole armor of God: the breast plate of righteousness, the sword of the spirit, the shield of faith, clothed in truth, and our feet shod with the preparation of the gospel and move forward in the army of the Lord...together!

THE SHEPHERD'S WAY

"He lets me rest in the meadow grass and leads me

besides the quiet streams. He gives me new strength.

He helps me do what honors him the most"

(Psalms 23:1-3)

LA Bible Students.

When we allow God our Shepherd to guide us, we have contentment. When we choose to sin, however, we are choosing to go our own way and we cannot blame God for the environment in which we find ourselves. Our Shepherd knows the "meadow grass" and "quiet streams" that will restore us. We will reach these places only by following him obediently. Rebelling against the Shepherd's leading is actually rebelling against our own best interests for future. We must remember this the next time we are tempted to go our own way rather than the Shepherd's way.

HEALTHY CRITICISM

There is a time for healthy criticism, when another person is living in open sin or engaging in a lifestyle that is not right. It is then that criticism can be healing or redemptemtive. When criticism is given, ask yourself if it was meant for hurt or healing. Proverbs 12:16-18 tells us the words of the wise brings healing. One can evaluate whether the criticism is coming from a person with a reputation for truth or lies. Consider it a privilege to be criticized for your faith in God. God has special blessings for those who patiently endure this kind of criticism (1 Peter 4:14). Constructive criticism should always be welcomed and a wholesome gift if given in love. Constructive criticism is always offered in love, to build up, and criticism is always responded to in love as well!

Those who do not accept constructive criticism and advise: (1.) A mocker stays away from wise men because he hates to be scolded... Prov. 15:12. (2.) A wise man is hungry for the truth, while the mocker feeds on trash...Prov. 15:14. (3.) If you profit from constructive criticism, you will be elected to the wise men's hall of fame. But to reject criticism is to harm yourself and your own best interests...Prov. 15:31. (4.) The Lord despises those who say that bad is good and good is bad...Prov. 17:15. Don't refuse to accept criticism; get all the help you can.... Prov. 23:12. (5.) Don't fail to correct your children; discipline won't hurt them! Punishment will keep them out of hell...Prov. 23:13-14. (6.) Fools think they need no advice, but the wise listen to others... Prov. 12:15. (7.) Seek advice from those who are faithful, godly, honest, and trustworthy. They can be counted on to give you counsel that comes from God's Word... Titus 1:15-16. (8.) It is important to seek advice from those who love God and have good knowledge of the Bible. If you wander beyond the teaching of Christ, you will not have fellowship with God...2 John 1:9-10. (9.) The ability to give wise counsel is a gift from the Holy Spirit, not the result of intelligence. 1 Corth. 12:8.

THE SECRET OF JOY

"This is the day the Lord has made;

let us rejoice and be glad in it" (Psalm 118:24).

We can have contentment, serenity and peace and joy no matter what happens. This joy comes from knowing Christ personally, and from depending on His strength, rather than our own. Joy does not come from outward circumstances but from inner strength. We cannot allow or rely on what we have or what we experience to give us joy, but with the Christ within us. His joy is greater than life's trials. Philippians 4:4, 12 tells us, "Always be full of joy in the Lord. I say it again—rejoice...." James 1:2 states, "Whenever trouble comes your way, let it be an opportunity for joy." God does not promise temporary happiness; in fact the Bible assumes problems will come our way, but God does promise lasting joy for all those who believe in Him. This kind of joy stays with us despite our problems. We get real lasting joy when we keep our eyes on Jesus. He was willing to die a shameful death on the cross because of the joy He knew would be His afterward (Hebrews 12:2). Paul said, "Since I know it is all for Christ's good, I am quite content with my weakness and with insults, hardships, persecutions, and calamities. For when I am weak, then I am strong" (12 Corinthians 12:8-10).

Rejoice, rejoice always, is not an option, but a command to rejoice under all circumstances. It is possible because the joy is in the Lord. We can be inwardly joyful even when everything around us is dreary. Paul had learned this as he was imprisoned in Rome...the true secret of joy and peace is to imitate Christ and serve others. By focusing on Christ we too can learn unity, humility, joy and peace!

Proverbs 13:9 tells us "The life of the godly is full of light and joy, but the sinner's light is snuffed out." Goodness is from God, and God is light. When we live godly lives, we are lamps along the way, but when we live ungodly lives, lamps go out. The light of godliness brings true happiness. When Christians cultivate and promote the joy of the Lord among God's people it is a powerful source of spiritual strength: "Do not sorrow, for the joy of the Lord is your strength" (Nehemiah 8:10).

Our Savior came to reclaim the joy that sin had stolen away. His death and glorious resurrection have secured our joy forever! If we need more proof, we have Jesus' own words: "These things I have spoken to you, that my joy may be in you, and that your joy may be full" (John 15:11). All of our joy is rooted in our Savior's everlasting love! We can bask in that joy now, even as we look forward to its fullness in the courts of heaven!

Thank you, Jesus, for the joy your everlasting love brings into my life.

THE SACREDNESS OF HUMAN LIFE

A great controversy rages today concerning abortion, focusing on the issue of whether the unborn baby (or fetus) is truly a person. The arguments are whether the unborn is fully a human being and whether there are justifiable reasons for abortion. There are those who would argue that abortion is acceptable if it will save the life of the mother, or in the case of rape or incest, or if the unborn child is known to be brain damaged or deformed. Ultimately the core questions are: In the process of conception and birth, when does human life begin, and what value do we place on the developing unborn child?

In Psalm 51:5 it says…I was born a sinner—yes, from the moment my mother conceived me. Sinfulness was present not only at birth but as far back as conception. As Christians we understand God is actively involved in our development before birth. As Christians we take all God's Word as face value. As an example, Psalm 139:13-16 states, "You made all the delicate, inner parts of my body and knit them together in my mother's womb. Thank you for making me so wonderfully complex! Your workmanship is marvelous—and how well I know it. You watched me as I was being formed in utter seclusion… (the white bones, blue veins, and red arteries which were all woven together)." God is present continuously during the nine months of pregnancy, forming, watching, creating, and even scheduling each day of the unborn baby's life. God had a personal relationship with the unborn baby. Jeremiah 1:5 states that God said, "I knew you before I formed you." God knew each person before they are born as we were developed in our mother's womb! "Before you were born, I set you apart and appointed you as my spokesman to the world." God knew each of us as we were being formed. He established a purpose for us before we are even born.

So, yes, it is a sin to have an abortion according to God's Word. Some have made their choices and left the path of their purpose. But it's never too late to get back on track by asking God for forgiveness. God can forgive someone who has had an abortion and restore them, if they confess their sin. In Isaiah 1:8 it states, "Come now…says the LORD. No matter how deep the stain of your sins, I can remove it. I can make you clean as freshly fallen snow. Even if you are stained as red as crimson, I can make you white as wool. No sin is beyond God's forgiveness. No matter what you may have done in the past, God can restore you to wholeness."

Psalm 139:1-4: "O Lord, You have searched me and known me. You know my sitting down and my rising up; you understand my thoughts afar off. You comprehend my path and my lying down, and are acquainted with all my ways. For there is not a word on my tongue, but behold, O LORD, You know it altogether."

Psalm 139:13: "For You formed my inward parts; You covered (interwoven) me in my mother's womb."

Psalm 139:15-17: "My frame was not hidden from You, when I was made in secret, and skillfully wrought in the lowest parts of earth (is a metaphor for womb). Your eyes saw my substance being yet unformed. The days were fashioned for me, when as yet there were none of them. How precious also are Your thoughts of me, O GOD! How great is the sum of them!"

THE RESURRECTION

Often when life seems bleak and hopeless, something happens that puts things in a new perspective. It happened with the death of Jesus. Imagine what must have been going through the disciples' minds as they witnessed (or heard about) the crucifixion of their Master. All their hopes and expectations—lifeless as the corpse that Joseph of Arimathea took away and laid in his tomb. Dead, broken and crushed…along with the dreams of the Twelve and many others who had truly believed that Jesus was the Messiah who would lead Israel to freedom, and now he lay rotting in a tomb. If that were the end of the story, you would never have heard of Jesus, or Christianity. Jesus' followers would have disappeared like the followers of dozens of other would-be Messiahs. If that were the end, you wouldn't be holding the Bible in your hands, reading it as countless millions of others have, and basing your life on its principles. There would be no churches. But Jesus' death was not the end. It was only the beginning.

You probably are familiar with the story of the Resurrection. The bare facts are that Jesus was put to death by crucifixion; that his body was placed in a borrowed tomb; that Jesus' followers were scattered and dejected. But Matthew 28 tells us, Jesus didn't stay dead! On the Sunday morning following his death, some strange events took place around the grave. The strangest of all is that Jesus rose from the dead! We have a tendency to take the Resurrection story for granted. But we need to remember that people didn't vacate their graveyards 2,000 years ago in Palestine any more than they do today. The Resurrection of Jesus has made all the difference in eternity for countless Christians. When the early Christians, including the disciples, were called upon to defend their faith in Jesus as Messiah, they didn't point to his great moral teachings and ethical principles. They didn't even refer to his miracles. They pointed to one rock-solid proof: his death and resurrection. Jesus himself pointed to his resurrection as his calling card, as proof that He was who He said He was. If it hadn't taken place, we would have reason to doubt the rest of his claims. Because Jesus really came back from death, it stands to reason that the rest of what he told us is true: that He is the way to the Father, that anyone who puts his or her faith in Christ can live forever with him in heaven; and that no matter how dark it looks right now, He will conduct us safely to the Promise Land. You can be sure that Christianity did not fizzle out and never will.

> "Early on Sunday morning, as the new day was dawning, Mary Magdalene and the other Mary went to the tomb. Suddenly there was a great earthquake; for an angel of the Lord came down from

heaven and rolled aside the stone and sat on it. His face shone like lightning and his clothing was a brilliant white. The guards shook with fear when they saw him, and fell into a dead faint. Then the angel spoke to the women. "Don't be frightened!" he said. "I know you are looking for Jesus, who was crucified, but he isn't here! For he has come back to life again, just as he said he would. Come in and see where his body was lying.... And now go quickly and tell his disciples that he has risen from the dead, and that he is going to Galilee to meet them there"
(Matthew 28:1-7).

THE REPROGRAMMING PROCESS

Almost every school in America is equipped with computers. Most businesses remain competitive because they're able to access and store large amounts of information. Computers are serving nearly every segment of society. But they have one flaw—they depend on the programs and information put into them.

Our minds work like a computer. If it's programmed to think about crud, that's what will happen, if it's programmed to think about things that are healthy, we will think healthy thoughts. It's as simple as that. The hard part comes in trying to keep out the unhealthy thoughts. It doesn't take much to pollute a mind.

So what's God's solution? Reprogram the mind! For this job, there are no shortcuts. The more exposure to things that have polluted us, whether from bad movies, magazines, TV, music, concerts, or just the everyday conversations of friends who don't care what they say, the longer it will take to clear our minds and reprogram them.

The reprograming process begins when we realize that destructive thoughts and images are trying to get a foothold in our minds, so kick them out: "For the weapons of our warfare are not carnal but mighty in God for pulling down strongholds, casting down arguments and every high thing that exalts itself against the knowledge of God, bring every thought into captivity to the obedience of Christ" (2 Corinthians 10:4-5). The word "obedience" here signifies, attentive hearing, to listen with compliant submission, assent, and agreement. The next step, as we see from Philippians 4:8, is choosing to dwell on what is true and good and right…pure and lovely, and…fine.

Christians must choose whose methods to use, God's or man's. God's mighty weapons are prayer, faith, hope, love, God's Word, and the Holy Spirit, these are powerful and effective! Also check Ephesians 6:13-18, which tells you to put on all the Armor of God. When dealing with pride that keeps people from a relationship with Christ, we may be tempted to use our own methods. But nothing can break down Satan's barriers like God's weapons!

REJECTION

Rejection comes with being a Christian, because our life and beliefs go against the flow of the rest of the world. Growing closer to God will naturally make you grow further away from the world. If you read Acts 7:54-59 you will see Stephen took a stand for Christ which cost him his life, and if you read further in Acts 8 and 9 you will see what the results of a fearless faith can be. If Stephen had known what his death would accomplish, he would have died smiling. Paul who once persecuted the Christians had his life turned around and he became a follower of Christ. Paul sadly had watched Stephen die and Stephen's reaction helped bring Paul to Christ.

People are watching Christians. They are seeing how we respond to rejection and verbal abuse. People want to believe in something true and worth living for no matter what the cost. When they find it, they may make an incredible impact in their world for Christ!

What do they learn from watching you?

THE NEWNESS OF LIFE

"They that wait upon the Lord shall renew their strength; they shall mount up with wings as eagles; they shall run, and not be weary; and they shall walk, and not faint"

(Isaiah 40:31).

The Bible tells us that God created man with the ability to know Him, and respond to Him. But at the beginning man broke that contract, and when he did, he died spiritually and handed on that spiritual death to all his descendants. The very inmost part of us is called our "spirit" or pneuma in Greek. Our spirit was created for one main purpose, to know God and the love He has for us. When man fell, his spirit died and ever since operated from his soul and body (Gen. 2:17). This is why human history is recorded of hate, bloodshed, cruelty, and confusion. If this situation isn't corrected, it obviously means...HELL. It's very real, whether one believes it or not; it is a fact. It's a place where one is eternally lost, in the dark, frightened, hateful and separated from God forever and sharing in the endless destruction of the devil and his angels.

But, PRAISE GOD, Jesus met the requirements for justice and made a way for man to once again be united to God and cause our spirit to have life again. Jesus was totally free from any sin or guilt. He was innocent and satisfied justice on our behalf of all the sins that man had committed. When He died, He rose again and opened the way for the Father to send the Holy Spirit through whom God's life was able to come and live in us. The only requirement is for us to recognize we have sinned, so we must ask Jesus to come and live in us and be our Lord and Savior.

The new life created by the Holy Spirit in us is called "eternal life," which means, God's life in us, the kind of life that never runs down, never gets tired, or bored, but always is joyful and fresh. This continually renewed freshness expresses the kind of life God wants to give us... "Behold I make all things new! We as born-again believers are promised that we shall walk in "newness of life," continually being refreshed and replenished.

One receives this newness of life by realizing they have been wrong and have sinned and is lost; going in the wrong direction and willing to go God's way. Then ask the Father to take away your guilt and sin. Ask Jesus Christ, God's only begotten Son to come into your life and become your Savior. Now believe Jesus has come the moment you ask Him to and thank Him for saving you and giving you the newness of life.

If you have done this now, your spirit which comes alive through Jesus Christ is in a place far deeper than your emotions. Whether you feel anything or not, you are different and Jesus will do what He promised...you have the newness of life! God is now living inside of you by the Holy Spirit: "If any man be in Christ, he is a new creature" (2 Cor. 5:17).

Now that you received Jesus as your Savior, your spirit came alive, and YOU have the newness of life. God has accepted YOU just as you are! Yield your spirit to the Holy Spirit to change you and allow your spirit to take its rightful place as head over your soul (intellect, will and emotions) and your body (your physical part). Your soul and body was accustomed to "running the show" but now your spirit must become in control. You no longer need to live by the demands of your soulish worldly thoughts, feelings and wrong desires. You may not feel different but deep inside of you, you are different.... You have God's own Spirit who will lead you in the life you were meant to have! Now you have the privilege of walking and fellowshipping with God through prayer, by reading His Word and fellowshipping in love with others, answered prayer and learning and growing spiritually and worshipping God within your church, and learning about all the blessings and promises that are for YOU from your Heavenly Father!

THE MIND OF CHRIST

"Let this mind be in you

which was also in Christ Jesus"

(Philippians 2:5)

Jesus chose to lay aside His divine form and adopt the lowly form of man. Even as a Man He did not choose wealth, power, or worldly position, but came as a servant, died the death of a criminal. In everything He humbled Himself, trusting God to exalt and establish His name. We are to adopt the same attitude that Jesus had of unselfishness, servanthood, humility, and obedience, having unity, treating others higher then ourselves, and walking in love and peace. Our attitude should be the kind that was shown by Jesus Christ. He did not demand and cling to his rights as God, but laid aside his mighty power and glory, taking the disguise of a slave and becoming like men. And he humbled himself even further, going so far as actually to die a criminal's death on the cross (Phil. 2:5-8).

Christ showed true humility, He poured out his life to pay the penalty we deserve. He laid aside self-interest, which is essential for us as well in all our relationships. We are to take Christ's attitude in serving others and not be concerned about our personal recognition. When we give up the need to receive credit and praise, we will be able to serve with joy, love, and kindness. Christ also suffered and died so that we might have eternal life. Christ gives us power to lay aside our personal needs and concerns. To utilize his power, we must imitate those leaders who deny themselves and serve others. We dare not be self-centered, or complaining, and as believers, we need to be united in love and work together as a team, keeping our focus on the model of Jesus Christ. We can become mature by being so identified with Christ that his attitude of humility, love, peace and sacrifice rules us. Developing the mind of Christ and our character begins with God's work in us, but it also requires discipline, obedience, and continual concentration on our part.

Jesus said, "Take My yoke upon you and learn from Me, for I am gentle and lowly in heart, and you will find rest for your souls. For My yoke is easy and My burden is light" (Matt. 11:29-30). Jesus was telling us to adopt his attitude of unselfishness, servanthood, humility and obedience. He is calling for us to take on his yoke which is easy and an open, free, loyal relationship with Him, which will be useful, pleasant, good, comfortable, suitable and serviceable.

You know the world is watching our every move, so we should be conducting our life as a gospel sermon for the world to see. We may be the only Bible someone may hear or see. Those who observe a godly life see what God is like. This is one of the church's primary functions. Focus on Christ Jesus as Mentor and Model and let his mind be in us!

THE REAL JESUS

"You are the Christ, the Son of the living God"

(Matthew 16:16).

Who is Jesus? Observing the ways He is portrayed these days, it's almost impossible to recognize Him as the Jesus of the Bible. Some groups add to what the Bible says about Him, while others diminish Him to simple humanity, claiming that He was merely a wise teacher or a master moralist. Some would like to make Jesus disappear altogether.

But this is nothing new. It's been happening for nearly 2,000 years. Thomas Jefferson wrote the U.S. Declaration of Independence and he went through the New Testament Gospels with scissors and cut out all references to Jesus' deity and the supernatural. This is known as The Jefferson Bible. Even recently, people have approached the Gospels in similar ways.

When Jesus asked His disciples what people were saying about who He was, some answers were Elijah, Jeremiah, and John the Baptist, but these answers were all inadequate. Peter was correct when he said, "You are the Christ, the Son of the living God" (Matthew 16:16).

Don't be deceived by fuzzy, watered down, or false descriptions of Jesus that you read, see, or hear about. Stick to the Bible! When people try to minimize His identity, tell them in no uncertain terms who is the real Jesus is! TO KNOW JESUS IS TO KNOW GOD.

All glory to Jesus, begotten of God
The great I AM is He;
Creator, sustainer—but wonder of all,
The Lamb of Calvary!

THE "ME" FACTOR

"The more you think of yourself, the harder it is

to find eternal life" (Matthew 16:25).

In these last days, we know we will have difficult times for the Bible tells us so. We are seeing it come about by the crimes, selfishness, and the disobedience of children to their parents and the lust for money power and sex. Nothing seems to be sacred. The hearts of people are cold and hard. Even friends betray friends and they are lovers of pleasures rather than God. Pride has overcome humility, and honesty and integrity have fallen in the back ground. The main fact is, the world is saying, "It's all about Me, who is going to take care of Me if I don't?" It is an age of self-help; "taking care of number one," making oneself the center of all things. Their main goal is to become self-sufficient and confident in self and taking pride in all that they accomplish.

The Bible warns us about the seductive power of selfishness. Selfishness can destroy relationships, even families. To think more highly about ourselves than others is called pride, which the Bible calls a deadly sin. The Bible's message is simple—God values us highly because He loves us deeply. But we must not think we are sufficient without God! Our sufficiency is in the Lord! Our value is tied to the value He places on us. It is because of God's power within us, we are capable of doing far more than most of us have dared to dream. Jeremiah 1:5 states, "I knew you before formed you in your mother's womb. Before you were born I set you apart and appointed you as my spokesman to the world." Also Jeremiah 29:11-14 tells us God has a future and a hope for us. God made us with great skill; He crafted us with loving care. He showed how much value He placed on us by the way He made us.

When we become selfish by thinking only about our own affairs and not caring for others, it can cause us to abuse even the power of the Holy Spirit (Acts 8:9-24). The more you think of yourself, the harder it is to find eternal life: "For whoever desires to save his life will lose it, but whoever loses his life for My sake will find it." It means to die to self is to live! To deny oneself is not to assume some false, external asceticism, but to put the interests of the kingdom first and foremost in one's life; to renounce self-centered ambitions, Seek first the kingdom of God and his righteousness, and all these things shall be added to you" (Matthew 6:33). The Scripture is stating, rather than being preoccupied with material things, our ambition should be to seek first God's kingdom and Himself with covenant faithfulness to respond. Don't seek victory and success, seek Jesus and his fellowship, and then you will experience blessings and prosperity.

Although the Bible warns us of a society that is barren of virtue and abounding with evil and people will be characterized by all kinds of self-centered and unnatural perversions and false teachings, we must maintain godly living and faithful servanthood, because a godly life testifies against godlessness in others. Devote yourself to Spirit-filled living, and become a committed servant of God's Word. We all need to be prepared at any time whether convenient or inconvenient to proclaim the Word with love and patience. We as disciples, dedicated students, and followers of the Lord Jesus Christ have been anointed by God's Spirit, and have the command to go and tell the Good News (Mark 16:15)! Remember, Jesus didn't come for the righteous, but the sinners. Let us as Christians fulfill our calling of truth to a dying, rebellious and disturbed world! Don't have the "Me Factor attitude," it won't get you blessings or rewards!

THE LAMB OF GOD

Isaiah 53:1-12 (Life Application Bible)

In God's eyes Jesus was like a tender green shoot, sprouting from a root in dry and sterile ground. But in our eyes there was no attractiveness at all, nothing to make us want Him. We despised Him and rejected Him...a man of sorrows, acquainted with bitterest grief. We turned our backs on Him and looked the other way when He went by. He was despised, and we didn't care. Yet it was our grief He bore, our sorrows that weighed Him down. And we thought His troubles were a punishment from God, for His own sins! But He was wounded and bruised for our sins. He was beaten that we might have peace; He was lashed...and we were healed! Every one of us, have strayed away like sheep! We who left God's paths to follow our own. Yet God laid on Him the guilt and sins of every one of us! He was oppressed and He was afflicted, yet He never said a word. He was brought as a lamb to the slaughter. He stood silent before the ones condemning Him. From prison and trial they led Him away to His death. But who among the people of that day realized it was their sins that He was dying for...that He was suffering their punishment? He was buried like a criminal, but in a rich man's grave; but He had done no wrong and had never spoken an evil word. But it was God's good plan to bruise Him and fill Him with grief. However, when His soul has been made an offering for sin, then He shall have a multitude of children, many heirs. He shall live again, and God's program shall prosper in His hands. And when He sees all that is accomplished by the anguish of His soul, He shall be satisfied; and because of what He has experienced, my righteous Servant shall make many to be counted righteous before God, for He shall bear all their sins. Therefore, I will give Him the honors of one who is mighty and great because He has poured out His soul unto death. He was counted as a sinner, and He bore the sins of many, and He pled with God for sinners.

THE IMPOSSIBLE DOESN'T EXIST!

The church is an occupational force and our mission is to enforce the victory of Calvary. The power of Calvary is God's love and the violence of Calvary is our prayers.

God requires the church to recognize that the kingdom of God should be regarded with our highest commitment and to understand that the kingdom is worth more than any pursuit. The kingdom of God is an internal rulership, and cannot be observed by the natural eye. We as the church should be aggressive about serving Christ...be violent in determination (Matt. 11:12-14; 20-21).

Prayer is a spiritual weapon that impacts our life and the lives of others (Eph. 6:10-13). Through prayer we bring forth God's promises and blessings, and come against the wiles of the devil. Prayer is the key to victory, and the pathway to God's power! Prayer can change anything! Through prayer, the impossible doesn't exist! Whenever hell has a pathway to bring people in, we the church can pray to God and He will tear down that gate, for heaven is the power and the church has the given authority through the Name of Jesus (Luke 10:19).

Church, we need to get violent for the things of God through prayer! When we pray, we turn on the light which makes the devil flee. We are an occupational force! When we pray, the gates of Hades cannot prevent the advance of the kingdom, nor claim victory over those who belong to God (Matt. 16:18). Jesus was aggressive, not passive, for He came to break those bondages that held people captive! His ministry was to get the "good news" out, and He passed the same ministry down to the disciples and the entire church (Luke 4:21).

The church's mission is to be violent in prayer, to enforce the victory of Calvary and bring forth violent loving-kindness.

God answers the sincere, bold, confident, fervent prayers of the believer, but we need to pray for Him to move. The kingdom comes about with determined prayer. Our motivation should be to pray, tear down the kingdom of darkness, and see what Jesus will do! Prayer is more than a destination. It is an intimate relationship with God, our heavenly Father. Prayer is a spiritual weapon and an instrument of praise to a worthy God! Praise in prayer will bring the presence of God, for He inhabits the praises of His people. The presence of God reverses what the devil meant for destruction.

God doesn't wait for us to become perfect, or until we "get it together to answer our prayers, for we are all imperfect people, who do things imperfectly." Prayer sets us and others free and gives us victory, success over defeat and failure. Prayer is a lifelong journey, a way of life, and an intimate relationship with our Heavenly Father.

Remember, with the prayer of faith,
the impossible doesn't exist....
"For with God nothing will be impossible"
(Luke 1:37).

THE IMPORTANCE OF EACH GOSPEL

MATTHEW: To prove that Jesus is the Messiah, the eternal King, Jesus is revealed as the King of kings. His miraculous birth, his life and teachings, his miracles, and his triumph over death show us who he really is. He is the supreme ruler of time and eternity, heaven and earth, men and angels. Jesus was the Messiah, the One for whom the Jews had waited, who was to deliver them from Roman oppression. Yet, tragically, they didn't recognize him when he came. They didn't understand that the true purpose of God's anointed deliverer was to die for all people, to free them from sin. Jesus came to earth to begin his Kingdom. The way to enter God's Kingdom is by faith. Jesus teaches us how to prepare for life in his Kingdom by living properly right now. When Jesus rose from the dead, he rose in power as the true King. In his victory over death, he established his credentials as King and his power and authority over evil. The Resurrection shows that Jesus is all-powerful; even death could not stop his plan of offering eternal life. People who believe in Jesus can hope for a resurrection like this. Our role is to live and share the message of his victory with those who do not yet know Jesus is ALIVE.

MARK: To present Jesus' person, work, and teachings. In Mark, Jesus demonstrates his divinity by overcoming disease, demons, and death. In Mark we see him as both Son of God and servant to man. Jesus did not come as a conquering king; he came as a servant. Jesus helped mankind by telling about God, showing compassion, and healing. His ultimate act of service was for giving his life as the sacrifice for sin. Mark records more of Jesus' miracles than his sermons. Jesus did miracles to confirm his message and to teach the disciples his true identity as God. Jesus crossed national, racial, and economic barriers to spread his Good News.

LUKE: To present an accurate account of the life of Christ and to present Christ as the perfect Man and Savior, Luke describes how God's Son entered human history. Jesus lived as the perfect Man. After a perfect ministry, he provided a perfect sacrifice for our sin so we could be saved. He offers forgiveness to all who will believe that he says is true and accept him as Lord of their life. Luke put a great emphasis on dates and details. Luke's devotion to accuracy gives us confidence in the reliability of the history of Jesus' life. Even more important, we can believe with certainty that Jesus is God.

JOHN: To prove conclusively that Jesus is the Son of God and that all who believes in him will have eternal life. John shows us that Jesus is unique as God's special Son, yet he is fully God. Because Jesus is fully God, he is able to reveal God to us clearly and accurately. Because Jesus is God's Son, we can perfectly trust what he says. By trusting him, we can gain open mind to understand God's message and fulfill his purpose in our lives. In John, we see Jesus revealed in power and magnificence even before his resurrection. Jesus offers eternal life to us. We are invited to live in a personal, eternal relationship with him that begins now. Although we must eventually age and die, by trusting Christ, we can have a new life that lasts forever. John records eight specific signs or miracles that reveal the nature of Jesus' power and love. We see Christ's power over everything created, and we see his love for all people. These signs encourage us to believe in him. Believing is active, living, and having trust in Jesus as God. When we believe in Jesus' life, words, death, and resurrection, and when we commit our life to him, he cleanses us from sin and empowers us to follow him.

If you have not made Jesus the Lord of your live by inviting him into your heart and life and believing that he IS the Son of God who died on the cross for your sin, NOW is the time!! Let Jesus change your life and give you purpose and allow the blessings and promises that are in His Word give you the abundance of life and eternal life. Then continue to learn about your Lord and Savior through reading the Word and going to a Bible-teaching church.

THE HURRY-UP SYNDROME?

Do you find yourself saying, "I don't have time," or, "There are not enough hours in a day?" Are you hurrying through life with time always running out? Do you feel like you are on a merry-go-round? If so you definitely need to get off that ride! God does not want His children filled with anxiety, stress, worry, frustrations, and confusions. Those are all the tools for the devil to prevent us from being the image of Christ and being an effective witness of God's Word. We can't glorify God in this state of mind. These are some of the reasons why the worldly and lost will not see who Jesus is. Why would they want any more issues than they already have? People are looking for a way out of their bondages; they are looking for peace and comfort and a better way of life. How are they going to know that there is a way; that Jesus is the way! And He is there for them and wants to release them from their burdens, give them hope, value and purpose if we as Christians don't get our act together!

When we are good stewards of the time, we will start the morning off with prayer and asking for God's direction and desires for the day. We would ask to place our priorities in order. We would pray for the sensitivity of the Holy Spirit so we could be led where the Lord would have us go. We would pray to be a blessing to someone He would place in our path for that day. We would pray for wisdom and insight and pray we walk in love and in the Spirit. This will help us to be prepared for the day ahead of us. If we do not take the morning prayer seriously, we may not fulfill our purpose for the day, or we could miss a blessing, or a warning of the day. We would not be prepared to be the image we need to be as a witness. Plus we are putting God first before we begin the day. We are showing the Lord we need Him, love Him and want to take time to praise Him. When we take time to pray for the day, time has a way of allowing us to get what needs to be accomplished finished. It also will go more smoothly.

If we do not take the time to honor God and seek His face in the morning we are opening the door for pressure, and overload which will cause worry and we will not produce fruit for that day. It might have been a day you could have led someone to the Lord and saved them from hell! When we are too busy we do not allow God to be God in our life. We will not sense His presence or guidance.

God wants us to be kings and priests, not scatterbrains. Time is a gift from God and if we are good stewards of time it will be a blessing and not a curse for us. God does not want us to waste time and be too busy for righteousness.

It is vital as Christians to be aware in these evil days and stay prayed up… keep oil in our lamps (Matthew 25:1-13) and watch and pray! Don't allow yourself to fall into the devil's trap of frustration, overcommitted, worry or anxiety or the cares of the life! Allow the Lord to direct your steps, your energy, your plans and your time, your total life!

THE HOLY SPIRIT IS OUR DAILY PARTNER

Besides the angels that God has sent to minister to us, God has sent the Holy Spirit. We received the Holy Spirit when we made Jesus Christ our personal Savior and Lord of our life. The Holy Spirit has been given to Believers to help them walk out their salvation with power and truth. Before we were born-again, the Holy Spirit was there to lead us and guide us to our salvation and the understanding of being "saved." After being born-again, He comes to dwell in us, and reveals the truth of the Gospel; helping us to walk in the understanding of God's ways. He changes our heart attitude, makes our heart tender and teachable with the Truth. He is always there to comfort us, teach us, help us pray and give us guidance, and wisdom. The Holy Spirit has "sealed" the believer which means, He is the One who marks us to be present on that day when salvation from sin will be complete. So as a believer, we must do our part and renounce our old ways, submit to the Holy Spirit and agree with God's ways. If we do not, we will grieve the Holy Spirit, and cause Him sorrow by the way we live. Grieving the Spirit clearly reveals that we want our own way, and not His. As we clearly and completely turn over the control of our life to the Lord in devotion, commitment, and obedience, we then begin to walk in the fruit of the Spirit which is, love, joy, peace, longsuffering, kindness, goodness, faithfulness, gentleness, and self-control (Gal. 5:22).

As Christians learn to walk in the Spirit; become kind, tenderhearted and forgiving, our nature will change and then will line up with the character of God and His image. This is how He has called the Body of Christ (the Church) to be. With this new nature we have the spiritual capacity of understanding revelation, wisdom and knowledge. The important key to remember is to stay in fellowship and partnership with the Holy Spirit daily! We are to depend and seek out His leading, guidance and direction daily. We need to daily seek the Lord's face with all our heart and we then will receive the blessings and power of the helping hand of the Holy Spirit. Those who seek and desire the quality of the fruit of the Spirit will walk in a spiritual dimension, the presence of the Lord and the blessings and reward of abundance now and for eternity. They will also become mature Christians with open hearts. They do what God shows them to do, and will be conscious of the Holy Spirit, plus having the capacity to understand God.

Believers, make the decision now to know and fellowship with the Holy Spirit. Make Him your daily partner and seek the fruit of the Spirit. The Lord desires us all to walk in power and spiritual dimension. Ask the Holy Spirit for His help, for God has sent Him for that very reason. He is our helper!

THE HOLY SPIRIT FREES US FROM SIN

"For to be carnally minded is death, but to be spiritually minded is life and peace" (Romans 8:6).

"For the weapons of our warfare are not carnal but mighty in God for pulling down strong holds, casting down arguments and every high thing that exalts itself against the knowledge of God, bringing every thought into captivity to the obedience of Christ" (2 Corinthians 10:4-5).

Throughout our life a conflict goes on between the new nature and the old, but there is a way to victory: Christ and His redemptive work frees (Jesus sets believers at liberty from domination of sin) us to live in the power of the Holy Spirit. Christians are free from God's judgment. But we must yield to the Holy Spirit and walk according to the Spirit and not the flesh. To walk in the flesh is to allow the fleshly, selfish desires to nominate us. When we walk in the flesh we cannot please God ("So then, those who are in the flesh cannot please God" (Romans 8:8)). Those who do not believe and have not received Salvation and or made Jesus Lord of their life cannot please God. In Romans 8:5 Paul expects that Christians ordinarily will live according to the Spirit. This involves holiness, not only in our action and words, but also in our thoughts that fill our minds each moment through the day. Growing spiritually is a progression which will reach its completion when we leave this world ("being confident of this very thing, that He who has begun a good work in you will complete it until the day of Jesus Christ…" (Phil. 1:6). It does not happen overnight. Paul also warns that Christians who are in the Spirit can from time to time live according to the flesh. We as Christians are able to choose to be righteous rather than be bound to the old nature. Obedience to the Word of God gains a new nature of holiness. Be clear that any hostile or disobedient tendency of words, action, or thoughts toward God's Word comes out of your fleshly nature. When this happens repent and get right with the Lord!

By allowing the Holy Spirit to guide us and empower us and to "think" good and godly thoughts, and bring every thought into captivity to Christ, we can win the battle over the mind and the thoughts that are fleshly. It's the mind the devil wants for it will open the door for spiritual death. Also walking in the flesh will stop your spiritual growth. The Bible teaches us, "...whatever things are true, whatever things are noble, whatever things are just, whatever things are pure, whatever things are lovely, whatever things are of good report, if there is any virtue and if there is anything praiseworthy meditate on these things" (Philippians 4:8). You can't sin if you don't think it! If you refuse to defeat a wrong thought, you will find other evil thoughts creeping in also.

Don't let your mind become so much a part of day to day life that you pay little attention to it. We have the choice to make every decision or action or our thoughts and words to be either fleshly or spiritual. Remember too, every thought will create a good action or a bad one. Reject those thoughts that are unfitting for a child of God! It always starts with a thought! So pay attention to your thoughts. If you keep the Presence of the Lord close and put good, positive and godly things in your mind, good things will be your outcome. Ask the Holy Spirit to help you control your thoughts. He is our helper!

THE FALSE CHRISTIAN

Pretending is fine if you're a child at play, but some people pretend about pretty serious things. In Acts 5:1-11, Ananias and Sapphira pretended to give all the money they received for their land to the Lord, but they actually kept part of it. It cost them more than they wanted to pay. They fell dead. You just can't pretend to God! He knows all! Delilah pretended to care for Samson, Judas Iscariot pretended to be a friend to Jesus, look what it cost him.

There are people now, who pretend to know God. They pretend to be Christians. What does the Lord say about those who pretend? Matthew 7:21-3: "Not everyone that saith unto me, Lord, Lord, shall enter into the kingdom of heaven; but he that doeth the will of my Father which is in heaven. Many will say to me in that day, Lord, Lord, have we not prophesied in thy name? and in thy name have cast out devils? And in thy name done many wonderful works? And then will I profess unto them, I never knew you: depart from me, ye that work iniquity." What a price to pay!

Yes, the world is full of pretenders. Satin is pleased when he can keep someone playing this deadly game. But the great pretender, the devil, will have an end someday as well (Rev. 20:10).

It is so dangerous to pretend with your soul! Do you really want to play games with your destiny? You will never win God's heart, or salvation by pretending to be a Christian. God desires our true heart, our love, obedience, faith and trust! He desires to adopt you into the family, bless you and give you eternal life. Why would anyone reject this by pretending?

Don't pretend with your soul. You don't have to pretend when you have the real thing. Be sure you are saved. Jesus says, "For whosoever shall call upon the name of the Lord shall be saved" (Romans 10:13). So stop pretending and trust Christ as your Savior! The only thing you give up is your sin! There is real life with Jesus! "Verily, verily, I say unto you, He that believeth on Me hath everlasting life" (John 6:47). "As newborn babies, desire the sincere milk of the Word that ye may grow thereby" (1 Peter 2:2) and "Study to shew thyself approved unto God, a workman that needeth not to be ashamed, rightly dividing the Word of truth" (11 Timothy 2:15).

If you repented and sincerely asked the Lord into your heart, then you are saved! The first step in your new life is to find a Bible believing church, be baptized, then begin serving the Lord in love, living a clean life and being an example of our Lord Jesus. You will not have to do this alone, for now you will have the help of the Holy Spirit, teaching and guiding you. Don't worry about you being not being good enough, for the Lord, He will accept you just as you are right now. He will help you live a good and blessed life.

THE FAITHFUL, THE UNFAITHFUL AND THE REBELLIOUS

"Behold, I am coming quickly, and My reward is with Me, to render to every man according to what he has done" (Revelation 22:12).

Having finished His work on earth, Jesus returned to heaven to receive His kingdom. You and I are living in the time period between His ascension and return, and He has given us a job to do. We do not know when He shall return, but we know that when He does return He will deal with three kinds of persons: the faithful, the unfaithful and the rebellious. Each believer individually, and the church collectively, has the great responsibility of "doing business" with the Gospel. Everything else that we do is secondary to the great task of world evangelization.

Jesus, however, has given us many promises that ought to encourage us to be faithful until He comes. We ought to be faithful simply because Christ has commanded us, but the promised rewards do encourage us. When we consider all that Jesus has done for us, we should be glad to serve Him just to show our appreciation. The work we do today is preparation for the work He has planned for us tomorrow. Faithfulness is the secret of growth. When Jesus comes again, He will reckon with His servants to see how faithful they have been. He will reward the faithful ones with responsibilities in the eternal kingdom. We do not know all that is involved in our future service for the Lord, either during His kingdom or in the new heaven and earth. But we need to be faithful so that He can trust us with work to do for His glory.

Being unfaithful is sin. For us to fail to do the work Christ has assigned to us is to slight His Word and insult His person. Jesus asks, "And why call Me Lord, Lord, and do not the things which I say?"(Luke 6:46). Our words can never substitute for deeds. If we have the love and the proper fear of the Lord, it will mobilize us to serve our Lord. Love and faithfulness go together, just as it does in a marriage. Christians who love their Lord will want to be faithful and do the work the Lord calls one to do. Unfaithfulness will cause the loss of our reward. What we do with today determines what will be done with us tomorrow. The Lord tells us to be faithful: "Watch yourselves, that you might not lose what you have accomplished, but that you may receive a full reward" (2 John 8).

When the Lord returns, it will mean reward for the faithful, but a loss of reward for the unfaithful, and terrible judgment for the unbelieving, rebellious people who rejected Him. They shall be punished with everlasting destruction from the presence of the Lord, and from the glory of His power" (2 Thessalonians 1:8-9). Remember this...this is now a time of grace and not judgment and any rebellious person can be saved because the Lord is longsuffering and is not willing that any should parish but come to repentance (2 Peter3:9). Make the right choice. "I have set before you life and death, blessing and cursing: therefore choose life, that both you and you descendants may live..." (Deuteronomy 30:19).

THE DARKEST HOUR IN THE HISTORY OF HUMANITY THAT BROUGHT VICTORY

Jesus died a horrible death and in a gruesome way for you and for me. The cross has inspired endless debates, wars, books, songs, and lives through the centuries. We are all sinners; we all played a part in putting Jesus to death. Because humans are all sinners we've broken God's laws, so we stand guilty before God and deserve punishment. The Good News is that God is gracious and will forgive us and give us new life through His Son. Consider this: God made Himself vulnerable to human beings one time, and we murdered Him. Because of our sinful nature, we are incapable of pleasing God, or doing anything on our own to change the situation. We were dead in our sins (Ephesians 2:5; Colossians 2:13). We desperately needed help from someone who could please God, who could do something about the desperate state of our souls. Jesus, by virtue of his sinless life, is that someone! We deserved God's anger and punishment, but God took the wrath we deserve and poured it out on Jesus, on the cross: "For He made Him who knew no sin to be sin for us, that we might become the righteousness of God in Him" (2 Corinthians 5:21). Jesus took upon himself our sins…every mean, dishonest, disgusting thought or action and was transformed from the perfect, holy, righteous Person He was into utter sin itself. Then in exchange, He poured God's goodness into us!

The Bible tells us that under Levitical law, an animal had to be offered every year to atone for the sins of the people. That word atone means "to cover" and it's used continually throughout the Old Testament. It's never used in the New Testament. The Greek word used to describe what Jesus did for us on the cross is a different word altogether. It doesn't mean "to cover"—it means to "remit; to do completely away with something." Do you know what this means? It means there is no longer a sin problem. Jesus solved it! As the perfect God-man, Jesus was in a position to receive the punishment our sins deserved. He stood in the chasm between God and man, which was created by our sins, and brought us back together by his blood. As horrible as the physical agony must have been, the spiritual agony of this transformation and punishment was worse. Jesus was deserted by God so that you and I never have to be. No wonder He cried out, "My God, My God why have You deserted Me?" Jesus died for YOU! Take it personally.

When you make Him your Lord, He didn't just cover your sins, He put you into right-standing with God and recreated you by the Spirit of God as if sin had never existed. But some believers are still caught up in sin consciences. They keep thinking of themselves as sin stained instead of blood-washed. They claim, "I'm just an old sinner saved by grace." No, you are not! You were an old sinner, but grace changed you forever into the very righteousness of God. You are now His workmanship, created in Christ Jesus! As far as God is concerned, your past life is forgotten. It died the death on the cross. So for those who think they are just an old sinner, saved by grace, receive the freedom from sin that's yours in Christ Jesus. Receive the righteousness that only the LAMB OF GOD can give.

"This is the covenant that I will make with them after those days, saith the Lord. I will put my laws into their hearts, and in their minds and their sins and iniquities will I remember no more" (Hebrews 10:16-17).

THE DANGER OF COMPLACENCY

Complacency means thinking too little of something great...a casual attitude toward God, toward a great problem confronting us. Also it's being lazy or at ease when you should be hard at work, when the time is late, it's when your full involvement is needed. Dangers could be on the horizon, but you may not even see them such as...military, social, personal, or spiritual. Satan is pleased when we fall into complacency and he is now ready to strike, but you don't even know he is there. These are all examples of complacency...smug attitudes of self-satisfaction, attitudes that say, "Everything is just fine because I'm happy and comfortable." God has some very strong words about complacency, especially complacency toward Him, and complacency toward sin, both are dangerous and puts us at great risk! God loves us to much to lose us to complacency without a fight!

What causes us to grow complacent? When we are in need, we usually take God more seriously. But when we are well fed, comfortable, and prosperous, it is easier to become complacent about God. It's the wise person who remembers God daily in times of both need and prosperity (Hosea 13:5-6).

It is a sin to be complacent. It is a sin to know what you ought to do and then not do it (James 4:17). God takes righteousness seriously and we as his people need to also. To know what is right and then be complacent about it or unwilling to do it is sin! Complacency leads to indifference, which leads to idleness. To stand for nothing is to stand against God. That's why complacency is so dangerous.

Complacency can lead to sin as Samson found out (Judges 16:16-17). Samson told Delilah his secret after she nagged him day after day. Samson had become so complacent about his God-given responsibility as a leader that he gave in and told her the secret to his strength. He thought it wouldn't matter; he thought everything would still be fine. Samson's complacency was a sin, because he disobeyed God's command not to tell anyone, and he let down his entire nation! In first King, the Eleventh chapter, verse one through four, King Solomon was instructed by the Lord not to intermarry with those nations. Yet Solomon insisted on loving them anyway...and sure enough, the women led Solomon's heart away from God. Solomon's complacency toward God and His commandments led to sin.

We must never be complacent about God or what He calls us to do or His ability to help us! Don't allow yourself to fall into a casual attitude toward God, thinking too little of Him and His Word or His ways, otherwise you may not see the dangers lurking on the horizon.

"For you closed your eyes to the facts and did not choose to reverence and trust the Lord, and you turned your back on me, spurning my advice. That is why you must eat bitter fruit of having your own way and experience the full terrors of the pathway you have chosen. For you turned away from me to death; your own complacency will kill you. Fools! But all who listen to me shall live in peace and safety, unafraid."

Proverbs 1:29-33 (Life Application Bible…students)

THE DEFILEMENT OF THE WORLD

"For all that is in the world, the lust of the flesh, the lust of the eyes, and the pride of life, is not of the Father, but is of the world" (1 John 2:16). "And the world is passing away, and the lust of it; but he who does the will of God abides forever" (1 John 2:17).

The world does not refer to the physical creation, but to the sphere of evil operating in our world under dominion of Satan, living in the world without partaking of the world is the Christian's call. When we truly set our affection on God, the lusts of the flesh (which is our sin nature) is reduced as a problem. Unlike Lot's wife, who regretted the loss of the world, let us look ahead to the glorious hope of love, life, and light where God rules eternally!

There is a great deal of evidence that God wants us to be holy. Because the world endeavors to incite us to be evil, we as Christians cannot love that system and still say we love God. The distinguishing mark of a Christian is that he or she does not want to sin. Rather, he desires to be holy. We must not allow ourselves to be attracted to the things of this world.

There are three areas in which Satan incites people to sin through his worldly system. The word, in the Greek text is epithumia it is a kind of lust and broader than sexual immorality…it generally has an evil connotation, referring to a strong desire for satisfaction that is evil. The "flesh" is the part of man that is prone to sin, which man has required from Adam when he rebelled against God. The flesh produces all kind of terrible things as Galatians 5 lists as the manifestations of the flesh, such as, immorality, idolatry, interpersonal relationships and indulgence.

Morality, the works of the flesh are manifested as: these: adultery, fornication, uncleanness, and lasciviousness. Fornication would include any type of sex outside of marriage, including homosexuality, which the world takes lightly and ignores! Besides sexual sin, the flesh also produces "uncleanness," which refers to impurity in thought and action, and "lasciviousness" which means "sensuality." A person characterized by the latter would be living only to please his or her pleasure sensitive appetites.

Idolatry is also of the flesh that not only touches the sexual area but the religious. Galatians 5:20 also mentions "idolatry" and "sorcery" which in the

Greek is pharmakia. The latter is revealed to occultic practices and drugs, which have always been a part of pagan idolatry.

The flesh tends to destroy our interpersonal relationships with others. Verses 20-21 mention "hatred, strife, jealousy, wrath, factions (dissention), seditions (disorder, rebellion), heresies (any persistent rejection of any article of faith by a member of the church, any belief or theory that is strongly at variance with established beliefs), envying and murder."

Indulgence is the flesh that cannot be under control or restrained, for its desires can result in "drunkenness, revelings (wild parties), and the like."

Verse 21 says that those who habitually indulge in the works of the flesh, "shall not inherit the kingdom of God." Paul is saying that if you continue to do those kind of things, you could not possibly be a Christian. It is impossible for a Christian to regularly practice those things, because he is a child of God.

Furthermore, a true Christian is indwelt by the Spirit, who gives him victory over the flesh. The Christian will hate sin. When you were saved, you became a partaker of the divine nature, which imparts the desire to do what pleases God. Satan attacks us at the point of our weakness...the flesh. He uses his system to incite our flesh. He also incites us to sin through our eyes...the lust of your eyes, and the pride of life. Jesus talked about the lust of the eyes in Matthew 5:27-29 (it's important that one reads these Scriptures). One can lust even with a thought, which is as bad as lusting with your eyes. If one has a problem with the lust of the eyes, you may have to take some drastic measures to change what you're looking at. If you are reading or watching immorality, you are opening yourself up to becoming programmed to lust, and porno (a very hard strong hold to overcome). Satan wants us to desire things that are beyond what God wants us to have, not because God is being mean, but because He knows what things will harm us. Psalm 119:37 states: "Turn away my eyes from looking at vanity".

The pride of life which in the Greek is alazoneia and refers to being proud when you really have nothing to be proud about, such as one who brags about something he doesn't have. People often live beyond what they can afford because they want others to think they have more than they have.

The Word states, "And the world passeth away, and the lust of it; but he doeth the will of God abideth forever." It is the Christian who does the will of God! God's will is that people be saved! Those who are saved will abide forever, but the world and its followers will pass away! We can't love the world because of its destiny. We are eternal, and the world is passing. The two principals of life and death can't operate together. The church is an eternal living people; the world is a dead system.

We often wonder now how much longer our civilization can last. The world is going to self-destruct because sin produces death. The world is a dying system. Its institutions are crumbling little by little...the family, the judicial system, and the government. Everything is breaking down because the world is plagued by sin, which operates on a death principal. The world has become defiled... (unclean, polluted with sin, to violate chastity of, make foul, dirty, taint...evil), so why would any Christian want to love this world? Christians are not to love the world and the things in it!

If you're a Christian, you have overcome the world. So act like it! If you're not a Christian, you are a part of a system that is self-destructing. You are being victimized by Satan, the god of this world. But understand Jesus Christ can change your life if you put your faith in Him and accept what He's done for you. He will take you out of this world's evil system and give you eternal life. That's His promise!

"For God hath not called us unto uncleanness, but unto holiness"
(1 Thessalonians 4:7).

THE BRIDE OF CHRIST

Look long enough in the eyes of our Savior and, there you will see a bride.... He sees her, He awaits her, and He longs for her. And who is that bride? Who is this beauty who occupies the heart of Jesus? YOU are. YOU have captured the heart of God. "As a man rejoices over his new wife, so your God will rejoice over you" (Isaiah 62:5).

The challenge is to remember that and to meditate on it, to focus on it. We must allow His love to change the way we look at ourselves. We have been chosen by Christ. We have been released from our old life in our old house, and He has claimed us as His beloved. You ask, "Well, where is He? Why hasn't He come?" There is only one answer, His bride is not ready. She is still being prepared.

Engaged people are obsessed with preparation. The right dress, the right weight, and the hair and tux has to be just right. Why? So their intended WILL marry them? No, just the opposite. They want to look their best because their intended IS marrying them.

The same is true for us. We want to look our best for Christ. We want our hearts to be pure and our thoughts to be clean. We want our faces to shine with grace and our eyes to sparkle with love. We want to be prepared. Why? In hopes that He will love us? No, just the opposite, because He already loves us.

We are spoken for. We are engaged, set apart, called out, a holy bride. We have been chosen for His castle. Don't settle for one-night stands in the arms of a stranger. Be obsessed with your wedding date. Guard against forgetfulness. Be intolerant of memory lapses. Write yourself notes. Memorize verses. Do whatever you need to do to remember and aim at what is in heaven. Think only about the things in heaven (Colossians 3:1-2). We are engaged to royalty, and our Prince is coming to take us home!!

THE BRIDE AND THE GROOM

The Lord illustrates the restoration of His intimacy with His people through the analogy of the bride and the bridegroom. The passage in Revelation 19:7-9 depicts the wedding feast of the Lamb, Jesus, when He claims His bride, the church, after she has made herself ready for Him. In his letter to the Ephesians, Paul explains how the bride will prepare herself: by submitting to God and allowing herself to be cleansed by the washing of His Word, so that she may be presented to the Bridegroom without spot, wrinkle, or blemish (Eph. 5:25-27).

When the bride is prepared and Jesus returns for her, the intimacy broken in the Garden will be completely restored, and man will again become one with Christ and with God, as Jesus prayed in John 17. But, as in the first "marriage," the bride must be bone of His bones and flesh of His flesh—that is, she must be like Him. He will not return for a defiled, defeated bride. In these days of restoration, God is preparing the bride with beauty and power and dressing her in His glory.

The church will display the kind of love Jesus demonstrated during His ministry on earth. Restoration also means the release of God's power without measure through the church. That release will come through His people as the gifts of the Spirit operate without restraint or restriction under the direction of the Holy Spirit-and in the Holy Spirit of God's love. As the church becomes a spiritual house (Eph. 2:20) inhabited by a holy priesthood, offering up spiritual sacrifices acceptable to God through Jesus Christ (1Pet. 2:5), all men will be drawn to Him; the world will at last see the glory of God through this restored church.

> "You also, as living stones, are being built up a spiritual house, a holy priesthood, to offer up spiritual sacrifices acceptable to God through Jesus Christ"
> (1 Peter 2:5).

THE ANSWER IS CALVARY'S CROSS

"God forbid that I should boast except in

the cross of our Lord Jesus Christ"

(Galatians 6:14).

Many heart-touching stories were circulated after the terrorist attacks on the World Trade Center on September 11, 2001. None seems more spiritually significant than that of ironworker Frank Silecchia. As he was helping to recover bodies, Frank noticed two steel beams in the shape of a cross standing upright in the middle of all the debris.

Appointing himself as the curator of that striking symbol of God's love, he often took heartbroken visitors to see it. Many of them were comforted by the silent testimony of the divine Presence in the worst tragedies. One day when journalist Barbara Walters came with tearful friends who had lost a son in the catastrophe, Frank simply led them to the cross.

The answer to the world's terrible pain and evil is not a philosophical argument or a theological treatise. The all sufficient answer is Calvary's Cross, where in fathomless grace, Jesus, the incarnate God, took upon Himself the burden of our sins and bore them "in His own body on the tree, that we… might live for righteousness" (1 Peter 2:24).

If you have not been to Calvary's cross, let me take you there. He suffered and died for you and then rose again. Believe in Him and you will be saved… "For since, in the wisdom of God, the world through wisdom did not know God, it pleased God through the foolishness of the message preached to save those who believed" (1 Cor. 1:21). Then start attending a good Bible-teaching church and learn more about God, His righteousness, His love for you, and the wonderful life He had planned for you with great purpose.

The pathway to heaven begins at the foot of the cross.

THE BIBLE IS YOUR SURE DEFENSE

Every believer knows the Bible is not the product of elevated human consciousness or, enlightened human intellect, but is directly "breathed" from God Himself (2 Peter 1:20). This means all Scripture is the product of God's creative breath. Therefore, being God's own utterance, it is called "The Word of God." Because it is inspired and trustworthy, we as believers read it carefully with the intent of applying it to our lives. We know the Bible can help us in every situation we encounter. It is also our standard for testing everything else that claims to be true. It is our safeguard against false teaching and our source of guidance for how we should live, regardless of circumstances. The Bible is our only source of knowledge about how we can be saved.

The Bible tells us in the final days before Christ returns; there will be false teachers, spiritual dropouts, and heresy (people professing opinions independent of the Truth). The false teacher will bring in destruction doctrines among us, even denying the Lord. The false teachers, having experienced the cleansing power of Christ, will now reject Him and will return to their former lifestyle and are worse off than before.

In these last days, there will be lovers of themselves, lovers of money, boasters, proud, blasphemers, disobedient to their parents, unthankful, unholy, unloving, unforgiving, slanderers without self-control, brutal, despisers of good, traitors, headstrong, haughty, lovers of pleasure rather than lovers of God, having a form of godliness but denying its power. FROM SUCH PEOPLE TURN AWAY (2 Timothy 3:1-5)! People will be characterized by all kinds of self-centered perversions. Some will maintain an outward pretense, speaking the vocabulary of Christianity, but refusing the reality that Christian faith expresses the power they deny is the heart of Christianity... the fact of a risen Redeemer, the truth of the inspired Word and the indwelling and overflowing of the Holy Spirit, working within believers and transforming their lives.

Because of deception and false teachings, we must be disciplined and ready to reject error by knowing God's Word. Knowing the Bible is your sure defense against error and confusion.

If our faith is strong, we needn't fear what lies ahead! We should not be afraid when we see evil increase, for God is still in control; He will be victorious. We must ready ourselves for Christ, spreading his good news to help others to be prepared also. Christ will return and bring total victory to all who will be ready! If we are ready, we don't have to be concerned about when He will return! God will bring victory to his faithful followers, and He will judge those who persecute them!

"Be diligent to present yourself approved to God, a worker who does not need to be ashamed, rightly dividing the word of truth" (2 Timothy 2:15)...this does not mean to segment the Word, but to rightly discern its truth by capturing the spirit of the word. (Heb. 4:12; 1 Cor. 2:13, 14; John 6:63).

THE BEST PART OF YOUR LIFE IS NOT BEHIND YOU

"Rejoice and exult in hope; be steadfast and patient in suffering and tribulation; be constant in prayer" (Romans 12:12).

Gray hair is supposed to be a crown of glory, but growing old doesn't always feel very glorious. We remember the precious time the Lord has given us and the wonderful memories. But at times we feel trapped by aching joints, and a frail body as well as lost abilities. It seems our best days are behind us and we feel we don't want to be a burden to others. We wonder, since we are still alive do we still have a purpose? We want to do so much more but now we are limited! Now would be the time to pray and ask the Lord to strengthen our hope and to help us recognize the blessings around us and ahead of us so we can continue to rejoice in this season of life.

The Lord will answer our prayer by reminding us, hope is a golden cord connecting us to heaven. This cord helps us to hold our head up high, even when multiple trials are buffeting us. Jesus reminds us, "I will never leave your side, and I never let go of your hand." But without the cord of hope, our head may slump and our feet may shuffle as our journey goes uphill with the Lord. Hope lifts our perspective from weary feet to the glorious view we see from the high road. We are reminded that the road we're traveling together is ultimately a highway to heaven. When we take time to consider this glorious destination, the roughness or smoothness of the road ahead becomes much less significant. The Lord is training us to hold our heart in focus of His continual Presence and our eyes fixed on heaven and continue walking the Word. As we bask in the beauty of His Presence, worshipping the Lord, new hope will grow within us. The Word reminds us, no matter how hopeless our situation may seem the Lord assures us that "all things are possible with God." Also Jesus is the Truth, and therefore He is true to all his promises. They provide a rock-solid foundation on which we can live and move and have our being.

Jesus is our risen, living Savior! Through his resurrection we have been born again to an ever-living hope. It is vital for us to remain hopeful, no matter what is going on in our life! The hope the Lord provides for us is an anchor for our soul, firm and secure even in the most troubling waters. A good way to remain anchored in the Lord is to whisper as often as needed: "Jesus, You are my Hope." This affirmation strengthens our hopeless situation into victory, and keeps us connected to Jesus. Those who hope in the Lord will not be disappointed.

Our hope is not only for the future; eternal life begins when we believe in God and join his family. If we sincerely believe in the Almighty God and we believe we are actually a blood bought child of God we will lift our heads up because of who we are and we will walk in hope! The eternal life we now have gives us hope and enables us to live with confidence in God (1 Peter 3:6).

"May the God of hope fill you with all joy and peace as you trust in Him, so that you may overflow with hope by the power of the Holy Spirit" (Romans 15:13).

TAKE NOTHING FOR GRANTED

We as the children of God should never take anything for granted, not even the rising of the sun! We live in such a fast pace world and as we arise each morning we plunge headlong into our activities. Before we put our feet on the floor our minds are already organizing our daily duties of the day. Our mind goes into neutral and our thoughts flow freely, we then tend to feel anxious and the focus becomes problem solving! This should be a warning to us to get our minds back into gear, turn around toward the Lord who has been waiting to say, "Good Morning, My Child, let Me help you with your day. Come in the Light of My love."

Before Satan tempted Eve in the Garden of Eden, thankfulness was as natural as breathing. Satan's temptation involved pointing Eve to the one thing that was forbidden her. The garden was filled with luscious, desirable fruits, but Eve focused on the one fruit she couldn't have rather than being thankful for the many good things freely available. This negative focus darkened her mind, and she gave in to temptation.

When we focus on what we don't have, or on situations that displease us, our mind also becomes darkened. We take for granted life, salvation, sunshine, flowers, and countless other gifts from the Lord. We look for what is wrong and refuse to enjoy life until that is "fixed." We need to count our blessing instead of our problems.

It's important to start our day with prayer and thanksgiving, asking the Lord to be Lord of our day, and asking to be alert for the many blessings that come our way throughout the day! It doesn't matter how much, or the duties we have before us, what is important is that we start the day with the Presence of the Lord, His guidance, and to ask the Lord what He would have us do for Him this day and to give thanks and appreciation of the day! A successful day is a day staying in touch with Jesus! When we approach the Lord with thanksgiving, the Light of His Presence pours into us, transforming us through and through. Walk in the Light with the Lord practicing the discipline of thanksgiving which brings many blessings. An important key to entering into the presence of God is to come humbly with abundant praise and thanksgiving. "Let us come before His presence with thanksgiving; Let us shout joyfully to Him with psalms" (Psalm 95:2).

To thank, means yadah to revere or worship with extended hands: to praise, give thanks. Yadah is an important word for "praise" or "thanksgiving," and occurs more than 100 times in the OT, more than half of these in the Book of Psalms. So many times we hear people say, "Yadah, Yadah, Yadah," but they don't realize the special and real meaning of this word. Every time we give thanks to the Lord, we are acknowledging that He is our Lord and Provider.

When we thank God during a difficult day, we are assuming the proper stance of a child of God. Also when we persevere in this thankfulness, resisting the temptation to grumble, we will find joy and peace in the midst of our struggles. "Give thanks in all circumstances, for this is God's will for you in Christ Jesus" (1 Thessalonians 5:18).

THE ROYAL ROBE

How do you view yourself? Do you see yourself robed in righteous, or do you see yourself as a failure and always missing the mark? You may find it easier to view yourself when you think you are living up to your standards of performance for God. But we can never live up to God's standards...in this life! God wants his children to see themselves as He sees us; clothed with garments of salvation, setting us free from the condemning law of sin, death and condemnation. We need God's righteousness every day. We need to remind ourselves every day, that we are clothed in the royal garment of righteousness! Don't fall into the pitfall of thinking you can manage life without God when everything is going well for you! And do not make the mistake of forgetting that the Lord's salvation-clothing is sufficient to cover all your sins. God has arrayed us in a robe of perfect righteousness. The more consistently we see ourselves clothed in God's royal garments, the more we can rejoice in His Presence. Christ Jesus wants us all to enjoy the riches of our salvation, free from condemnation, knowing that nothing and no one can strip you of that covering! "Therefore there is now no condemnation for those who are in Christ Jesus. For the law of the Spirit of life in Christ Jesus has set you free from the law of sin and death" (Romans 8:1-2). As Christians, we are chosen royalty, that's right; we are a chosen royalty, belonging to Jesus our Savior... "But you are a chosen race, a royal priesthood, a holy nation, a people for God's own possession, so that you may proclaim the excellencies of Him who has called you out of darkness into His marvelous light" (1 Peter 2:9).

Christians know in their acceptance of Jesus Christ, that we have received God's grace and mercy, we are now "in Christ" by virtue of the new birth, so there is absolutely no condemnation in you or toward you from God: "There is therefore now no condemnation to them which are in Christ Jesus, who walk not after the flesh, but after the Spirit" (Romans 8:1). You are free from fear, and liberated from guilt...no matter what you have done or where you have been. Since you are not condemned, you have no need to condemn others. Jesus accepted the sin of the world along with its punishment; judgment is passed ("But now he has reconciled you by Christ's physical body through death to present you holy in His sight, without blemish and free from accusation" (Colossians 1:22). God is not holding the sins of the world against the ungodly. He is offering reconciliation (forgiveness and pardon) to all who accept His Son. What a freedom to see others reconciled to God and to tell them about the Good News!

Although we as Christians have learned not to condemn ourselves or focus on our failures, we at times do forget we have the royal robe of righteousness.

By daily confessing this Scripture…we are covered in righteousness and it will help remind us and to be deeply rooted in this truth within our heart…

"Therefore there is no condemnation
for those who are in Christ Jesus"
(Romans 8:1).

THE CASUAL SOVEREIGNTY OF GOD IS DEADLY!

"Therefore, since we are receiving a kingdom which cannot be shaken, let us have grace, by which we may serve God acceptable with reverence and godly fear. For our God is a consuming fire" (Hebrews 12:28-29).

Our country has forgotten the sovereignty of the Almighty God! We have casually despised His sovereignty, taking Him and his power, wisdom, thankfulness and grace for granted. We find ourselves depending more on ourselves than God who is Omniscience (all-knowing), omnipresence (present everywhere), and omnipotent, (all powerful). He has no beginning or end. He is a Spirit yet, a person who is totally self-aware… "I AM"; totally moral; and totally self-assertive… "I WILL." He is also a righteous judge and totally fair and just. He sustains the whole universe. He causes everything to be! He has the ability to be everywhere at all times! Do you know anyone or any other god who is like our God? Of course you don't!

But yet we as a nation think we can run it without Him, or depend and trust God for the well-being of our country and ourselves! We think we can make decisions without His help! Or we pray and expect God to answer our prayers just the way we want, when we want! We expect blessings and favor when we have not obeyed, honored, or even took the time to pray and acknowledge His presence, or thanked Him throughout each day for His love, guidance, and the Holy Spirit. Have we trusted and depended on Him moment to moment? Have we even notice our neediness?

Our awareness of God creates a strong connection to His Presence. His power gives us strength to take the next step and to resist discouragement, and despair. Only God's power, wisdom, love, and grace enable us to live abundantly in the mists of our situations and limitations. God says, "When we are weak, we are strong," and "My grace is sufficient for you, my strength is made perfect in weakness" (2 Corinthians 12:9-10). God's grace is sufficient for us, but its sufficiency is for one day at a time. Plus God's Grace is sufficient for every situation! Our part is to recognize our neediness and receive it: "Those who look to him are radiant; their faces are never covered with shame" (Psalm 34:5). GOD IS THE CREATOR and Sustainer of time and space; HE IS OUR GREAT COMFORTER, FRIEND, AND REDEEMER! He desires to bless us, prosperous us, not harm us; He wants to give us a victorious plan for each of us for our life (Jeremiah 29:11-14). God loves us (John 3:16).

Knowing all this about our Heavenly Father God, His Word, and love for us and the world, we have to ask ourselves, "Why would our country, the government, or any individual, dare to take our Sovereign God Almighty, our Creator for granted, or casual; having no reverent fear for Him? Why would we depend on ourselves and choose our ways above God's? Why do we think we have all the answers; trusting ourselves and our decisions, especially after seeing our country falling apart, families becoming dysfunctional, our economy failing and government corrupt from our choices?"

God and his ways are the only way for the good-will to happen! The sooner we all acknowledge God for who He is and come into agreement on this, the sooner people and life will have value!

WHAT MATTERS TO YOU, MATTERS TO GOD

"For our high priest is able to understand our weakness. Let us, then, feel very sure that we can come before God's throne where there is grace. There we can receive mercy and grace to help us when we need it" (Hebrews 4:15-16).

You probably think that's true, when it comes to the big stuff, it matters to God, and you know that God really cares. But what about the smaller things? What about broken dishes, late flights, tooth aches, or a crashed hard disk? Do you think that God cares then? Does these matter to God? We think He's got a universe to run, and the planets to keep in balance, presidents and kings to watch over. He's got wars to worry about and famines to fix. You ask yourself, "Who am I to tell him about my ingrown toenail?" Well, I am pleased to tell you who YOU are! In fact, let me explain who You really are! YOU are an heir of God; You are eternal; You have a crown; You are a holy priest, You were chosen before creation. But more than any of the above—more significant than any title or position is the simple fact that YOU ARE GOD'S CHILD! "The Father has loved us so much that we are called the children of God. And we really are his children" (1 John 3:1). If you are still thinking, "No, not me, maybe Mother Teresa or Billy Graham, but not me." "You really are God's Child," that's why John added that phrase.

As a result, if something big or small is important to you, it's important to God! So go ahead, talk to God about anything. He won't think it's silly or not important. Does God care about the little things in our lives? You better believe it. If it matters to you, it matters to God!

The God who is good gave us the invitation to call upon Him… "Call to me and I will answer you, and I will tell you great and mighty things, which you do not know" (Jeremiah 33:3, NASB). He then promised to answer in a way that was beyond what we asked for: "Now to Him who is able to do exceedingly abundantly above all that we ask or think, according to the power that works in us" (Ephesians 3:20). The word great in this Scripture means "considerably above average." He follows the word great with the word mighty. Mighty means "inaccessible." God has given us access to the inaccessible. It is out of the reach of our skills, character, or qualifications! But

God gave us the key to the inaccessible...He Himself is that key. He invites us to call upon Him, giving Him the open door to answer in a way that is above our expectations and imagination. There is no goodness apart from Him, so our journey is a discovery of the person of God...the One whose inaccessible goodness is now accessible by an invitation with His promise to be found by us.

PRAYER OF PURSUIT

Lord, You have invited me to pursue You.

Even though you live inside of me, in full, I am experiencing You in part.

I see in part, taste in part, encounter in part.

This doesn't discourage me; it fuels my hunger to experience more of You.

Father, I ask you to come right now and overwhelm me with the revelation of Your goodness.

Your greatness is unsearchable.

Your goodness is beyond comprehension.

Help me to live mindful of these truths.

Even though Your goodness is beyond my comprehension, it is not beyond my experience.

I will experience in part while living on earth, but every experience gives me a greater glimpse.

Every experience in Your Presence gives me a richer taste.

Every experience satisfies the deepest parts of my heart and also leaves me hungry for more.

Thank You, God, for the gift of hunger!

It's this gift that draws me into unexplored realms of Your Presence and goodness.

A PRAYER OF INVITATION

Lord, I receive your invitation. I seek You with the expectation of finding You. You invited me into a place of discovering Your goodness and experiencing Your Presence. This means I should set out on this journey expecting to meet you. Holy Spirit, may I be ready and willing to obey as I seek You. May I be ready and willing to follow You. I say "yes," God. I say "yes" to this quest of discovering You. And I say "yes," to whatever you ask of me. In His Name I pray…Amen.

"THIS CUP"

When God made covenant, Abraham knew there was no longer any reason to doubt God and His promises. For in Abraham's day, covenant partners exchanged their valuable and personal belongings. During the ceremony they would exchange weapons and coats or armor confessing loyalty to one another, even to death. Entering covenant meant you were giving all that you were and all that you had with your covenant partner. It also consisted of cutting of blood and combining it together to signify becoming as one, sealing the pact, covenant was taken seriously. It still should be taken seriously!

Taking the Blood of Jesus is also serious. We are to partake in a "worthy" manner, which means, to attribute the full worth of Christ's redeeming work. We are to "partake" with faith in His full forgiveness, full acceptance and the full power to restore, strengthen and heal. Failing to take this seriously and unworthily and abuse its meaning could have you in your affliction or suffer premature death (1Corth. 11:30).

Just as the act of water baptism outwardly confesses an inward experience of salvation through the blood of Jesus, each observance of the Lord's table is a powerful occasion for faiths confession. It is saying we as Christians confess before all heaven that we believe in the "New Covenant" and the power of Christ's Blood through His death. The outward act of faith as we partake of the cup and bread is outwardly proclaiming, "I lay hold of all the benefits of Jesus Christ's full redemption for my life—forgiveness, wholeness, strength, health and sufficiency."

The Lord's Supper is not just a simple ritual of remembrance, but an active confession, by which you actively will call to memory and appropriate today all that Jesus has provided and promised through the cross. We partake with humility and examining of our hearts, and confessing of any sin, and then worship and give praise and thanks for God's love and for the covenant that cannot be dissolved. When you realize the significance of the "New Covenant" that was established in the Blood of Jesus you will have the same confidence Abraham had that made him the Father of faith. There will be no room for doubting God and His word and promises. You will not waver but be convinced once and for all that there is power in the Blood of Christ. When Jesus became the sacrifice that ratified your covenant with God.

THE FOUNDATION OF OUR MORALS AND VALUES

Our foundation of a good and prosperous life was set before us many years ago. God gave Moses the principals, the way of life we were to live as God commanded, called the Ten Commandments and sent him forth to deliver them to the people. These Commandments signified, respect, peace and security, unity for the people and obedience, faith, reverence, love and devotion for God. As you know, people couldn't keep them. The first four Commandments are related to one's relationship with God. The next six Commandments have to do with human relationships. When you are right with God it compels one to be right with one's neighbor. Some people think the Ten Commandments were meant for that time. But they convey duties for everyone and reveal to us the basic morality required by God.

When Jesus came He did not come to destroy the Law, but to fulfill it (Matt. 5:17-20). That is, Jesus moved the understanding of the Law from its external, legalistic meaning to its spiritual one. He moved to a deeper level of meaning, to the spirit behind the Law which God intended from the beginning. So behind all the Law had stood two great principals of love for God and love for your neighbor. The commandment to love had been there all along; Jesus simply emphasized them in a way that would never change how we should look at them.

God had also commanded people to teach them to their children so life would continue as He had willed. But as we know, our foundation of morals, values, and way of life now are far from God's will. The fear (reference) and love of the Lord and taking His Name in vain is not respected, having no other image one worships is violated by drugs and other addictions, observing the Sabbath (Sunday) day as holy, as long been gone. Stores still stay open and people still work on that day. Honor your mother and father is sadly rejected, do not murder or commit adultery, or steal is an everyday activity for many people. Do not covet your neighbor or his belongings happen daily. We can see clearly that the Ten Commandments and the love and fear of the Lord for many are not taken seriously.

But the ones who reject God's will fail to realize He is a Sovereign God, which means God will have His will over them in whatever way He chooses. Are there consequences one will face by not observing God's will and choosing to go your own way? The promises and blessing within the Bible cannot be received. Perhaps the most important blessing in the entire Bible is that "…the Lord will establish you as a holy people to Himself…keep the commandments" (Deut. 28:15-68).

"I call heaven and earth as witnesses today against you, that I have set before you, life and death, blessing and cursing, therefore choose life, that both you and your descendants may live; that you may love the Lord your God, that you may obey His voice and that you may cling to Him, for He is your life and the length of your days..." (Deuteronomy 30:19).

WHAT WILL YOU CHOOSE?

THE CHRISTIAN'S WORLD

To be a Christian is, in a sense, to be a man without a country. If you take the Scriptures to heart, have genuine faith and love for God you will attempt to live what the Scriptures teach and try to obey God. But of course you will have to be prepared to come into conflict with the world. You now belong to no one but Christ, while those in the world give themselves to people, possessions, institutions, and idols other than Christ. To be a Christian is to stand apart and yet to remain within—to dare to be different. You look at everything through the prism of Scripture, and things look different when viewed biblically.

Success in the world means power, influence, money, prestige. But in the Christian world, it means pleasing God. This quest for obedience may lead you to do things that are wholly contrary to what the world wants and rewards.

Obeying God's commandments means reading and understanding Scripture, then determining that you are going to live exactly as Scripture teaches which is not going to be easy, for it is almost impossible not to be caught up every day in some of the ways of the world. But you can make an effort. This is how the process of sanctification works…learning how to obey God, how to listen for his commands in your life. It is reading the Scripture and allowing it to soak into you. It is all about understanding the requirements of God's commandments and then gradually, day by day allowing that understanding to control the actions of your life.

One thing that might cause failure to obey God would be that we figure God's time is our Bible study, our prayer time, the prayer group meeting, or Sunday church service. That is just not true! God's time is every moment of our lives! We don't put Him on and off like a suit of clothes…if we would wear Him all day long, we would discover obedience becoming a reflex action. Obedience out of love for God is vital. God wants us to obey him for our own safety like any good father wants for his children so they will live in peace, joy and hope of the future. But as any good father, God at times, out of love must discipline his children. But He always gives fair warning and time to change our ways when we head down the wrong path. God wants us to be faithful to Him. It hurts Him to see us wander away in disobedience. We cannot be perfect, but we can strive for maturity and we always have the Holy Spirit to guide us and help us to stay on the right path, Let us not be as those people He has something against:

> The Lord has this against you who live in the land: The people are not true, not loyal to God, nor do those who live in the land

even know him. Cursing, lying, killing, stealing and adultery are everywhere. One murder follows another. Because of this the land dries up, and all its people are dying. Even the wild animals and the birds of the air and the fish of the sea are dying" (Hosea 4:1-3).

UNITED WE STAND...DIVIDED WE FALL

Our country has been under much turmoil and disasters this year. The hardships of people who have lost family members, their homes, their jobs, and all of their belongings were hard to bare.

Some people think God has brought these adversities upon us to discipline us, or get our attention. Some think the devil was behind it all, and some just believe it was all from nature. Whatever the case is, God is not unaware, or mad, or has forgotten us or stopped loving us! His promise never to leave us still stands, and his Word that says "Do not fear for I have overcome the world" also still stands. GOD IS STILL IN CONTROL! What God does want is...the church, the Christians, his children, to depend and trust in Him! We are too busy focusing on the tragedy instead of Jesus. In our weakness, his power plugs in! We are to live life and work in collaboration with God. His reasons for allowing these adversaries may be shrouded in mystery, but His continual Presence is an absolute promise! In the closeness to the Lord, we are safe, and in the intimacy of His Presence, we are energized. We are to do everything in dependence on Him. The desire to act independently...apart from Him—springs from the root of pride. The Bible tells us... "Apart from Me, you can do nothing:" that is, nothing of eternal value. Together with God we face whatever each day brings. Nothing is wasted when it is shared with the Lord, for "He can bring beauty out of ashes, and we know that all things work together for good to those who love God...."

Through the hurricanes, tornados and floods, people united together in love, compassion and help. Now that's how we should act. We shouldn't have to wait for a disaster, to be kind, caring and helpful, united in purpose with others and God! Love is our bond daily, if we are the children of God!

VENGEANCE

"Instead of plotting revenge, we are to live at peace whenever possible" (Romans 12:14-21).

Revenge belongs to God! (Deut. 32:35). If vengeance is God's, then it is not ours. God has not asked us to settle the score or get even, ever! Judgment is God's job. To assume otherwise is to assume God can't do it.

When we are mistreated, our animalistic response is to go on the hunt. Instinctively, we double up our fists. Getting even is only natural. Which, incidentally, is precisely the problem. Revenge is natural, not spiritual. Getting even is the rule of the jungle. Giving grace is the rule of the kingdom.

X-ray the soul of the vengeful and behold the tumor of bitterness: black, menacing, malignant and Carcinoma of the spirit. Its fatal fibers creep around the edge of the heart and ravage it. Yesterday you can't alter, but your reaction to yesterday you can. Revenge is irreverent. When we strike back we are saying, "I know vengeance is yours, God, but I just didn't think You would punish enough. I thought I'd better take this situation into my own hands. You have a tendency to be a little soft."

To forgive someone is to display reverence. If left unchecked our anger and thirst for revenge can destroy our life. Forgiveness is not saying the one who hurt you was right. Forgiveness is stating that God is fair and He will do what is right. Is there a situation or relationship in your life that you are holding out for some revenge? Now is the time my friend to let it go and "let God be God."

After all, don't we have enough things to do without trying to do God's work too?

GUILT

"There is therefore now no condemnation to them which are in Christ Jesus, who walk not after the flesh, but after the Spirit" (Romans 8:1).

Sometimes your shame is private. Maybe you were pushed over the edge by an abusive spouse, or seduced by a compromising superior. No one knows but you, and that's enough. Or maybe you were branded by a divorce you didn't want, or have a contaminating disease you never expected, or marked by a handicap you didn't create. Whether private, or public, shame is always painful, and unless you deal with it, it is permanent. You will need to invite Christ into your journey, and let Him stand beside you as you retell the events of the darkest nights of your soul. He will be listening and have compassion and understanding. Then you listen carefully, as He is saying, "I judge you not guilty." Now watch, carefully, He's writing and leaving you a message, not in sand, but on the Cross. Not with His hand, but His Blood. His message has two words: Not guilty. So now you can confess: "There is no condemnation in me. I refuse all guilt and shame over past sins and failures. I am free in Jesus for I have received God's grace!"

VENGEANCE IS MINE, SAITH THE LORD!

"Vengeance is Mine, and recompense; their foot shall slip in due time; for the day of their calamity is at hand" (Deuteronomy 32:35).

People seem to have ignorantly forgotten there is a much greater law we need to be obedient to, besides being accountable to manmade laws. But in the last past years, many people have decided God's Word, and His way of a peaceful living, and having a purposeful life could be placed in the hands of man. Since when does man know better than God! But unfortunately the church has a lot to do with the down fall of righteousness. We as the church have ignored our responsibility, devotion and righteousness. We did not stand up for the needed prayer, the Bible, and our freedom to worship when and where! We allowed God to take the back seat to morality and peace and the love for our country and others. The Commandments and the Golden Rule faded into the shadows. Now it is being said we can no longer say, Happy Thanksgiving Day, we are advised by some of the schools to say, Happy Fall Day, because they don't want to offend anyone. Don't they realize Americans are offended because it's our history and heritage? During Christmas season we are not to say, Merry Christmas, so we don't offend anyone, we are advised to say, Happy Holidays. We cannot take Christ out of Christmas! It is because of Christ we have Christmas! The world has made Christmas a frustrating, stressful, money-making day! What will the world be saying during Easter...Resurrection Day? When God is ignored and the honor for God's Kingdom is no longer important to people we can expect our world to crumble and become corrupt and filled with violence. When man takes things into their own hands, the judgments and choices become distorted and perverted. Without God as the head of our life, there is no peace, or right judgments! Isaiah 59:1-9 says...It is because of all this evil that deliverance is far from us...God promises to condemn all violence. A life of violence brings its own destruction. According to Jesus, violence is to be replaced by a willingness to love even our enemies. Romans 12:14 21 explains, instead of plotting revenge, we are to live at peace whenever possible. We have totally ignored God's Word: "But above all these things put on love, which is the bond of perfection, and let the peace of God rule in your hearts, to which also you were called in one body; and be thankful" (Colossians 3:15). Church, we desperately need to adopt and practice diligently every form of relational righteousness: love compassion, humble attitudes, self-giving behavior, freely flowing forgiveness, and patience with others! Choose peace to govern all your relationships. Human relationships were designed to be fueled and filled by righteousness. As we practice those things God commands, our relationships will become a sampling of heaven on earth. Faithful believers, if we don't take a stand for our history, heritage, prayer, Bible and God's standard for right living, the generations after us will not know the truth of our Nation, or learn of our Spiritual journey, God's Promises, Salvation, Calvary, and having One True God who loves us, and what it is like to have an intimate relationship with Jesus and the Holy Spirit.

Church, we can make a serious change, and we are responsible for spreading the Gospel! If we don't step up and let our voice be heard everything good and godly will fade into the shadows. Only by showing the world that God has all the answers to make our lives and this nation and world a better place to live, there must be change! If there is no change in the Christian's life, how will the world see the love, power and peace that the Lord wants all of man-kind to have?

We are entering a New Year; let our pledge to make a change in our homes, communities, our churches, and our nation that brings glory to God. If everyone does their part we can turn the world upside down…Jesus did! Take this challenge seriously, especially if you say you are a faithful and devoted believer…prove it! If you want to make a difference, your heart will be inspired to take action that will give a positive influence.

We all have seen the violence and destruction that was caused in Ferguson and other states as well as other countries when men take matters into their hands, excluding God. What did they accomplish?

People, we need to lift up our voices and examples to schools, our communities, our governor and even our President. We can even state our opinions to what wholesome TV shows we prefer for our families and the movies. If we don't make a stand now for righteousness, who will? Most importantly our godly character and examples must be displayed within our own homes, not just in public. We can start with prayer. Pray for our families daily, our communities, our Church and Pastors, and our leaders. We must live and share God's Word and the Gospel! Remember, God's Word never returns void! Also keep in mind: much prayer…much power, more prayer…more power! As Christian believers we all have been given spiritual gifts, so let's put them to work for the Kingdom of God and the peace and love for the world. Leave the vengeance to God!

"THOSE WHO LOVE YOUR LAW HAVE GREAT PEACE AND DO NOT STUMBLE"
(Psalm 119:165)

WITHOUT GOD

Have you ever thought what it would be without God? I have. To me it would be living in a dark emptiness without purpose or value, being hopeless, afraid having no worthwhile future. We all would be walking around following what everyone else is doing instead of being an individual with their own journey in life, making the same mistakes and decisions, love would become lust and friendship would become insecure and false…meaningless. Lies would become the truth, and good would be bad and bad would become good. We would not have an eternal life of joy, peace and incredible love. We would live life for ourselves being selfish; making many more mistakes and wrong decisions with so many negative consequences. We would not care what was right, or wrong as long as it made us happy. Everyone says, "Do what makes you happy." Striving for bigger and better material things would be the goal in life. When we go through troubles, pain, sickness and hard times, we might not know what to do because who would even truly care to help, or guide us in the right direction; I believe we would feel heartless, hopeless and insecure with no conscience. Would your friends, that you thought were your friends, be there for you? Is this a life really worth living? Does all this sound too familiar in our world right now? Don't you want more…better out of life and after?

To me this is a very dark world to live in! Everyone is too busy for you, families become broken homes, and no one can trust anyone and actually no one truly cares about family life or friends. People choose entertainment rather than church. There would be much more crime because people would not have, or even cares about values, or character, or integrity. Evil would run rapid! This is a very scary analogy, but so true! I am not saying everyone is living a life without God but many are.

We need God in our life, in our families, in our government and in this county! If we are to live a life of security, peace, value, honor, respect, love, guidance, joy, wisdom and have eternal life in heaven, WE NEED GOD IN OUR LIFE! God wants to be there for us to love and care for us, guide us, and give us a life with value and He has a purpose for each and every one of us. He wants to share his best with us and help us become the men and women He had planned for us to be. He has given us many promises and blessings in his Word to be fulfilled as we walk with Him! There is only "light," no "darkness" when you follow Jesus. Life is truly worth living and the journey with Jesus is always adventurous. It is not without trials but the difference is Jesus is always there to see you through! I could not live without Jesus in my Life!! I know those who have already given their heart to Jesus are very happy, fulfilled and secure with their decision.

If you want a better and valuable life with purpose and haven't yet asked Jesus Christ into your heart and life, this is right time, right NOW! Don't settle for a life that is not going anywhere but hell! Pray this prayer with sincerity: Dear Jesus, My life is worthless without you, for I am a sinner. I know you are the Son of God who died for my sin. I ask You now to forgive me and come into my heart and change my life. Help me to live for You and the life you had planned for me and not be selfish and live carelessly just for myself. Help me to learn about you and your ways and love. I want to be fulfilled in this life, and when I come home to You, Jesus. Thank You, Jesus, for caring and loving me enough to die for me. Thank You for saving me! Amen, You are now "saved" and adopted into the family of God!

If you have prayed this prayer, continue on by going to a Bible-teaching church and learn of the Lord and his Word and the undying love He has for you. Read your Bible and allow the Holy Spirit to transform you and your life. This is the most important decision you have ever made in your entire life! God Bless you!

WITHOUT CHRIST...THERE IS NO CHRISTMAS

"You shall have no other gods before Me" (Exodus 20:3).

Has the legend of Santa Clause replaced the "sweetest story ever told"? What has happened to the hearts of America? Can the pagan legend of Santa Claus substitute the true story of God's love, the giver of every good and perfect gift? One cannot say that the legend of Santa Claus has stolen the hearts of many children and is a harmless tradition! It has been embedded in the children's hearts that Santa Claus is the god of Christmas, who brings cheer and is the children's friend. It is being told that Santa is all-seeing and all knowing. He sees what all the children do and makes a "Book of Remembrance" of the names of good or bad children and their actions. It is said Santa comes down from the sky with wonderful gifts. He rewards all good children. Santa gives them everything they want. Is it any wonder that the children's reaction is to open their hearts, to strive to please Santa so they can get what they want to dream about him, talk about him, watch for the stories about him on TV, and wait eagerly for him?

It is as a thief; Santa Claus has stolen the hearts of many children. Have we as parents and family members allowed this by standing by and offering no resistance while he stole the hearts of childhood? We have not stood up and lifted our voice loud enough in protest as Santa corrupted the minds and hearts of children everywhere with this false image and lying imagination. It might have seemed like a harmless tradition, but doesn't the devil work in discreet subtle disguises to deceive children and parents? It seemed like a charming story which always brought joy, but has it really?

We have not lifted the standard of Jesus, the true God, the gift giver and tender Friend of children, who is not willing that "one of these little ones should perish" (Matthew 18:14).

"You shall not make for yourself a carved image-
any likeness of anything..." (Exodus 20:4).

"You shall not bow down to them or serve them.
For the Lord your God, am a jealous God..." (Exodus 20).

WHY WE NEED TO WALK IN HUMILITY

"Haughtiness goes before destruction;

humility precedes honor" (Proverbs 18:12).

Pride is our enemy when it involves wanting too much recognition, taking too much credit, wanting our own way, thinking our way is best. In summary, thinking too highly of ourselves is destructive. The Bible tells us pride has great power to damage our relationships with others and with God (2 Timothy 3:2-5). Remember, Satan was cast from heaven because of pride. Pride will harden our hearts which in turn leads to an arrogant disregard of God and sin. Pride leads to ignoring God and a life of disobedience (Psalm 10:2-11). Second Chronicles 26:16-20 says: "But when he had become powerful, he also became proud, which led to his downfall." An inflated estimation of our past successes leads to prideful behavior and, ultimately, judgment. Pride renders us blind to our own sin (Luke 18:10-11). Our spiritual lives are infected and will divide the church if we walk in pride. God hates pride and will judge it severely. God sets Himself against the proud, but shows favor to the humble (James 4:6).

So you can see it is important to avoid pride and seek humility. Humility is true strength, for it reaches into the Kingdom of Heaven. Pride is true weakness, for it reaches no further than our own ego. Humility is the first step toward wholeness. Unfortunately, when we prosper and all is well, we may fall into pride, thinking we have achieved it all. But when we are put down financially, physically, or in other ways, we suddenly find it necessary to ask for the Lord's help. Even when we are doing the work for God, the most holy and wonderful work of all, we are to work humbly, as Matthew 6:1 warns us, "Take care! Don't do your good deeds publicly, to be admired, because then you will lose the reward from your Father in heaven." It would be easy to do the Lord's work with great pride. After all, His work is the most wonderful work in the entire world. But the Apostle Paul recognized that doing God's work is serving, which takes humility. Those who are proud are not good at serving (Acts 20:19). God wants us all to be humble and gentle, and to be patient with each other, making allowances for each other's faults because of your love and for the unity of the church. Humility is the path to greatness (Psalm 18:27). God has promised to bless humble people (Psalm 18:27; Isaiah 57:15). You must understand humility is not effacing oneself. It is not destroying one's sense of self-worth. It is honest recognition of our own worth, our worth as God sees us. Pride elevates us above others, and often God himself. But to destroy one's sense of self-worth is also unacceptable, for it denies the value God placed upon us when He created us in His image. To see ourselves as God sees us, that is our goal! Jonathan Edwards wrote, "Nothing sets a person so much out of the devil's reach as humility." Let us pray this prayer together: Heavenly Father, thank you for helping me find humility in my life. I fully realize that without Jesus I can do nothing. I will not let anything I do be done through strife or vain glory, because I want to have the mind of Christ at all times. With your help, Father, I will serve you with all humility of mind. Help me Father to be clothed with humility. I humble myself under your mighty hand, knowing that you will exalt me in your perfect timing. Thank you for the power of humility in my life, Lord. I pray in the Name of Jesus...Amen.

WHY PRAYER IS IMPORTANT

To understand the importance of prayer we first must know what prayer is. Prayer is a conversation of the heart with God. Through prayer we align ourselves with our Creator, and His presence is revealed to us. As we grow in our love and worship of Him we are united with our Lord through prayer and our lives become fuller, richer, more joyous, and more peaceful.

The importance of having a spirit of prayer is one of the most important factors in our walk with Christ. A good prayer life is being aware of God's presence and being transparent with Him. Don't ever be afraid to be open and honest about yourself or your circumstance, for He already knows everything about you and what you are going through. Honesty shows respect for who He is and real love means you don't have anything to fear from your Heavenly Father.

Prayer helps us reexamine our relationship with our Creator and helps us focus on our relationship with others, for we will be judged on how we relate to others on a godly basis. We need to ask ourselves whether our relationships at work or at home are godly.

Prayer helps us know the heart of our Lord and His desires for our lives. When we are constantly seeking our Lord in prayer, we align ourselves with His wishes and desires. We are no longer programmed to see what we want, but we see what God wants. We turn over control of our lives to Him and do His will. In prayer, we pour out to Him our joys, our anguish, and petitions for others and ourselves.

Prayer should be as a bolt to lock at night, and our key to open the day. Prayer is the single most important action we can take to know God. If we don't have a good prayer life, our priorities get mixed up. Prayer must have priority. If we neglect our prayer life, we lose sight of our Lord, and become proud and arrogant people who think we don't need God, Prayer, therefore, sets us straight and keeps us safe in our Lord. How we view God and pray to Him indicates where our priorities are. As we open our hearts and allow the Lord to rule our lives, He will develop us in ways far beyond anything we, on our own, have ever attempted.

Our Lord commands a relationship of love with Him reflected in our prayer lives. Without love, our prayers are meaningless...a series of empty words. Without love, our walk with God is a ritual. Without love, we cannot truly know and worship Him. He seeks a relationship of love and adoration in which we can talk together and experience Him with us at all times. Prayer honors God, aligns us to GOD and prayer meets our needs. Prayer is an act of worship and praise. We must get serious about worship if we want a lifestyle of prayer. How can we pray to God if we don't first acknowledge Him as our Redeemer and Lord? In worship, as in prayer, we align ourselves with God. Also we humble ourselves before God so that we become totally dependent on Him. We need to seek His will in all that we do every day and in every decision of our lives. A lifestyle of prayer leads us to the realization that without Him we can do nothing of lasting value. The more we pray, the more we realize how dependent upon God we are.

Praying meets our needs. When we ask of God in the name of Jesus, we pray for the same things He desires to give us, as outlined in His Word. Prayer, therefore, involves agreeing with God. Praying God's promises ensures victory and God's blessings upon us.

Prayer helps us make sure we are constantly focused on our Redeemer and Lord. It is our means of communication with Christ; worshiping the risen Lord. It should be faithful, fervent, and focused. Our job is to integrate our whole life with Christ...our work, our play, and our families, so that everything we do, every choice we make is based on our subconscious awareness of the Person of Jesus Christ. A life of prayer helps to develop the life of God in each of us. We grow more dependent on God, more faithful to Him and we love Him and others more as we spend more time in prayer.

Making time for prayer is not an option; it is a necessity for those of us who are serious about our relationship with our heavenly Father and our spiritual walk with the Lord. One can pray anywhere and at any time, out loud or silent, God will hear our prayers and answer.

> "Ask and it will be given to you; seek and you will find; knock and the door will be opened to you. For everyone who asks receives; he who seeks finds; and to him who knocks, the door will be opened" (Matthew 7:7-8).

WHY ME, GOD?

When hard times and suffering comes our way, we at times have the tendency to ask God, "Why me, God? I have been doing all the right things according to your Word. So why did you let this happen to me?" We start complaining and revaluating His faithfulness. Tough times seem to drag on at times and the situations around us seem to refuse to get in line with the promises of God, but this is not the time to reevaluate God! He is not missing it, and He's not failing. In the Book of Job, he too started to complain about his suffering and boldly confronted God and questioned God's ability, and asked, "Why, God?" Job thought he was doing everything by the Book too. Job assumed he knew everything until God questioned him, and asked him, "Do you know more than Me?" After God finished questioning Job, he realized the majesty, sovereignty, righteousness and holiness of God, and Job humbly repented, which made him also deeply aware of his sin and inability to justify himself. As we begin to see and understand the holiness and purity of God, we begin to understand our own need for holiness and purity. Job's circumstances made it appear that either Job had sinned or God was unjust. Job learned God's sustaining grace and experience God's merciful restoration.

The fruit of godliness will develop in our lives as we grow in our personal knowledge and understanding of God. Godly living turns from evil and seeks to understand God's perspective in every circumstance of life. We must recognize that simply hearing about God is not enough. Intimacy and personal encounter enable us to perceive and know Him for ourselves. We must believe God is always for us in the midst of intense trials and suffering and place our hope and trust in our Creator and Sustainer of all things; the loving righteous, all-powerful, and just One!

Don't doubt God's judgment, or His faithfulness, or complain about your suffering or hard times. Instead, reevaluate yourself and see where you might have failed. Walk in love with the situation which is, with patience, long suffering and bearing all things and not being touchy, as 1 Corinthians 13:1-8, because Love never fails. If you can't find out what the problem is, just pray and say, "God, I don't know what's wrong here, and I'm asking you to show me. But one thing I know, the problem is not with you, and I continue to be moved by Your Word and not by circumstances." Then if God reveals something to you, be quick to make changes. Understand that honest struggle on faith's journey is more honoring to God than religious-sounding talk or mere religious observance. Remember too, God does not do anything without love and purpose, and resulting in victory. He knows us all and knows what is best for each of us. Just trust Him and His love for you! Be encouraged to stand firm and keep honoring God with your words. The Lord is listening to you when the pressure is on. What is He going to hear?

> "My soul finds rest in God alone; my salvation comes
> from Him. He alone is my rock and my salvation;
> He is my fortress, I will never be shaken…"
> (Psalm 62:1-2).

WHY KEEPING YOUR OATH IS IMPORTANT

"A man who makes a vow to the Lord or

makes a pledge under oath must never break it"

(Numbers 30:1-2).

An oath is a solemn appeal to God or to some person or thing to witness one's determination to speak the truth or to keep a promise. Giving one's oath or promise is important because it means you are to give your personal word of truth, which includes commitment, free from deception and marked by integrity. Being honest reveals our character and brings a clear conscience. Dishonesty and deception is a form of bondage because we are always trying to hide our real motives. There is freedom in honesty because it allows for forgiveness, vulnerability, positive change, and healing. Also honesty evaluates our walk with the Lord which is the only way to keep growing in faith. God urges us to conduct our daily living with complete honesty. Being honest will inherit God's goodness. Proverbs 16:11 states, "The Lord demands fairness in every business deal; he sets the standard. God expects it." And, "Good people are guided by their honesty; treacherous people are destroyed by their dishonesty" (Proverbs 11:3).

Giving your oath or a promise to God or others means commitment which requires a decision of the mind followed by an act of the will. Commitment to the Lord manifests itself in obedient trust. Commitment is also being willing to suffer the consequences of obedience (Dan. 3:14-18). Commitment is more than intellectual agreement, it involves a sacrificial giving of the whole self which is never easy; at times it requires courageous perseverance. If we break an oath or promise to God or another person, we have broken a trust. Then the only thing to do is to admit the wrong, and ask for forgiveness. Understanding commitment and learning to commit our hearts, minds, and bodies is central to a life of faith.

Among the most oaths given is in marriages, and in court cases who have sworn on the Bible to tell the truth. Today, oaths are taken too lightly and meaningless and broken which then causes divorces and difficulties in solving crime in the court room from the truth not told. It also breaks the trust in our relationship with the Lord. Keeping a promise is the basic foundation for trust in any relationship. Our vows, oaths and promises to the Lord is important: "It is dangerous to make a rash promise to God before counting the cost" (Proverbs 20:25). Jesus said that our actions give away our value system. What we do shows what we really believe (Luke 6:45). What does your action show? Living by values of Scripture earns us a good reputation and makes us trustworthy. The Lord requires us to do what is right, to love mercy, and to walk humbly with your God (Micah 6:8). Matthew 15:19 tells us, "From the heart come evil thoughts, murder, adultery, all other sexual immorality, theft, lying and slander." The heart is the wellspring of moral or immoral behavior. Conduct is the fruit of character, and character is the fruit of belief. Breaking an oath, or a promise is losing the integrity of your word and your trust.

"But let your 'Yes' be 'Yes' and your 'No' be 'No'" (Matthew 5:37).

Let your word be of integrity and truth, and if making a promise, consider the cost first. Don't make a vow, oath or promise you can't, or won't keep! Wise living involves learning to assess the relative value of choices you make.

WHY DID JESUS TEACH IN PARABLES?

Jesus used parables to hide the truth so that He might reveal the truth. A parable would excite the concerned and stimulate them to learn more. The parable would also blind the careless, for they would not repent and receive forgiveness, also because of their condition of heart it would hasten their judgment. The purpose of the parables was to make spiritual truths clearer to hearers and to put truth in a form easily remembered, and to avoid offenses with hostile people who would not receive the truth. We must not criticize Christ because His parables brought judgment to some and salvation to others. This "gaining and losing" is a law of life. If we use what we have, we receive more; if we neglect to use it, we lose it. While this does not apply in every area of life, it is generally true. His disciples possessed saving faith, and therefore received more through an understanding of the parables. But the unbelievers in opposing the truth would lose, and their hearts would become harder. The parables were "born out of life," and therefore have a way of touching us in those areas where life is the most meaningful and significant. The parables are both mirrors and windows. As mirrors, they help us see ourselves. They reveal our lives as they really are. As windows, they help us see life and God. We need to look for the main truth that the parable teaches us. For example, the main message of the parable of the prodigal son is that God receives and forgives sinners. We must also ask God for the spiritual perception of the parable. He will give us the wisdom and understanding of the truth of the parable. The disciples were privileged to understand the hidden truths, and therefore they had a great responsibility to put these truths into practice. We also have that responsibility to do so also, "For unto whomever much is given, of him shall be much required" (Luke 12:48). We learn the truth so we can live the truth! The truth becomes alive to us as we live it. The three responsibilities we have toward God's truth are: (1) the responsibility of learning the truth, (2) living the truth, and (3) sharing the truth. Our Lord did not invent the parable. You will find parables in the Old Testament as well (2 Samuel 12:1 4, for example), and the Jewish rabbis used them often.

In the parables, Jesus deals with subjects we cannot afford to treat lightly: salvation, forgiveness of others, love for minority groups, the right and wrong use of money, prayer, motives for service, and much more.

If you find yourself jolted by what you learn from these stories, give thanks to God and then apply the lessons to your life.

THE CHRISTIAN'S RACE

"Let us run the race that is before us and never give up"

(Hebrews 12:1).

The Christian's race is not a jog but rather a demanding and grueling, sometimes agonizing race. It takes a massive effort to finish strong. So many are sitting on the side of the trail. They used to be running and there was a time when they kept the pace. But they got weary and discouraged; they didn't think the race would be this tough. They may be Christians. They come to church, put their buck in the plate and warm the pew, but their hearts are no longer in the race. They retired before their time, they gave up...how sad is that!

"We have around us many people whose lives tell us what faith means. So let us run the race that is before us and never give up. We should remove from our lives anything that would get in the way and the sin that so easily holds us back. Let us look only to Jesus, the One who began our faith and who makes it perfect. Think about Jesus' example. He held on while wicked people were doing evil things" (Hebrews 12:1-3).

"You have become weak, so make yourselves strong again. Live in the right way so that you will be saved and your weakness will not cause you to be lost. Try to live in peace with all people, and try to live free from sin. Anyone whose life is not holy will never see the Lord. Be careful that no one fails to receive God's grace and begins to cause trouble among you. Be careful that no one takes part in sexual sin..." (Hebrews 12:12-16).

Although we may not feel strong enough to push on to victory, we will be able to continue as we follow Christ and draw upon his strength. We will also grow through endurance and discipline which will lead to maturity. Endurance also builds character and leads to victory. We can use our growing strength to help those around us who are weak and struggling. So don't throw in the towel or write off your future!

The church has far too many "baby Christians." Some have only been in Christ a short time, so that is understandable. But for those Christians who have been in God's family for years and act like "babies."...well, there is no excuse. Christians need to grow up in their spirituality and their relationship with Christ. Christians face a great risk by remaining a spiritual infant. The race may be difficult, but God expects us to handle difficult circumstances, trouble, and trials with our faith. Christians are called to be humble, patient, genuine, faithful, watchful, and responsible—assured of the risen Jesus' presence as they are expectant of His return when faith will give away to sight.

We have a Great Shepherd who leads us and has given us everything we need to be successful. We are never forsaken; Jesus is at our side every day to help us walk every step along the way of our journey, right to the end. So don't allow the devil to beat you down with discouragement or disappointments, depression or with any other of his deceiving tricks! Remember, God says you are an overcomer and victorious! So if you fall during the race, just pick yourself up by the bootstraps, and continue in the race; be determined to finish the race and receive the prize! Wouldn't it be great to hear the Lord say, "Well done, good and faithful servant" (Luke 19:17; Matthew 25:21)? Or will you be one who hears the Lord say, "Assuredly, I say to you, I do not know you" (Matthew 25:12; Luke 13:27)?

TRUTH OR DARE

"Truth stands the test of time; lies are soon exposed"

(Proverbs 12:19).

"Lying lips are abomination to the Lord..."

(Proverbs 12:22).

It's amazing but not surprising how many people lie and think nothing of it! We don't expect people in high places to lie, but it seems to be the trend. Actually God does not expect any one to lie. The lies lately heard on the TV and the media and our own government have caused so much chaos and insecurity in America through their lies. It's strange that our parents taught us never to lie, but now the parents seem to have won the blue ribbon in their marriages and their families, on the job, in the communities, in the court room, in the schools and in all walks of lives, from the top to the bottom of the working system...where does it all end? Who can you believe in this decaying world? Be grateful, for we can believe Jesus, He is truth: "I am the way, the truth and the life" (John 14:6). Jesus cannot lie, for it is not in his nature, for lying is a sin and Jesus is sinless.

Why do people lie or even distort the truth? Some want to make themselves look good, or become popular and others try to avoid trouble and punishment and some just don't ever want to appear wrong. Whatever the case may be lying is a deadly sin. The Bible states in Proverbs 6:16-19 that is six, no seven things the Lord hates: a proud look, a lying tongue, hands that kill innocent people, a mind that thinks up evil plans, feet that are quick to do evil, a witness who lies, and someone who starts arguments among families. The Bible has always stated that there is life or death in the power of the tongue! When we lie, we deceive God, others, or even ourselves. We as believers cannot follow the God of truth while we persistently tell lies...even small ones. Although, there are no small or big ones, a lie is a lie no matter what size and is judged the same. Those who are serious about following the Lord will hate and abhor all falsehood (Psalm 119:163), and those who are godly hate lies... (Proverbs 13:5). Colossians 3:9 tells us, "Don't lie to each other, for you have stripped off your old nature and all its wicked deeds." We should hate lies because they are part of the old sinful nature we had before we were Christians.

Lying is deceiving someone. It can be direct or indirect, such as telling only part of the truth when it benefits you to do so. But to fall short of truth, in any way, is to lie. If we walk in love as God has called us to do, then we do not want to deceive them in anyway. If we care about our example and character, we don't want to lie. If we want to please the Lord, we don't want to lie. If we want our prayers answered and blessings in our life, we cannot lie.

Pray for those who you know lie, or deceive others. If this Word of God convicts you, get right with the Lord, repent and be forgiven. Jesus would say, "Go and sin no more." Determine to always tell the truth in all matters no matter what the cost! Honesty brings a clear conscience. Don't be like those who dare to lie and don't know, or care it is a sin that God will one day judge them for it. Remember, we are accountable for every idle word we say that is unworthy and we will be judged for them.

"But I say to you that for every idle word men may speak, they will give account of it in the day of judgment. For by your words you will be justified, and by your words you will be condemned"
(Matthew 12:36).

SANCTIFICATION

For real sanctification (which means set apart for God) to occur in the Christian's life, absolute changes are necessary. There must be a change in our consciousness. There must be a change in our conscientiousness and in our convictions. Consciousness involves knowledge. We need to know God's commands and his desires; what pleases Him. We must move beyond consciousness to conviction. Conviction is a matter of depth and intensity. It is one thing to be aware that a certain action is right, but it is another to have a conviction about it. A conviction is knowledge that is settled. It has a firm hold on us. It goes beyond our brains and penetrates the conscience. Our conscience acts as a kind of governor upon our behavior. It is the inner voice that either accuses or excuses us. It monitors our behavior by way of approval or disapproval. For the conscience to function in a godly way it must be influenced by godly convictions. To gain consciences, our consciousness of what is right or wrong must be sharpened; which involves the brain. It is a matter of learning and knowing God's Word! Certain things no one can do for you. One of those things is spending time with God, and reading and knowing the Word, allowing it to become rooted within your heart so you would not sin against God (Psm. 119:11), that is, if you are really serious about changing your behavior, obeying and pleasing God...being sanctified, set apart for God. God's Word is the perfect standard of truth, values, reality and behavior. It is wholly sufficient for godly living. By grasping its powerful message, God's children can be pure.

THE WORD OF GOD

Psalm 119:1:11

Happy are those who live pure lives, who follow the Lord's teachings. Happy are those who keep his rules, who try to obey him with their whole heart. They don't do what is wrong; they follow his ways. Lord you gave your orders to be obeyed completely. I wish I were more loyal in obeying your demands. Then I would not be ashamed when I study your commands. When I learn that your laws are fair, I praise you with an honest heart. I will obey your demands, so please don't ever leave me. How can a young person live a pure life? By obeying your word. With all my heart I will try to obey you. I have taken your words to heart so I would not sin against you.

THE WAY YOU SHOULD LIVE...EPHESIANS 4:17-32

In the Lord's name I tell you this. Do not continue living like those who do not believe. Their thoughts are worth nothing. They do not understand, and they know nothing, because they refuse to listen. So they cannot have the life that God gives. They have lost all feeling of shame, and they use their lives for doing evil. They continually want to do all kinds of evil. But what you learned in Christ was not like this. I know that you heard about him, and you are in him, so you were taught the truth that is in Jesus. You were taught to leave your old self—to stop living the evil way you lived before. The old self became worse, because people are fooled by the evil things they want to do. But you were taught to be made new in your hearts, to become a new person. That new person is made to be like God—made to be truly good and holy.

So you must stop telling lies. Tell each other the truth, because we all belong to each other in the same body. When you are angry, do not sin, and be sure to stop being angry before the end of the day. Do not give the devil a way to defeat you. Those who are stealing must stop stealing and start working. They should earn an honest living for themselves. Then they will have something to share with those who are poor.

When you talk, do not say harmful things, but say what people need—words that will help others become strong. Then what you say will do good to those who will listen to you. And do not make the Holy Spirit sad. The Spirit is God's proof that you belong to him. God gave you the Spirit to show that God will make you free when the final day comes. Do not be biter or angry or mad. Never shout angrily or say things to hurt others. Never do anything evil. Be kind and loving to each other, and forgive each other just as God forgave you in Christ.

LIVING IN THE LIGHT...EPHESIANS 5:1-5

You are God's children whom he loves, so try to be like him. Live a life of love just as Christ loved us and gave himself for us as a sweet-smelling offering and sacrifice to God. But there must be no sexual sin among you, or any kind of evil or greed. Those things are not right for God's holy people. Also, there must not be no evil talk among you, and you must not speak foolishly or tell evil jokes. These things are not right for you. Instead, you should be giving thanks to God. You can be sure of this: No one will have a place in the kingdom of Christ and of God who sins sexually, or does evil things, or is greedy. Anyone who is greedy is serving a false god.

TRY TO LEARN WHAT PLEASES GOD...Eph. 5:10

Attitudes of humility, gentleness, and patience should characterize Christians. We are told to accept each other in love. Take an inventory of your heart. Are you living in an overflow of God's love? How well do I love the people in my life? Does the way I treat people reflect God the way He has treated me? Conventional wisdom says that a lack of love implies a lack of effort, so we try harder, dig deeper and strain harder. Ask the Holy Spirit for his help.

"Thy will be done on earth as it is in heaven..." is the way God's children should reflect their heart and action so the world will know Jesus.

THE STRATEGY OF TEMPTATION

If we could destroy our enemy's ability to bring temptation into our lives, he would be powerless! What is the primary path by which a born-again believer moves from obedience to disobedience, from righteousness to unrighteousness? It's giving in to the lie of the temptation. We are all subject to temptation, which is not a sin until you put action to it. Even Jesus faced Satan's temptations, but Jesus rebuked Satan and revealed the very nature of his attack: "You shall not tempt the Lord your God."

Another word to describe a temptation is incentive. An incentive is something that motivates or incites a person to do something. Incentives can be good or bad. However, Satan will use incentives for evil to the point they become temptations. All Satan's temptations are an evil lie! The fall into sin is always preceded by the temptation, which is meant to overtake us. Every single temptation is rooted in at least one massive lie, which is promoted as the answer for what the person is looking for. With this understanding, also comes the power to resist temptation and break any authority it might have over us! Jesus has promised never to leave us nor forsake us and God is faithful, who will not allow us to be tempted beyond what we are able, but with the temptation He will make a way of escape, that we may be able to bear it.

Satan had incited (to urge on; stimulate, or promote to action) Eve's imagination with the thought of becoming like God stating, "You will be like God." Temptation always will breed doubt about the Word and the character of God. Also temptation always minimizes the real dangers and maximizes the imagined benefits. Temptation always incites lust to know and experience evil, which is forbidden by God, in the false pursuit of that which is good. Without any temptation or motivation, why would Adam or Eve ever have considered disobeying the Lord? Do you see the critical role of temptation in life? Without it, what could be the motivation for choosing sin?

Satan will tempt us throughout our life. Whatever sin we have committed was preceded by temptation, which we believed and then acted upon by disobeying God and willfully sinning. And there are those who might think, they can't be tempted. Wrong, wrong! First Corinthians 10:12 begins with a strong warning about temptations: "Therefore let him who thinks he stands take heed lest he fall." Which is better, to think you can't fall into sin or, know you can? The best answer is found in Proverbs 16:18: "Pride goes before destruction and a haughty spirit before a fall." When you think you can't fall, pride reigns. When pride reigns, destruction will soon follow. The correct attitude and action in the face of temptation is watchfulness, prayer, and active dependence upon the Lord: "Watch and pray, lest you enter into temptation. The spirit indeed is willing, but the flesh is weak" (Matthew 26:41). Our focus must always be upon our weakness and upon His strength. Pray daily that the Lord would keep you from temptation, but when it comes, that He would strengthen you in and through it. Remember, temptations seize, they grasp and hold us down until we finally sin. You will notice that when we have given in to temptation, it no longer exists.

The truth is that the Lord God will never leave you or forsake you in the face of a temptation. He will always, in every circumstance, sovereignly limit your temptations so they never exceed your ability to say NO. The Lord has His full attention on you and your ability. He may limit the temptation but not necessarily increase the strength. God enables you to obey by taking off the weights until He knows you can lift yourself up! The greatest lie about temptation is the lie that says, "I can't say no to this temptation no matter how hard I try."

UNCONDITIONAL TRUST

Having unconditional trust means putting no restrictions on God's actions in your life. It is knowing without a single doubt that you can trust God with your life no matter what you are going through, because God is completely trustworthy. He cannot lie, it is not in His nature and His promises are all true! Trust is a critical element of faith, without trust we cannot grow and mature and without faith we cannot please God!

At times we all go through difficult situations, or health issues, or setbacks, or discouragements and we blame God. We might even think He is punishing us for something and we can't understand why we are going through this trouble. You might be doing everything right, by reading the Word, going to church and praying and seeking God but you are confused by going through this difficulty and then you start doubting God and His Word. Or you have prayed and you can't understand why God has not answered your prayer. This is where your unconditional trust should take over! Remember, God IS LOVE! His nature can only be of love. God does everything out of love. He knows exactly what is best for us at all times. He is always in control of our life. At times God needs to stretch us for the growth of faith. Difficulties and trials strengthen our faith, as we all know; they are a stepping-stones to growth.

Each time we make it through a difficult time, we get stronger and there will be another trial on the way to keep us growing stronger for the Kingdom of God. God would never intentionally hurt His children! He loves us more than we can comprehend! We need to understand this and get it rooted in our heart! Just because God has not answered your prayer the way you would like, does not mean He did not answer it. He answered your prayer in the way that would bless you and what was best for you as any good father would. And just because you did not understand what was happening to you in a difficult circumstance does not mean you should doubt God and get discouraged, or give up, or turn to another person for the answer you want, or take up a bad habit! This is where unconditional trust takes over! You are to trust God in everything and in every situation!

Remember Abraham, who waited so long for a son, then God asked him to sacrifice his son? Abraham did not question God, but I'm sure he didn't understand and was disappointed and confused, BUT he never questioned God, he was ready to do it! That is unconditional trust and love! Remember the three young men, Shadrach, Meshack and Abed-Nego, they too faced a life going situation, but they trusted God to deliver them, they said even if they were not delivered, they would trust God for whatever was His will! Remember when Jesus was praying in the garden and asked God, "Father, if it is Your will, take this cup away from Me; nevertheless not My will, but

Yours, be done" (Luke 22:42)? That is unconditional trust and strong faith and love!

Somethings may be hard to go through, but the Lord has promised to be right there with us as we go through the valleys. We need to trust God above all else, because He wants us to know He IS trustworthy! He wants us to rejoice in Him within our hearts, and trust in His Holy name. Trusting God means to obey his commands even when we don't fully understand. It means trusting in Him and not ourselves. Trusting in God will bring peace, joy and set us free from worry, fear, depression and confusion:

"Though you do not see Him, you trust Him;
and even now you are happy..."
(1Peter 1:8).

UNITY CREATES BELIEF

Grace makes three proclamations. First, only God can forgive my godlessness.... Second, only God can judge my neighbor.... Third, I must accept who God accepts.

God has enlisted us in his navy and placed us on his ship. The boat has one purpose: to carry us safely to the other shore. This is no cruise ship; it's a battleship. We aren't called to a life of leisure; we are called to a life of service. Each of us has a different task. Some, concerned with those who are drowning, are snatching people from the water. Others are occupied with the enemy, so they man the cannons of prayer and worship. Still others devote themselves to the crew, feeding and training the crew members.

Though different, we are the same. Each can tell of a personal encounter with the captain, for each has received a personal call. He found us among the shanties of the seaport and invited us to follow him.

Though the battle is fierce, the boat is safe, for our captain is God. The ship will not sink. For that, there is no concern. There is concern, however, regarding the disharmony of the crew.

Unity creates belief. Disunity fosters disbelief. Who wants to board a ship of bickering sailors? Life on the ocean may be rough, but at least the waves don't call us names. Could it be that unity is the key to reaching the world for Christ?

WHO'S IN CHARGE OF YOUR LIFE?

"...casting all your care upon Him, for He cares for you"

(1 Peter 5:7).

Who is in charge of your life? If it is you then you have a good reason to worry. But if it is not you, then worry is both unnecessary and counterproductive. The Lord has promised to be with us and never to leave us or forsake us. His Light is like a cocoon around us and His presence is with us, whether we are aware of it or not, He has promised it! Many things can block this awareness, but the major culprit is worry. We tend to worry as an inescapable fact of life. However, worry is a form of unbelief. When we start to feel anxious about something; we need to turn the situation over to the Lord and back off and not take it back, and focus on Him with expectation and gratitude. We at times give the circumstance to the Lord and then take it back. If we have it again, the Lord no longer has it. When we give it to the Lord, He will take care of it or show us how to handle it. In this world we have problems, but we always have the Lord to go to if we don't lose sight of Him and His presence.

"These things I have spoken to you, that in Me you may have peace.
In this world you will have tribulation; but be of good cheer.
I have overcome the world"
(John 16:33).

WHO IS WEAK IN FAITH AND WHO IS STRONG?

We are all weak in some areas and strong in others. Our faith is weak if we have to avoid certain places in order to protect our spirituality. If we are strong, we will not fear we will be defiled by the world. Evil is prevalent in our fallen world. Just as the Bible stated, evil has become good and good has become evil in these last days. Many Christians have conformed to the world's way. But much has weighted heavy on them and they have gotten weary, confused and discouraged and afraid. Some give up and some just become lazy in their spiritual walk. Sin has slowly crept in and condoned by many Christians who have fallen asleep, which has made their hearts harden, blinded their spiritual eyes, seared their conscience and they became desensitized to the Lord. There is only a flicker of light left that the world could no longer see. Some have just fallen away from the faith as the Bible warned would happen. As Christians, we all experience a tug to give in to our sin nature, but our new nature moves us to resist. Sin wants to drive a hole in us and Christ wants to keep you unscarred by the effects of sin. When we walk in the Spirit (obeying the Word) then we won't give in to the flesh, If we stay close to the Lord and his Word our conscience will advise us when we stray off-course. We make choices to be obedient or rebellious each day. Evil has become rapid in the world of today, but God is able to turn it around for our long-range good. He wants to fulfill his purpose. Those who love and trust in God and his ways and not life's treasures, or the world's ways, are fitting into God's plans and promises. We are not to follow leaders, or a corrupt government who does not believe in God, and leads us astray from our faith. We do not have to except sin and should not because the government chooses to be corrupt and allows such sins as abortions, same-sex marriages, not allowing Christians to pray, or read the Bible when and where they want. God expects us, the Body of Christ to be faithful and devoted no matter what. Out refusal to conform to the world, however, must go even deeper than the level of behavior and customs. It must be firmly founded in our minds. We must keep our minds renewed by the new attitude Christ gives us through His Word. Renewing our mind is vital to our lifeline and is a daily process. If we do not do this, we become weak and weary, discouraged and afraid; ineffective Christians! If our character is like Christ's, we can be sure our behavior will honor God. When we take a stand for Christ, we can expect to face opposition, disapproval, ridicule, and even persecution. Satan is a crafty tempter, but we can take hold of the tremendous power that Christ is available to us. We have the Word and the Holy Spirit living in us to give us power and God at our back (2 Corinthians 2:14; Acts 1:8; Luke 1:37, 10:19; Romans 8:28, 8:37; Revelation 22:20, 22:12; 2 Timothy 3:1-7, 3:8)! PLEASE READ THEM!

America, we need to unite and encourage one another! It will make a big difference in country, and we won't fall apart or get discouraged or weary or give up! We need to be sensitive to other's need for encouragement and offer supportive words or actions. This is God's country and He is for us, so who can be against us!

Christians, we need to get back on our knees and repent for condoling sin, having half-hearted devotion, allowing our hearts to become hard, not trusting in God's control, being lazy in our spiritual growth and most of all the absence of prayer! We need to keep our faith strong and our morals godly and our righteousness in action at all times. We have failed to do these things and evil and fear got the upper hand. But it's not too late! We can PRAY for forgiveness and for revival! It should start first in our own homes and families! We need to ready ourselves and be self-disciplined for the coming of the Lord and help others to be prepared too. Christians, keep your courage and don't get weary of doing good (Gal. 6:9). No one knows when Christ will return. But in the meantime, we are to live moral and holy lives, ever watching for His coming. Believers must not neglect their daily responsibilities, but always work and live as unto the Lord. We are to live as though we expect Christ's return at any time. Don't be caught unprepared! Don't allow yourself to become fearful or numb to sin or let your heart be hardened. Keep a roaring fire in your soul for the Lord! Be the overcomer God says we are! So put on your daily Armor of God then face the day with victory, peace and gratitude in your heart and praise on your lips to our God! Our endurance will be rewarded! "Be diligent to present yourself approved to God, a worker who does not need to be ashamed, rightly dividing the word of truth" (2 Timothy 2:15).

"Therefore let us not sleep, as others do,
but let us watch and be sober"
(1 Thessalonians 5:6).

WHERE IS THE FAMILY VALUE AND MORALS?

The crime rate is so high these days and the lack of family values and morals play a big part of this increase of violence. Many families contribute to this problem. Families are not functioning in the way they were meant to be. Families were God's unique idea from the beginning. There is no greater institution, no better group of people to effect positive change in the world than the family. Families can also bring negative change as well, as we now are experiencing. There is no better place to learn the essential principals of life than the family, and nowhere can the truths of God's Word be more effectively taught and modeled. But how many families are teaching and being the example of Jesus within the home? How many families are stressing the importance of going to church together, or praying together as a family? Actually there is no other group of people with more power and ability to destroy a person than the family. Physical and verbal abuse, as well as neglect, can damage the emotional well-being of a child well into adulthood, and often for a lifetime. The failure of parents to teach spiritual truths to their children directly impacts their relationship with God and how they treat others. Family is the environment that shapes a child's lifetime direction. The Bible records the family as central and fundamental to the development of people and nations. It is our responsibility to "Teach your children to choose the right path, and when they are older, they will remain upon it" (Proverbs 22:6). Faith in God is the most important inheritance we can pass along to future generations.

Many parents these days don't have enough time to share with their children the vital love, guidance, security, bonding and devotion they need because of their work load. Many children are given a key to the house when getting home from school. They are alone to fend for their selves with no supervision. Many children have no one as an example for guidance or security and have to make choices and decisions on their own without having the ability to because of their age. Children learn a lot from example, so if the family is dysfunctional in morals and abuse, the child will be affected and guided in the wrong direction. Neglecting to teach your children spiritual truths and neglecting discipline have tragic consequences. If the parent does not show respect, or have integrity or good solid morals and principals within the family for one another, the children will not either. If the child does not receive guidance, recognition, encouragement, love, understanding, guidance, and patience they will look for it outside the home. This is where they can get with the wrong crowd.

Parents, your children are a gift from God and a reward from Him (Psalm 127:3) and He expects you to be a good example for them and love them and be responsible for them and their upbringing, and to teach them about the Lord and his ways in the home and at church. You will have to answer for this one day. As God abundantly cares for us, so we should joyfully care for our family.

"Finally, all of you should be of one mind, full of sympathy toward one another, loving one another with tender hearts and humble minds" (1 Peter 3:8).

WHERE ARE YOU AT?

"This is all the more urgent, for you know how late it is time is running out. Wake up, for our salvation is nearer now than when we first believed"

(Romans 13:11).

The decisions you make now will affect your future! Now is the time to wake up to the life God has for us! Many Christians are not moving forward and seem to be stagnate or asleep. They are not living for a purpose. God expects us as Christians to change the world around us. In order for us to truly accomplish the will of the Father, we must first make contact and connection with Him. We must have an intimate relationship with Jesus and exercise; activate our faith...use it!

Some Christians know the Word well, and know Jesus is real and He is the only way, but they only have head knowledge. The Word needs to be believed and rooted in their heart where it will come alive! Those who only have head knowledge and don't practice the Word and their faith, or spend time with Jesus in prayer, will drift for a while; they will still see Jesus as they go their own way but will start to stumble around. Eventually they will lose sight of Jesus altogether. Their feet will no longer be on the path of peace and have now lost their way. They walk in darkness, fear, doubt anxiety and compromise. But they still have a choice to turn their life around and connect with Jesus by repentance. No sin is too great for God, so one can humble themself and get back in the race with urgency and wake up to the life God has given us! Then there are those Christians who live in the reality of Jesus and the Word is alive and growing within their heart. They have taken the time to fellowship with Jesus intimately and they are well connected to Him. They took the Word seriously and meditated upon it until it got rooted within their heart. They are now growing and walking in love, peace and joy. They are free to walk out their life in God's Kingdom as an adventure as they continue to spiritually grow.

Then there are some Christians who have fallen into fear which will lead to failure and remorse. But failure is only an event, not a person. God can still accomplish his purpose within them. We all need to accept failure and mistakes, because we will make them, until we go home with the Lord. But instead of feeling bad, or remorseful, we have to step out of the boat, or we will miss

God. So whatever is hindering you from growing and fulfilling your life's purpose, give it to God, repent, activate your faith, and turn your life around, and don't look back! Even if you blow it a thousand times, bring it to God, don't run from Him but to Him! God gives us all grace to continue on.

God will also bring you back to your purpose as you draw near to Him. The decision you make will determine your future. Always remember people are not the failure, even if we do fail, failure is an event. Don't allow failure to cause fear! God does not make failures! God only creates good and perfect gifts! God is LOVE.

Where are you at? Are you connected with God? Are you plugged in and trusting God and exercising heartfelt faith? Is the Word in your heart, or head? Do you have an intimate relationship with Jesus?

Recognize your state! Examine your heart. Do you need to wake up from your sleep, climb out of your coffins; Christ will show you the light. These are desperate times so don't live carelessly, and unthinkingly! Make sure you understand what the Master wants!

(This message is shared and gleaned from Pastor Lou's Sunday's teachings.)

WHEN THOSE WHO ARE CALLED TO FISH... FLOURISH

"Follow Me and I will make you fishers of men"

(Matthew 4:19).

When those who are called to fish, don't fish, instead they fight. Instead of casting our nets, we cast stones. Instead of extending helping hands, we point accusing fingers and instead of being fishers of the lost, we become critics of the saved. Rather than helping the hurting, we hurt the help. The result... church scrooges... "Bah humbug" spirituality. Beady eyes searching for warts on others while ignoring the wart on our nose, and crooked fingers that bypass strengths and point out weaknesses. Then we wonder why we have split churches, poor testimonies, broken hearts and legalistic wars. What's up with that!! And sadly the poor go unfed, confused, go uncounseled, and lost and unreached. This is what happens when those who are called to fish, don't fish, they fight. You say you are not called? Then why was the Great Commission, "Go into all the world and preach the gospel to every creature" (Mark 16:15), written in the Word for Christians? Preaching means also living godly by example, and sharing the Word with those who will receive it. Christ seeks those who will serve without seeking recognition, selflessly and obedient to exalt Christ and make him known. Such servants establish their personhood and ministries by their devotion and obedience to Jesus, and their disposition to serve unselfishly. They do so wherever and however God sovereignly directs. They are the other side of the fish tale: When those who are called to fish, they fish...then the flourish!

Nothing handles a case of gripes like an afternoon service project, and nothing restores perspective better than a visit to a hospital ward. Nothing unites soldiers better than a common task. Leave soldiers inside the barracks with no time on the front line and see what happens to their attitude. The soldiers will invent things to complain about, bunks will be too hard, food will be too cold, and leaders will be too tough. The company will be too stale! Yet place those same soldiers in the trench and let them duck a few bullets and what was boring in the barracks will seem like a haven. The beds will feel great, the food ideal, and leadership will be courageous. The company will be exciting!

Church, we are the Body of Christ, and we are to be in unity; unity is the highest form of Christian relationship. Through the Holy Spirit, great diversity becomes dynamic unity. We are all one body, we have the same Spirit. God is the creator of true unity. The presence of the Holy Spirit in the church will bring unity and peace. God has created us differently, which means there will be differences of opinion, but our common goal is the same—to serve God. Serving God, and glorifying Him and being the image of Christ which also means being fishers of men! Remember, those who are called (Christians) to fishs…they flourish!

"Let there be real harmony so there won't be divisions in the church. I plead with you to be…united in thought and purpose…" (1 Corinthians 1:10-13).

WHEN SHOULD WE DISOBEY THE CIVIL GOVERNMENT?

"...We ought to obey God rather than men" (Acts 5:29).

When a civil government refuses people the liberty to worship and obey God freely, it has lost its mandate of authority from God. Then the Christian should feel justified in disobeying.

Thomas Jefferson believed that when a government began to be tyrannical, it was the right and even the duty of citizens to rebel against that government. The Christian, however, is called to bear with his government whenever possible. Jesus did not call for revolution against Rome, even though it was an oppressive conqueror of Israel. On the other hand, the apostles refused to obey an order not to preach and teach in Jesus' name (Acts 5:27-29). Whenever the civil government forbids the practice of things that God has commanded us to do, or tells us to do things that He has commanded us not to do, and then we are on solid ground in disobeying the government. Blind obedience to the government is never right. However difficult or costly it may be, we all must reserve the right to say to say "no" to things that we consider oppressive or immoral.

WHATEVER DOES NOT BEGIN WITH GOD WILL END IN FAILURE

The idea of self-help is popular because it supports the notion that we are in control. There are many books on the market referring to self-help. In the words of the poem "Invictus": "I am the master of my fate; I am the captain of my soul" supports the idea that we are in control, but we are not! It is contrary to everything Christian. Eventually something happens that reminds us how out-of-control life is, and no self-help book can help us make it right. To become a Christian requires that we admit our helplessness and acknowledge our total dependence on God. "Without Me, you can do nothing," said Jesus (John 15:5). There are times when we become quite proud of ourselves for accomplishing something, but in all actuality God has accomplished it through us. When we realize this, repentance is due and the glory belongs to God.

The ancient Israelites were always getting in trouble for trusting human strength rather than God's (Jer. 17:5). Yet even after their failures, the Lord said, "Blessed is the man who trusts in the Lord, and whose hope is the Lord" (v. 7).

When especially difficult circumstances or strong temptations invade our lives and remind us of our powerlessness, we have an all-powerful God who works on our behalf of those who trust Him. The Lord tells us to embrace all the circumstances that He allows in our life, trusting Him to bring good out of them. We are to view problems as opportunities to rely more fully on Him. When we start to feel stressed, we need to let those feelings alert us to the need for the Lord. Our needs become doorways to deep dependence on Him and increasing intimacy between us. Although self-sufficiency is acclaimed in the world, reliance on the Lord produces abundant living in His Kingdom. Actually we are to thank the Lord for the difficulties in our life, since they provide protection from the idolatry of self-reliance.

"Blessed is the man who trusts in the Lord, whose hope is in the Lord. For he will be like a tree planted by the waters, which spreads out its roots by the river and will not fear when heat comes; its leaf will be green and will not be anxious in the year of drought, nor will cease from yielding fruit" (Jeremiah 17:7-8).

"The Lord is my strength and my shield; my heart trusted in Him, and I am helped" (Psalm 28:7).

"I am the vine, you are the branches. He who abides in Me, and I in Him, bears much fruit; for without Me you can do nothing" (John 15:5).

"If you abide in Me, and My words abide in you, you shall ask what you desire, and it shall be done for you. By this My Father is glorified, that you bear much fruit; so you will be My disciples" (John 15:7-8).

A KINGDOM CAN BE DESTROYED!

Jesus said, "Every kingdom divided against itself is brought to desolation, and a house divided against a house falls" (Luke 11:17-18).

This is a universal truth. The best of all plans can be destroyed if we lack unity. When there is division, plans cannot succeed. This is the reason Satan does everything he can do to cause division among Christians. Because we are so divided, suspicious, and focused on each other's weak points, we are breaking the most important key for corporate success: unity.

Jesus said that the world would know that God had sent Him if his disciples were one (John 17:20-23). Unity is "exhibit A" to the world, showing the supernatural origins of the Christian church; with unity, the church can win the world! Without unity, the church is powerless. Evil men can find success through unity, as we see as proof of ISIS. Unity brings incredible strength! Nothing is impossible for people working in unity.

In the Old Testament times, when God desired to destroy the enemies of Israel, He sent division among them and caused them to fight themselves. Israel often did not have to go into battle to fight because the enemy destroyed itself. Any time an organization begins to fight itself, it will go down. Unless it moves in unity, there is absolutely nothing it can do…for good or evil. Think what God's people working in unity under His blessing can accomplish according to the law of His kingdom!

WHAT TO SAY TO THOSE WHO POINT TO THE HYPOCRITES

Unfortunately, even some Christians act shamefully. In fact, there probably is not a Christian alive who, at one time or another, hasn't betrayed God by his or her actions. The word "hypocrite" means "play act," to claim to be a certain type of person while acting like someone else. God is pretty upset at hypocrites, those who claim to be his followers but really aren't. The TV preachers who get into trouble or local pastor who molested someone are hypocrites who give the Christians a bad name and example.

Jesus said, "More than anything else beware of these Pharisees and the way they pretend to be good when they aren't. But such hypocrisy cannot be hidden forever. It will become as evident as yeast in dough. Whatever they have said in the dark shall be heard in the light, and what you have whispered in the inner rooms shall be broadcast from the housetops for all to hear!" (Luke 12:1-3).

When our world's final act draws to a close, some of the first to receive God's wrath will be those who have been playacting with God (see Isaiah 29:13-14). He is not amused or impressed; they will be judged.

Unfortunately, there is nothing you can do to prevent strangers from misrepresenting Christ. The only person you can prevent from being a hypocrite is you. Here are some ways to keep from being a hypocrite: 1. Watch your own actions closely (2 Corinthians 13:5). If what you say doesn't match what you believe, get ready to be called a hypocrite. 2. Don't come down on other people too hard. Remember, the only difference between you and those who aren't Christians is that you've received the gift of forgiveness. 3. Be quick to admit when you make a mistake. True humility is rare in our culture. For some reason, people are drawn to those who can readily admit their mistakes. It's called being genuine.

WHAT IS THE GREATEST VIRTUE IN THE KINGDOM?

"Therefore whoever humbles himself as this little child is the greatest in the kingdom of heaven" (Matthew 18:4).

If pride is the greatest sin—and it is—then humility must be the greatest virtue. Humility is recognition of our own worth, our worth as God sees us. Christ died for people He loved very much and those people have great worth and value in God's eyes. To see ourselves as God sees us…that is our goal. Humility is true strength. Humility is the first step toward wholeness. It takes humility to serve God. It is humility that allows us to acknowledge that God has a claim on our life, that we are a fallible, mortal creature, and that God is the Master of the universe. It is humility that says, "I am a sinner, and I need to be saved." Humility is the beginning of wisdom (Prov. 22:4). "The truths of the kingdom are only perceived by those who are humble. No one who is proud will ever gain anything from God, because God resists the proud, but gives grace to the humble" (James 4:6). Those who are humble receive the grace of God and are given the secrets of the kingdom, because they come as beggars. Jesus Christ said, "(Blessed are the poor in spirit) for theirs is the kingdom of heaven" (Matt. 5:3).

WHAT PART OF ALMIGHTY GOD DOES ONE NOT UNDERSTAND?

In the days of the Old Testament people of God acknowledged that God was mighty, sovereign, holy, and righteous and how much He demanded obedience. He was their protector and their lifeline! They knew how to worship and praise Him for who He was. They totally humbled themselves and they lived their life for God and died for God! They knew He was the One True God!

As Christians today we fail to realize all of God's attributes and how powerful, holy and mighty He is. We sing it, say it, but fail to realize His true Greatness and Glory. We fail to reckon with the reality of His limitless wisdom and power. It might be that we ourselves are limited and weak; we imagine that at some point God is too, and find it hard to believe that He is not. But the closer we draw to God, the more we are awed by His greatness and majesty. Our thoughts of God are too human. Our thoughts of God are not great enough. Some Christians try to mold God into their lifestyle and try to manipulate God. Others think of God as a Christian Santa Clause. Some think because God is so loving that He will allow things to slip by and He will understand. That is so far from the truth! One who sins without repentance, cannot expect God to answer their prayers. Or one cannot expect God to bless them when they don't even have time for Him, or be bothered to build a personal and intimate relationship with Him. Jesus requires absolute devotion and rejects lackadaisical, halfhearted followers. Zeal for the Lord is not optional for His followers. We as Christians are to give our love for Jesus first place in our life and avoid lukewarmness. Just going to church and going through the movement of worship, or any outward works do not always indicate a right condition of heart. A right condition of heart produces good works. Some people don't realize how vital fellowship with God is, or the wonderful benefits that result from a caring, sincere relationship with God can be.

There are people today falling away from the Lord as they did in the Old Testament because they are allowing the world and its ways into their life which will hardened their heart. They thought that just by observing certain rituals and speaking certain words, they could stay in favor with God. In the Old Testament, the Lord let them know that He despised their ritualistic worship and empty sacrifices (Amos. 5:21, 22), mock solemnity (Is. 58:4, 5), and lip-service devotion (Jer. 7:4). He had become sick of their singing, in which they only mouthed words that meant nothing to them (Amos 5:23). Be aware, He will again. The danger of falling out of love with Christ is no less present in our times, and it causes much grief now as it did then. Intimacy with God is a precious and fragile thing that must be carefully guarded. It is sad to see some people who come into the church on Sundays just to make a showing. They are not focused on God, nor do they have the humility, respect, or the knowledge that they are in the presence of a Holy God who is worthy and due our worship and our total heart with humility, and to be praised in truth and spirit. Many Christians of today could take the example of the church in the Old Testament. God has to be a living reality to worship Him from the depth of our hearts.

Repentance for being lukewarm is necessary for the individuals restoration and the restoration of the church. Restoration to the individual believer means LIFE. Paul speaks of "Christ who is our life." Restoration means the replacing of spiritual death with spiritual life (Ez. 36:25-28). To the church as a whole, restoration means more than becoming a reproduction of the New Testament church. It means becoming all God originally intended the church to be. Restoration also means the release of God's power without measure through the church. As the church becomes a spiritual house (Eph. 2:20), inhabited by a holy priesthood, offering up spiritual sacrifices acceptable to God through Jesus Christ (1 Pet. 2:5), then all men will be drawn to Him; the world will at last see the Glory of God through this restored church.

Believers, keep in mind, there is no way of being neutral in the Kingdom and the Lord cannot be taken lightly, or on our terms. He cannot be manipulated, He will not change, He will not tolerate pride, sin of any kind, or doubt; He is a SOVEREIGN HOLY GOD. One is either for Jesus, or against Him.

God's name reveals this truth. He is the "Great, I AM" (Ex. 3:14). God supplies all of our needs, our healing, all wisdom, our peace, our sanctification, provision, victory, and our salvation. It is only when you realize that you are needy daily; moment to moment, and realize how much you need Jesus, that's when you can truly experience Almighty God! Jesus is everything we need!

There is NO ONE greater than the Almighty God! He will not permit us to take Him lightly, or disrespect Him in any way! What He will accept is to love Him with all our heart, mind, soul and strength and allowing Him in every area of our life, and depending on Him for all our needs. We must stay in an attitude of gratitude; giving thanks day by day, moment by moment, and acknowledging His glorious Presence at all times, and staying in constant fellowship in prayer with Him. When we honor God, He honors us.

"I know your works, that you are neither cold nor hot. I could wish you were cold or hot. So then, because you are lukewarm, neither cold or hot, I will vomit you out of my mouth" (Revelation 3:15-16).

(Cold springs are refreshing; hot mineral springs are medicinal; lukewarm is nauseating.)

WHAT IS SALVATION

"Through faith, we must appropriate salvation for our minds, emotions, and wills by putting off the 'old man' (old nature) and putting on the new" (Colossians 3:9).

Salvation means the changing of your spirit, soul, and body into the image of Christ. Salvation from God's point of view means that you will become a complete person, because we put down our inabilities and take on the completeness of Christ. You will become totally the person God wants you to be. Salvation is not instantaneous for all parts of man. The spirit of man (the real you) is recreated within him at the new birth instantly (2 Corinthians 5:17), but the body of man will not be recreated until Resurrection Day. The body is a temple which contains the real part of you that literally has God in you. That is why, in Christ, race, gender, color, or class does not matter (Gal. 3:28). None of those things exist in the spirit realm. The soul of man must be changed progressively into the new man through day-to-day choices, through setting our wills under the authority of God and allowing Him to renew us totally—our minds, wills, and emotions. God is saying today, "Whatever thing, is hindering you or not helping you to become the kind of person, the total man that I want you to be, get rid of it! I want My people to stand up victoriously and boldly each day, calling on the name of Jesus." God does not want the work of Jesus to go in vain in any part of our lives.

For God to affect you in all three parts of your being, He has given you freedom of choice in each area. YOU must choose to be born again. It is the act of your will. Then the Holy Spirit creates a new spirit within you. It is YOUR will that you decide to read and study the Word of God. So you choose to allow God to renew your mind to His image. It is by choice that YOU decide to appropriate healing for the body and to walk in divine health. If you are born-again, Christ Jesus made it available to you for the life of God is now implanted within you. When your soul is renewed, the words of your mouth will be in line with God's principals. You will walk, and talk exactly like Jesus if He was in your situation. When you speak the Word out of a renewed soul, the devil will know, you are above and not beneath (Deut. 28:13), because you are speaking the Word of God. When you speak the Word of God, it shall come to pass. Heaven backs you up!

The believer by faith in God can change his world; can frame a new world in himself and his surroundings. By speaking God's Words in every area of your life, you will cause your present "world" to be framed into the way God wants it to be. Speak God's Word into your family, good health and prosperity. Speak the promises of God with faith and as you speak, your faith will grow. If you are going to be conformed to the image of God, you will have to come out of the shell of this world. Satan wants us to except things "the way they are" and feel defeated, to quit, give up. The devil wants us to think, "Everyone gets sick, or everyone gets depressed." NOT SO! The devil wants to destroy us! Jesus tells us when God's Word is spoken, nothing immediately happens in the natural but something immediately begins to happen in the spiritual realm (Mark 11:13-24). Things may look the same on the outside, but inside, things have already changed. We need to learn to persist in faith! The Biblical principal of speaking things in faith, or believing that what you say you will have…is true forever! It also is true of speaking negatively, you will surely get what you say and believe. What you believe will come to pass.

We understand that in the beginning God spoke out His Words and the world was framed. Words spoken are important. There is life or death in the power of words. So guard your mouth from negative or ungodly words. By faith, we are to understand that God has given us the chance and choice to frame our world…a godly world of faith and the Word. Faith is the total absence of self-dependability, and faith depends totally on God. He is totally dependable and we can trust Him with our being. If you want to frame your world, speak death to the world the devil has formed around you by operating in the God-kind-of-faith and speaking forth the Word in the Name of Jesus. Just as the centurion understood authority and the spoken word in Luke 7:6-10 and framed his world through his believe, God wants us to frame our world with Jesus, the written Word. We need to hold fast to Jesus and our confession. God is saying, "After I have done all these things for you, don't throw it aside. Beloved, hold your ground." This means, be ready to fight any enemy who comes to steal whatever precious thing you received from God. Many Christians are in danger of losing what Jesus rightfully purchased for them on the Cross. They have lost their deliverances, blessings or health because of sin.

The blessings came in the first place because of God's mercy, grace, tender love, and compassion, Whether you keep your blessings depends on you. If you are not living right or making Jesus the center of your life, you could lose those things God gave you: "For sin shall not have dominion over you: for ye are not under the law, but under grace" (Romans 6:14). God's Word tells us He has given us power not to allow sin to dominate us.

For victory to be complete, know who you are in Christ, and know what is rightfully yours. Know what you can do by the power and authority of the Name of Jesus. Speak the promises of God, your faith will grow, and as you speak them your faith will grow from a single seed planted to a large harvest of blessings.

So if you are going to improve your life and be conformed to the image of God, you must bring your body and soul (emotions, intellect, will), under the authority of the Holy Spirit. Your spirit (the real you) must take charge; you tell your soul and body what to do. Do not let them control you. If your soul and body are not yet in order, you will still not be able to walk in the completeness of your salvation. God's will is for you to be saved in all three components of your total being…spirit, soul and body. Receive in faith your healing, and it will be done. Obtain the promises by simply accepting Jesus as your Savior. God wants you well, free and out of bondage. Act upon the knowledge of truth and you will be free. God wants us in His image so that we can be blessings to the world. Choose to allow the Lord to "save" your soul, to conform your character through His Word and the Holy Spirit and conform your character to the image of Jesus.

After you read Mark 11:22, 23, confess this out loud: I am as Jesus. I accept my life and position in Christ. What He has said about me is true. He has made me a mountain mover. Jesus lives in me. I have His name, His Word, His Spirit, and His life. I believe in my heart that what I say with my mouth comes to pass. I have what I say because I am led by the Spirit. No obstacle can stand against me. They are removed in Jesus' name.

WHAT DOES GOD SAY ABOUT HOMOSEXUALITY?

"If a man also lie with mankind, as he lieth with a woman, both of them have committed an abomination: they shall surely be put to death; their blood shall be upon them" (Leviticus 20:13).

These days it is becoming more and more common to see same-sex marriages. It has gradually become condoled even in some schools. There are gay gatherings after school. The Supreme Court rules that U.S. Constitution guarantees the right for the same-sex couples to marry in all 50 States. It's Sodom and Gomorra all over again! Some gays say they were born this way. This is a lie right from the pit of hell! We are what we think, as the Bible says, "For as he thinks in his heart so he is" (Proverbs 23:7). What we think is sometimes determined by what we read and imagine, dream or are otherwise exposed to. God as our Creator doesn't make mistakes! The Bible says, "...as He is, so are we in this world" (1 John 4:17). God loves all people but cannot and will NOT condole any sin! God is a Holy God, and a Righteous God! Not much is being taught in the churches about homosexuality. We as Christians cannot just ignore or condole it for the sake of that person's soul. This sin has been put back up on the shelf which allowed it to come more alive! A sexual love affair between two persons of the same-sex or lusting after the same-sex, is referred to as gays and lesbians (female). It is a behavioral sin that creates tremendous emotional and social problems. The Word of God calls homosexuality an abomination because it is in rebellion to God's original plan of one man and one woman united together for life who are commanded by God to be fruitful and multiply, thus establishing the home and the priesthood in the home (Lev. 18:22; 20:13).

In 2 Timothy 3:3 the Bible warns us that in the last days men shall be "without natural affections." Unless the caller is repentant and under the conviction of the Holy Spirit, he or she will inevitable be angry and defensive of his or her lifestyle. As Christians we have the responsibility to stand up for the Word of God and speak the Truth to the unbeliever. God says the Truth will set you free.

If anyone knows of a person of such and cares about them and their soul, you can pray in the power of the Spirit and the authority of Jesus, binding lust and homosexual desire. Release freedom from lust, and victory and newness of life in Christ and the power of the Holy Spirit. Try to get this person into a Christian fellowship so he or she can learn the disciplined living required of the Christian (Rom. 6:7-23). Sometimes deliverance may be needed first. Try to encourage the person to come and be involved in a church family. It is very important that the person renew his or her mind (Rom. 12:2). Explain that it is also important to saturate one's self in Scripture. It is the lust factor that has to be dealt with which creates or heightens the propensity to sin. Also their patterns need to be changed as far as thoughts and routines. The old patterns need to be known so they are not repeated. An alternative and victorious act is praise and worship. Emphasize the praise principal to resist temptation. It's important also to emphasize the need to change one's preeminence and how praise does so. Above all, if this person is serious about a life changing process, assure him or her, you care and will be there for them. Be faithful and continue to pray for this person. God has guaranteed believers victory through Christ: "But thanks be to God, which giveth us the victory through our Lord Jesus Christ" (1 Cor. 15:57). God has made us overcomers (1 John 5:4, 5; Rev. 12:11), also God says, "I can do all things through Christ who strengthens us" (Phil. 4:13). Don't forget... "For with God nothing shall be impossible" (Luke 1:3). Share these Scriptures with the one you are mentoring and reassure and encourage yourself too!

WHAT DOES FREEDOM IN CHRIST MEAN TO YOU?

Yes, we are free in Christ; He brings the true freedom...freedom from sin. He has set us free to live a free life. In the Old Testament people were bound by the Law. But we as Christian believers are no longer bound by the old Law. If we could have been saved by Law then God would not have had to give us a different way to get out of the grip of sin. In the Bible, Paul is not saying the Old Testament laws do not apply to us today. He is saying certain types of the laws may not apply to us. The Ten Commandments still apply for us today. But the Old Law could not save us. It pointed out our need to be forgiven. The Old Testament Law still has value in that it points out proper guidelines for living, restrains people from evil, and reveals our sin to us. It helps us realize that we are all sinners and that it is impossible through ourselves and our works to please God. Thus the Law paved the way for us to welcome the Savior. Christ fulfilled the obligations of the Law for us. The Law can't save anyone, only by having faith in Christ will save us. Faith in Christ brings true freedom from sin and from the futile attempt to be right with God by keeping the Law. Christ is the only way of escape to all who will believe Him. Until Christ came we were guarded by the Law; kept in protective custody, so to speak, until we could believe in the coming Savior. Now we as believers are all children of God through faith in Jesus Christ. We are free to serve Him. But this is a willing service in a spirit of joy, and we do it in the power of the Holy Spirit. The Holy Spirit that indwells in us produces dramatic changes inside of us which is called... "The Fruit of the Holy Spirit," which is God's own character...love, joy, peace, patience, kindness, goodness, faithfulness, gentleness, and self-control (Galatians 5: 22:23). Freedom is a privilege to love and serve, not to do wrong! The whole Law could be summed up in this one command: "Love others as you love yourself" (Galatians 5:13-15).

Some people misuse this precious freedom. This freedom doesn't mean we do what we want, it does have certain limits. We must never allow our freedom from the Law to become an occasion for fleshly activity, for then we are cut off from Christ. We are also accountable for one another. If we obey the Holy Spirit's instructions we won't always be doing the wrong things our evil nature wants us to do. Also, being guided by the Holy Spirit we no longer force ourselves to obey the old Law of trying to be good and win God's favor. When we follow our own wrong inclinations, our lives produce evil results: impure thoughts, lustful pleasures, idolatry, spiritism (encouraging the activity of demons), hatred, fighting, jealousy, anger, and constant effort to get the best for ourselves and having complaints and criticism. There are some areas where the Bible is vague. For an example: the Bible doesn't specifically forbid watching or attending movies with certain vulgar language, violence, or sex, but by looking at a number of passages in the Word, it is obvious we should avoid those kind of movies. It is not rocket science to know from your heart and spirit what to stay away from when you love Jesus! Just ask yourself, "Would Jesus approve of this?" "Would Jesus do this?" We can count on the Holy Spirit, to tell us where to go and what to do, and then we won't always be going in the wrong direction. But one must be sensitive to the leading of the Spirit and listen and obey Him.

Reading the Book of Galatians will help you understand through Paul's teaching of the message of salvation, and that it was a gift from God and it could not be earned by obeying certain rules, or having to "qualify" for eternal life, that is called legalism. Paul teaches you can only be saved by faith in Christ; all we have to do is except it. So if we long to be free, truly free, that desire will point us to Christ. Only through Jesus and his gospel can we be truly free from sin, free from the demands of the Law, and joyfully serve our Lord with the kind of life we want and He wants us to have.

"For I through the law died to the law that I might live to God. I have been crucified with Christ; it is no longer I who live, but Christ lives in me; and the life which I now live in the flesh I live by faith in the Son of God, who loved me and gave Himself for me. I do not set aside the grace of God; for if righteousness comes through the law, then Christ died in vain" (Galatians 2:20-21).

WHAT DO YOU HAVE YOUR MIND SET ON?

"Let this mind be in you which was also in Christ Jesus"

(Philippians 2:5).

In the Book of Romans 8:1-15 Paul presents two ways of life: walking according to the flesh or walking according to the Spirit. To walk in the flesh is to follow the sinful desires of one's old life of sin which can never please God as unbelievers. To walk in the Spirit is to follow the desires of the Holy Spirit and live in a way pleasing to God. Walking according to the Spirit involves holiness, not only in actions and words, but also in the thoughts that fill our minds each moment through the day. Those who are in the flesh characterize people's very nature.

All Christians have the Holy Spirit within them. Anyone who does not have the Holy Spirit within is not a Christian. Though Paul says that Christians are in the Spirit, he also warns they can from time to time live according to the flesh. Christians have the ability and choice to either walk in the uncharacteristic of the flesh or in the Spirit. He also warns them not to walk in the flesh. To walk in the flesh is death and to walk in the Spirit is peace and life. As Christians we are to actively work at growing in holiness and to "put to death" any sin in our hearts and minds, as well as our words and deeds.

Our mind, as we have learned, is a battleground that we need to be in control of. The devil wants to manipulate our thought life. He will plant seeds in our mind and hopes we will mediate on them until we agree with him and do what he wants us to do and then take action on these thoughts. Every thought always takes action. God can also plant seeds in our minds that will take a positive action that will agree with Him and His ways. But God also gives us a choice to make our own decisions, because He wants us to follow Him in love not as a robot. How we think forms patters and perceptions.

How we perceive things is important for as we see them we form our choices, whether it is negative or positive. We then carry out our actions of our choices, either in the flesh or in the Spirit. Our actions will determine our character of who we are.

We have to win the battle of the mind as it will determine the perception of the way we live. We must defeat the wrong thoughts. To know God is to know the right thoughts and the ways that please God and the success of life. We can be sure to do the right thing if our mind is thinking the Word, and talking the Word which in turn will do the right thing. If we meditate on the Word and understand it and use it and it will then take root within us and be as second nature. To control our thoughts is to truly love God, know His heart, and be obedient to His ways and Word, allowing the Spirit to be in control of our life. Remember, there is no such thing as half obedience! Our thought life is very valuable for it will determine not only our character but it will represent the enemy, or Jesus. It also will determine…life and peace or death. Christians value your thought life; live according to the Spirit!

"And if Christ is in you, the body is dead because of sin, but the Spirit is life because of righteousness. But if the Spirit of Him who raised Jesus from the dead will also give life to your mortal bodies through His Spirit who dwells in you" (Romans 8:10-11).

WHAT ARE YOUR PRIORITIES?

"Thus says the Lord of Hosts:

'Consider your ways!'"

(Haggai 1:7)

In the Book of Haggai it explains how the problems of Judah became confused. Like Judah, our priorities relating to work, family and God's work are often mixed up. Friends, possessions, and fun may rank higher on our list of importance than God.

God had given the Jews the assignment to finish the Temple in Jerusalem when they returned from captivity. But after fifteen years, they still had not completed it. They were more concerned about building their own homes than about finishing God's work. Haggai told them to get their priorities straight. Haggai was the first of the postexilic prophets, God sent Haggai to remind the Jews of what is really important in life. God refuses to be forgotten. He demanded priority in the Jews' life, and He demands priority in our life. God blesses those who make Him number one. Haggai also encouraged the people as they worked, assuring them of the presence of the Holy Spirit, of final victory, and the future reign of the Messiah.

It is easy to make other activities more important than doing God's work. But God wants us to build His Kingdom. Don't stop and don't make excuses. Set your heart on what is right and do it. Get your priorities straight by centering them on Christ. If God gives you a task, don't be afraid to get started. His resources are infinite. God will help you complete it by giving you encouragement from others along the way.

Remember, God has chosen you…each of us have been chosen by God. We did not choose Him, He chose us! This truth should make us see our value in God's eyes and motivate us to work for Him. When you feel down, remind yourself, "God has chosen me!"

Haggai also relayed the message from the Lord to the Jews that holiness will not rub off on others, but contamination will. The people needed to understand that activities in the Temple would not clean up their sin; only repentance and obedience could do that. If we insist on harboring wrong or "toxic" attitudes and sins, or maintain close relationships with sinful people, we will be contaminated. Holy living will come only when we are empowered by God's Holy Spirit.

The Book of Haggai is a very small Book but very big on importance! Haggai issues a clear call to his own people and to us that we should set ourselves to the task assigned to us by God. We should not allow difficulties, enemies, or selfish pursuits to turn us aside from our divinely given responsibilities. We are to make the work of God priority, both with our time and with our money (Haggai 1:1-4). The challenge to faith is the same in every generation; seek first the things of God and trust Him to provide the daily necessities of life. The glorification of any work we pursue comes by the presence of God in it. God calls us to commit what we are, what we have, and all that we do to Him.

WE SHAPE TOMORROW'S WORLD BY WHAT WE TEACH OUR CHILDREN TODAY

"That they may arise and declare (God's law) to their children, that they may set their hope in God" (Psalm 78:6-7).

In 19th-centry Scotland, a young mother observed her three-year-old son's inquisitive nature. It seemed he was curious about everything that moved or made a noise. James Clerk Maxwell would carry his boyhood wonder with him into a remarkable career in science. He went on to do groundbreaking work in electricity and magnetism. Years later, Albert Einstein would say of Maxwell's work that it was "the most fruitful that physics has experienced since the time of Newton."

From early childhood, religion touched all aspects of Maxwell's life. As a committed Christian, he prayed: "Teach us to study the works of Thy hands… and strengthen our reason for Thy service." The boyhood cultivation of Maxwell's spiritual life and curiosity resulted in a lifetime of using science in service to the Creator.

The community of faith has always had the responsibility to nurture the talent of the younger generation and orient their lives to the Lord, "that they may arise and declare (God's law) to their children, that they may set their hope in God" (Ps. 78:6-7).

Finding ways to encourage children's love for learning while establishing them in the faith is an important investment in the future.

Our children are a gift from God
On loan from heaven above,
To train and nourish in the Lord,
And show to them His love.

WE CAN FACE ANY FEAR

BECAUSE THE LORD IS WITH US!

A mother asked her five-year-old son to go to the pantry to get her a can of soup. But he refused and protested. "It's dark in there." Mon assured David, "It's okay. Don't be afraid, Jesus is in there." So David opened the door slowly and seeing that it was dark, he shouted, "Jesus, can you hand me a can of soup?"

This humorous story of David's fear reminds us of Gideon. The Lord appeared to Gideon, calling him "a mighty man of valor" (Judg. 6:12) and then telling him to deliver Israel out of Midian's hand (v. 14). But Gideon's fearful reply was, "My clan is the weakest in Manasseh, and I am the least in my father's house (v. 15). Even after the Lord told Gideon that with His help he would defeat the Midianites (v. 16), he was still afraid. Then Gideon asked the Lord for signs to confirm God's will and empowerment (w. 17, 36-40). So, why did the Lord address fearful Gideon as a "mighty man of valor"? Because of whom Gideon would one day become with the Lord's help.

We too may doubt our own abilities and potential. But let us never doubt what God can do with us when we trust and obey Him. Gideon's God is the same God who will help us accomplish all that He asks us to do. The Lord provides the strength we need to follow and obey His will. So we don't need to be afraid that what He asks we can't fulfill. We can face any fear when we know the Lord is with us.

WAKE UP, AMERICA!

What happened to America the Beautiful? What happened to America the peaceful, the respected; land of opportunity? Where is the freedom to read the Bible, pray or the display of the Ten Commandments and the Pledge of Allegiance (which stands for the loyalty to our country)? Oh, America, what have we done? Or should it be said, what have we not done? As children of God, we have become ineffective by compromising God's Word, being too complacent and self-centered with our own individual life. We have not held up our responsibility as examples of our Lord and Savior. By allowing our own interests and desires to come first and not God's, we have fallen back from His standards and ways of life. Our nation is living proof of this! We have not stood up for righteousness and morals. For many the daily hope for an abundant, prosperous, peaceful, and moral life lies on a shelf covered in dust...the Holy Bible. Whether or not people believe the Bible is the most definite true Word of God and the standard of a rich and fulfilling life is not up for debate. For every word in the Bible is true and factual and is the living inspired Word of God! So to believe it is rewarding and fulfilling and a life of success. By not believing in the Bible does not cancel the fact that it is the Truth and without it there is failure in family life, business, finances, health, leadership, morals and standards, for victory or salvation and spiritual, intimate relationship and growth.

Our nation's foundation was built on the Bible and the standards of God. Because of that fact America became a great, honorable and prosperous nation. People put God first; they honored Him and his ways in prayer, worship and lived the Word daily. Family life was important, loving, and respectful and valued integrity. These qualities branched out from the family home into their jobs, communities, and leadership and government. Once God is omitted from our life, crime, corruption, hate, respect and integrity, health and financial difficulties arise like a growing infectious disease affecting all of society and the whole nation. Once we no longer honor God, He no longer honors us. We all desire honor and respect, so why should God not expect it as well? So should we as a nation be devastated because there is so much crime and corruption and dysfunctional morals? Absolutely not! We have ourselves to blame because each of us have our responsibility to be a living example of Jesus, to walk in love, faith, kindness and peace and uphold the standard of life God expects from His children who call themselves Christians...Christ-like people. God is expecting His children to raise the standard of godly living and not blend in with the dying world.

It's not too late to repent and allow God to heal our nation. We can stand up for righteousness and morality. But we must stand in unity. Then we can call

America the Beautiful once again. By putting God first in all areas of our life we can bring back respect, peace, kindness, compassion for others and integrity!

Parents should be teaching their children about Jesus for the next generation. Families should be praying together as a family. Have you heard families who pray together stay together? Praying over your children and blessing them will keep them safe and guided. Do you teach your children to pray and the importance of going to church? Are you a good example for your children? Do your children have their own Bible and see to it they read it? Children also learn quickly by what they see. Are you and your spouse loving and respectful to each other? Do you monitor what is seen on the TV? Are we kind and helpful to our neighbor? Remember, life begins in the home. Home life is so important for it to permeate into the world. The second step in reviving our nation starts in our home! The first step is putting God first and His desires and cause! A godly-life will snowball into effect and reflect to others. So let's get serious about our life and our nation and the concern for a dying world.

Pick up your Bibles, blow the dust off and read it like your life, your future, your children's life and future, and the generations to come and our Nation and world depend on it...because it does! Also start praying for your families, your communities, your work place, leadership and the morals of this country. Pray IS powerful. More prayer...more power...much prayer...much power. Let your voice and godly example be seen and heard! As individual Christians.... We can make a difference! Remember, it's never too late to do the right thing. It is wrong to do nothing! Jesus walked this earth as a Man and He and the Holy Spirit turned the world all around. We as believers have the same opportunity for we too have Jesus and the Holy Spirit. We have God's very own Spirit!

America, if we don't wake up, we will be helping to turn our Nation's destiny worse than Sodom and Gomorra. Peace, love, freedom and most of all God and His Word will be lost and not be there for the generations to come to support and prosper them with a fulfilling life. WAKE UP, AMERICA!

FAITH... Faith is holding on to the faithfulness of God and, as long as you do that, you cannot go wrong. Faith does not look at itself or at the person who is exercising it. Faith looks at God... Faith is interested in God only, and it talks about God and it praises God and it extols the virtues of God. The measure of strength of a man's faith, always, is ultimately the measure of his knowledge of God. He knows God so well that he can rest on the knowledge. And it is the prayers of such a man that are answered.

"Jesus answered and said to them, 'Have faith in God'"
(Mark 11:22).

WHAT ATTITUDE WILL YOU CHOOSE?

Maybe you've heard the saying, "Attitude is everything." Our attitudes are so important because they make the difference between having a miserable life or a life of joy and peace. It is also the difference between a worldly person, and a Christian. The attitude of Jesus is forgiving, enduring, and selfless. The Israelites spent 40 years in the wilderness all because of their bad attitude. They thought their enemies were the problem, but in fact it was their bad attitude. Here are a few common bad attitudes that keep people stuck going around the mountain and drying up in the wilderness.

1. BASING THE FUTURE ON THE PAST
   The Israelites based all their expectations on what happened in the past and what they saw in their present circumstances. They lacked positive vision. If you are dwelling on a painful past, decide to believe in faith… "For I know the thoughts that I think toward you, says the Lord, thoughts of peace and not of evil, to give you a future and hope" (Jeremiah 29:11). When you speak God's Word over your circumstances, it unleashes His power and provision in your life.

2. SOMEONE ELSE NEEDS TO TAKE RESPONSIBILITY
   You might have been hurt so you think it is someone else's job to get you out of the mess you are in. Be encouraged to stop looking for others to fix your problems. Instead be a responsible person and believe God has empowered you to overcome and handle it through prayer. Know you have God's nature, ability and power to overcome every obstacle you face. "But thanks be to God, which giveth us the victory through our Lord Jesus Christ" (1 Corin. 15:57).

3. MAKE IT EASY FOR ME
   You might think it's just too hard for you and you feel you can't take it anymore. But you must realize you are stronger than you think. Don't let the enemy convince you that you are helpless! God's Word says: "I can do all thinks through Christ who strengthens me" (Phil. 4:13).

4. GRUMBLING AND COMPLAINING, FAULT-FINDING
   Don't be one who ignores all the good qualities in people and only sees their faults. As Christians we are to have a humble,

> unselfish, thankful attitude that puts people first. You need to claim… "I am born of love, love fills my very being. I will walk in the fruit of the Spirit of love. I no longer fear people because love has made me consistent. I am fearless and loving in every circumstance and love is my way of life!" "There is no fear in love; but perfect love casteth out fear…" (1 John 4:18).

Don't let self-pity waste your time, it won't change a thing! You can be pitiful or powerful! You can't have both. God wants to give you beauty for your ashes. So surrender your ashes. People can take a lot of things away from you, but no one can take away your good attitude. Even if you're dealing with a lifetime of negative or destructive attitudes, it's not too late to change. Through the power of the Holy Spirit, you can succeed. It's never too late as long as you let God be God and let Him be in charge of the process.

WE ARE GOD'S CHILDREN

1 John 3:1-10

"The Father has loved us so much that we are called children of God. And we really are his children. The reason the people in the world do not know us is that they have not known him. Dear friends, now we are children of God, and we have not yet been shown what we will be in the future. But we know that when Christ comes again, we will be like him, we will see him as he really is. Christ is pure, and all who have this hope in Christ keep themselves pure like Christ.

The person who sins breaks God's law. Yes, sin is living against God's law. You know that Christ came to take away sins and that there is no sin in Christ. So anyone who lives in Christ does not go on sinning. Anyone who goes on sinning has never really understood Christ and has never known him.

Dear children, do not let anyone lead you the wrong way. Christ is all that is right. So be like Christ a person must do what is right. The devil has been sinning since the beginning so anyone who continues to sin belongs to the devil. The Son of God came for this purpose: to destroy the devil's work.

Those who are God's children do not continue sinning, because the new life from God remains in them. They are not able to go on sinning, because they have become children of God. So we can see who God's children are and who the devil's children are: Those who do not do what is right are not God's children, and those who do not love their brothers and sisters are not God's child."

John wrote that Christians should become more like Jesus. Their actions should prove that they unite in love as the church of God. John is not teaching perfectionism. John is saying sin is natural to the children of the devil, but unnatural to children of God who cannot sin without the Spirit's conviction. Love for others is a sure sign that God lives in us and that we are in the fellowship of His love. Recognize that hate for others means that you are in the darkness. Also recognize that only those who obey Jesus really know Him. Understand that obedience is the first evidence of love for God, and know and believe that only those who are learning to live like Jesus know and love Him. One who is born again (1) loves other believers, and (2) obeys the Word of God and the Holy Spirit. If you know your brother or sister is in sin...pray for them (1 John 5:1-8; 5:16, 17). The enemy seeks to destroy the unity of the body of Christ. When Christians refuse to forgive or they judge their brother or sister they are choosing strife instead of vital unity and they are causing division as the devil desires. So be aware that the devil will try to bring all separation and division among the body of Christ...the church of believers (1 John 2:18-19).

WHERE IS THE HOLINESS IN OUR CHURCHES... THE RESPECT AND THE FEAR OF THE LORD WITHIN THE HOUSE OF THE LORD?

"You must be holy because I, the LORD your God, am holy" (Leviticus).

There seems to be a lack of holiness, reverence and respect, within the sanctuary of churches nowadays. Holiness means wholly dedicated, devoted to God distinct and separate from the world's way of living and the presence of righteousness, purity and godliness. Holiness here on earth is not perfection; it is striving for purity. There is complacency...a casual attitude of the awareness of the holiness of God and for the house of God. Complacency means thinking too little of something, being lazy. Satan is then ready to strike and we wouldn't even know he was there. Complacency leads to indifference, which leads to idleness. To stand for nothing is to stand against God. That's why complacency is so dangerous. Revelation three, verse fifteen to seventeen states, "I know all the things you do, that you are neither hot nor cold. I wish you were one or the other! But since you are like lukewarm water, I will spit you out of my mouth!" God is saying He does not tolerate a mediocre spiritual life; He can't stomach lukewarm faith. He is angered by a religion that puts on a show but ignores the service...this is hypocrisy. God does not want us to compromise His Word, His ways or our Christian life for this too is to negotiate away that which is holy. We are most likely to compromise in areas where we are weak. Jesus said that our actions give away our value system, so what we do or don't do shows what we really believe in (Luke 6:45).

The dress code has now changed from "dressing appropriate for God" to "casual dress and flip-flops" which also affects your attitude to be casual. Then there are women who dress provocative and some Pastors won't even pray for them as they come up for prayer, because they don't want to look at them; Pastors get embarrassed. No one would go to see the President in shorts and flip-flops, or go to a wedding in such attire, so why would we stand in the Presence of the Most Holy God in casual apparel with a casual attitude? Although clothing restrictions for church have been greatly relaxed in recent years, the correct dress is still conservative.

We come to church to worship our Great and Mighty God together as the body of Christ with our whole heart giving praises, prayer, and with an attitude of gratitude of His Word, blessings and promises and, for all that He is, for He is so worthy of all our praises with our whole heart. Reverence is the quality that guides one's behavior and attententiveness, and dignity. Only a heartfelt, right attitude, and respect will prepare a place for God and welcome the Holy Spirit to move among us. But if the church has gone from Christ-centered to manmade, expecting to be entertained, and catered to self-centered feelings, instead of being in a sacred place of worship and a place of prayer, we hardly can expect to welcome God and expect the Holy Spirit to want to move without our love and reverence for God. Instead of the church transforming the world, the world seems to be transforming the church.

Jesus warned us, "My house shall be called the house of prayer..."

WHY DOES GOD ALLOW SUFFERING AND EVIL?

So many people ask this question. Why does God allow suffering and evil? Why do horrible things happen to good people? The book of Job addresses these questions more than any portion of Scripture. For reasons unknown to Job, a series of crushing catastrophes hit him, leaving him to ask, "Why me, God?" And God responds (chap. 38-41) with his longest unbroken speech in the Bible—but He never tells Job why. He basically tells Job that as God He can do whatever He wants, and that's all the answer Job needs. God reminded Job who He is. We all have asked that question from time to time forgetting that God is a Sovereign God. He is all powerful and wise. Why seems to be a question we can ask, but God is not bound to answer. Sometimes He will and other times He won't. We must trust his judgment. He is all knowing and knows what's best for us because He loves us. Although we may not be able to understand fully the pain we or others experience, it can lead us to rediscover God. He is always present, even in suffering.

Remember, we live in a broken world of sinful people. When you are tempted to blame God for your suffering, think of it like this. It's like giving a fragile, priceless treasure to a child and he breaks it. But he is mad and says, "Look what you have done! Look at this piece of junk you gave me!" The child is wrong; you gave him a treasured possession and he ruined it. God also gave us a perfect world; we too have ruined it and turned it into the chaos it is today.

Also remember, being a Christian, or a good person does not exempt one from pain and suffering. Jesus even guaranteed us in John 16:33 that we will experience trials and heartache. Storms will come, but the test is how we respond to them, God has not promised his children happiness. God wants us filled with the joy of the Lord but, He does not promise happiness, there is a difference. He is more concerned with our holiness, and that involves pain and sacrifice. Worthwhile things come with great cost. Following Jesus is no exception. But Jesus overcame suffering and we can too.

God does not like seeing his children suffer. He just wants us to imitate His Son, even when it's not all fun and games. No one hurts more than God when you or someone suffers. He's a good, good Father and it pains Him deeply when we hurt. We can't always understand what God does, or doesn't do, we must just trust Him, for we know He loves us very much and He is so much wiser than us. Man's wisdom is always partial and temporary. Plus God knows the future and has planned each step. He is always in control! Since we are locked into time, unable to see beyond today, we cannot know the reasons for everything that happens. We often must choose between anger and trust. We must trust God for our unanswered questions. So the next time you wonder why bad things happen remember we have a devil on the rampage, and he has those who want to follow him and do evil in this world. Remember, God has given us all free will to make our own choices, so don't blame God. We never doubt that God does not love us, for He got personally involved in our struggle—He became a man and suffered and died for us! Who do you know who would lay down their life for you and the world? God knows everything and sees everything and cares about everything! At times He seems far away. This may cause us to feel alone and doubt his care. We should serve God for who He is, not for what we feel. God's solution to an unfair world is to guarantee life with Him forever. No matter how unfair your present world seems, God offers the hope of being in His Presence eternally.

WE AREN'T GOOD ENOUGH TO JUDGE

"If you think you can judge others, you are wrong. When you judge them, you are really judging yourself guilty, because you do the same things they do. God judges those who do wrong things, and we know that his judging is right. You judge those who do wrong, but you do wrong yourselves. Do you think you will be able to escape the judgment of God?" (Romans 2:1-3) "God judges everyone the same way" (2:11).

It's not our job to hold the gavel. It's one thing to have an opinion. It's quite another to pass a verdict. It is one thing to be repulsed at an act, and another entirely to claim that I am superior or he is beyond the grace of God.

It's our job to hate sin, but it's God's job to deal with the sinner. God has called us to despise evil, but He's never called us to despise the evil doer. Besides, judging others is the quick and easy way to feel better about ourselves. We can boast, "Look God, compared to them who are really evil, I'm not bad." But the problem with that statement is, God doesn't compare us to them. They aren't the standard. God is. Compared to his standard… "There is no one who does anything good" (Romans 3:12).

WHAT SHOULD WE BE DOING WHEN CHRIST RETURNS?

What should we, as His stewards, be doing when Christ comes? We should be watching (Matt. 24:42), be ready (Matt. 24:44), and be about our Father's business!

Christ will come again, but not as a meek child in a manager. Christ…the HOLY ONE shall come in all His glory (Rev. 19-20). The radiance of the risen Christ will reveal the sinfulness of man and will expose to us what kind of life we have been living. Jesus came the first time to die. This time He comes to judge. We do not know when He will come (Luke 12:40) but we are to be ready. I Thessalonians 5:2-4 (illustration) says, He will come as a thief in the night. How will some Christians feel…ashamed (I John 2:28).

Life is too short to be wasted; in fact, the most precious possession we have is TIME, although some seem to disagree. God wants our lives available to Him, that He might use us to do His will.

When Christ returns, we as Christians will be judged for our works: "If any man's work shall be burned, he shall suffer loss: but he himself shall be saved; yet so as by fire "(I Corth, 3:12-15). All Christians must appear before the judgment seat of Christ (II Corth. 5:10). Romans 14:12 says, "So then every one of us shall give an account of himself to God." It has been said that in times of peril just before an accident, a person sees his life pass before him. Would we be pleased with our lives as we are now living if we knew that we had only a few minutes or hours left to live? The urgency of the hour demands Christian discipleship. We know not when Christ will come, so we must live every day as if it were our last. Are you ready to say with the writer of Revelation, "Even so, come, Lord Jesus?" Are you a faithful steward, and ready for your Master's return?

For what do Christians receive rewards? I Timothy 4:8…A crown of righteousness, granted for loving the appearing of Christ. I Thessalonians 2:19…A crown of rejoicing, granted for souls won to Christ. James 1:12…A crown of life, granted for loving Christ and enduring temptation. I Peter 5:4…A crown of glory, granted for being an example to the flock of God.

Dr. J. Sidlow Baxter gave this illustration of the second coming of Christ: A Scotchman and his two sons were returning from a fishing trip. The younger son said: "I can see her now, my precious wife, waiting at home for me…oh, yes, she is indeed a faithful one." The elder son said: "My wife will not only be waiting, but she will be perched on a window sill watching for me to come home. That is what I call faithfulness." The father Scotchman said, "Sons, I can show where your mother, bless her dear heart, excels them both. She will not only be waiting and watching for me to come home, but she will be fixing my dinner as well!"

We should be watching, waiting and working until our Lord comes. How about you?

THE NEW BIRTH

God made everything when you were born. He made everything new the first time and He will make everything new the second time. If you belong to Christ, you are a new creation… "The old things have gone; everything is made new!"

(2 Corinthians 5:17).

At our new birth God remakes our souls and gives us what we need. New eyes so we can see faith. A new mind so we can have the mind of Christ. A new strength so we won't grow tired. A new vision so we won't lose heart. A new voice for praise and new hands for service. And most of all, a new heart that has been cleansed by Christ.

We have soiled what He gave us the first time. We used our eyes to see impurity, our hands to give pain, our feet to walk the wrong path, our minds to think evil thoughts. All of us need to be made new again....born again.

The first birth was for earthly life; the second one is for eternal life. The first time we received a physical heart; the second time we received a spiritual heart. The first birth enabled us to have life on earth. The second birth enables us to have life eternal.

Salvation is God's business. Grace is his idea, his work, and his expense. He offers it to whom he desires, when he desires, Our job in the process is to inform the people, not screen them.

No rules are given, no system was offered and no code or ritual God said, "Everyone who believes can have eternal life in Him." The motive behind this gift of the new birth is...love...." "God so loved the world so much that he gave his one and only Son so that whoever believes in him may not be lost, but have eternal life" (John 3:16).

If you have not been born-again, pray now and repent and be forgiven of your sins, and invite Jesus into your heart so you too can live a life that pleases God, and have the promise of eternal life.

YOUR VOICE MATTERS IN HEAVEN

For we do not have a High Priest who cannot sympathize with our weaknesses, but was in all points tempted as we therefore come boldly to the throne of grace, that we may obtain mercy and find grace to help in time of need (Hebrews 4:15-16).

You and I live in a loud world. To get someone's attention is no easy task. He must be willing to set aside everything to listen; turn down the radio, turn away from the computer, and set the book down and shut the TV off. When someone is willing to silence everything else so he can clearly hear you and concentrate and give you his undivided attention, it is a privilege!

You can talk to God because God listens. God wants to hear from you because what matters to you also matters to God. He takes you very seriously. Whether it is a very important matter, or even a small problem, it's important to God, because you are His child. So go ahead and tell God what hurts, talk to Him. He won't turn away. He always has time for His children and desires to hear from us. "For our High Priest is able to understand our weaknesses." No need to fear that you will be ignored. God is concerned with everything about you and what you have to say, even if what you have to share impresses no one, it will impress God and He will listen. He listens to the painful plea of the elderly in the rest homes. He listens to the gruff confession of the death-row inmate. When the alcoholic begs for mercy, when the spouse seeks guidance, when the businessman steps off the street into the church, even when a child shares his heart, God listens. Intently and carefully each prayer is honored as precious jewels...your words do not stop until they reach the very throne room of God. You may not know the mystery of prayer, but you can know the power of prayer that can change a situation, a life, meet a need, bring healing to a body or a relationship, bring delivery and draw you closer to Jesus in an intimate relationship. Actions in heaven begin the minute someone prays on earth. What an amazing thought! Let us always feel confident to boldly come before our heavenly Father God's throne room sharing our heart and knowing He will always listen and care. If it matters to you, it will matter to Him.

BETTER THAN HAPPINESS

"The fruit of the Spirit is...joy" (Galatians 5:22).

Real joy is a fruit of something, or someone, much greater than happiness. According to the Bible scholar Ian Barclay, "Happiness is not a biblical word at all. It is derived from the root to happen. Clearly, what happens to us will affect our happiness." Joy, on the other hand, is a fruit of God's Spirit and is not affected by good or bad happenings. Joy is not dependent on our circumstances. It is dependent, as we ourselves need to be, on God Himself who dwells within us. Those who know the joy that comes from God don't need happenings to keep them happy. They learn how to develop inner joy because they know that no matter what happens, God offers hope and promise.

We should desire to have this joy in our lives, without chasing after it. Let's live and walk in the Spirit so that the fruit of joy will naturally burst forth. "The joy of the Lord is your strength" (Nehemiah 8:10).

HAPPINESS DEPENDS ON HAPPENINGS; JOY DEPENDS ON JESUS.

ANGER

Anger is a sin because it violates God's commandment to love. It is a dangerous emotion that always threatens to leap out of control and lead to violence, emotional hurt, increased mental stress, and other destructible results. There is spiritual damage as well. Anger keeps us from developing a spirit pleasing to God. Self-control is good. Christs wants us to practice thought-control as well. Jesus said we will be held accountable even for our attitudes...

"But I warn you-unless you obey God better than the teachers of religious law and the Pharisees do, you can't enter the Kingdom of Heaven at all!" (Matthew 5:20).

RIDICULE

Isaiah 51:7

Isaiah encouraged those who served God to discern right from wrong and to follow God's laws. He also gave them hope when they faced people's scorn or slander because of their faith. We need not fear when people ridicule us for our faith because God is with us and truth will prevail. If people make fun of you or dislike you because you believe in God, remember that they are not against you personally, but against God. He will deal with them; you should concentrate on loving and obeying Him.

THE FEW PRECEDING BIBLE BOOKS

ARE EXAMPLES OF YESTERDAY

HISTORY AND FOR TODAYS

UNDERSTANDING OF SPIRITUAL WISDOM

EZEKIEL... "GOD STRENGTHENS"

The author, Ezekiel, whose name means "God Strengthens," is identified as the priest, the son of Buzi (1:3). A bright light, a dazzling fire...that is what the glory of the Lord looked like to Ezekiel (1:13-28). He fell to the ground, overwhelmed by the holiness of God and his own sinfulness and insignificance. God gave Ezekiel specific instructions about what to say and how to say it. Each detail had a special meaning. Often we ignore or disregard the smaller details of God's Word, thinking He probably doesn't care. Like Ezekiel, we should want to obey God completely, even in the details. Eventually every person will kneel before God, either out of reverence and awe for his mercy or out of fear of his judgment. Based on the way you are living today, how will you respond? Ezekiel's message was addressed to a demoralized remnant of Judah exiled in Babylon. Ezekiel prophesied in the captivity in Babylon, as Jeremiah prophesied just before him. Ezekiel was given the difficult responsibility of presenting God's message to the ungrateful and abusive. Sometimes we also are called to be an example or share our faith with people who may be unkind to us. Just as the Lord told Ezekiel not to give up, He tells us not to give up. You can only be faithful in delivering it. You are not witnessing for their sakes alone, but out of faithfulness to God. You cannot make others accept your message; you can only be faithful. The people ignored Ezekiel's message. When people mock your witness for Christ or fail to take your advice, don't give up. Each individual is responsible for his or her own sin. The Book of Ezekiel is easily divided into three sections, Judah's judgment (chs. 4:-24), the heathen nation's judgment (chs. 25-32), and future blessings for God's covenant people (chs. 33-48).

Three very important personal, relevant lessons can be learned in Ezekiel. First is the importance of individual moral responsibility. Although it is true that God still blesses and corrects entire local churches (Rev. 2; 3), His primary dealings are with individuals. Second, Ezekiel teaches that though God is reluctant to discipline his people severely, He must. He is a righteous and jealous God as much as He is merciful and forgiving (12:-16). Third, Ezekiel assures us that God will ultimately triumph in history. His enemies may be winning now, but future judgment will totally destroy them (35:1-15).

Ezekiel focuses on the common failure of God's servants. This results from their gauging their success by man's approval rather than God's standard.

In scene after scene, God revealed to Ezekiel the extent to which the people had embraced idolatry and wickedness. God's Spirit works with us in a similar way, revealing sin that lurks in our life. Rationalizing makes it easier to commit sin, but it doesn't influence God's promise to punish (ver. 9:9-10). It is easy to point a finger at Sodom, especially for its terrible sexual sins. If we do not commit such horrible sins as adultery, homosexuality, stealing, and murder, we may think that we are doing all right. But what about sins like pride, laziness, gluttony, and ignoring the needy. These sins may not be as openly shocking as the others, but they are just as deserving of punishment!

The Book of Ezekiel begins by describing the holiness of God, which Israel had despised and ignored. As a result, God's Presence had departed from the Temple, the city, and the people. The Book ends with a detailed vision of the new Temple, the new city, and the new people…all demonstrating God's holiness (ver. 48:1-35). The pressure of everyday life can persuade us to focus on the here and now and thus forget God. That is why worship is so important; it takes our eyes off our current worries, gives us a glimpse of God's holiness, and allows us to look toward his future kingdom. God's Presence makes everything glorious, and worship brings us into his presence.

Ezekiel wrote of his vision revealing God's moral perfection. Ezekiel also wrote to let the people know that God was present with them in Babylon, not just in Jerusalem. Because God is morally perfect, He can help us live above our tendency to compromise. He can give us the power to overcome sin and to reflect his holiness. Moral purity is an important part of Christian discipleship.

Israel sinned, so God punished them. The fall of Jerusalem and the Babylon exile were used by God to correct the rebels and draw them back from their sinful way of life. Ezekiel warned them that not only was the nation responsible for sin, but each individual was also accountable to God. We cannot excuse ourselves from our responsibilities before God. We too are accountable to Him. Rather than avoid God, we must recognize sin for what it is…rebellion against God. Be assured you will not be saved by another's righteousness or be judged for another's sin (14:15-20).

Ezekiel consoled the people by telling them that the day would come when God would restore those who turn away from sin. God would be their King and Shepherd. He would give his people a new heart to worship Him and establish a new government and a Temple. Knowing that they will eventually be rescued and restored should encourage believers during difficult times. But we must be faithful to God because we love Him, not for what He can do for us. Our faith must be in Him, not in possible future benefits.

An angel gave Ezekiel a detailed vision of the new Temple. God's holy Presence had left Israel and the Temple because of sin. This ideal Temple now pictures the return of God's Presence when God will cleanse his people and restore true worship. All God's promises will be fulfilled under the rule of the Messiah. The faithful followers will be brought back to perfect fellowship with God. To prepare for this we must focus on God's holiness, and making needed changes in our lives.

Ezekiel said, "The power of the Lord was upon me and I was carried away by the Spirit of the Lord to a valley full of old, dry bones that were scattered everywhere across the ground. He led me around among them, and then He said to me: Son of dust, can these bones become people again? I replied, Lord; You alone know the answer to that. Then He told me to speak to the bones and say: "O dry bones, listen to the words of God, for the Lord God says, 'See! I am going to make you live and breathe again!" So I spoke these words from God, just as He told me to…and suddenly there was a rattling noise from all across the valley, and the bones of each body came together and attached to each other, just as they used to be…. The bodies started to breathe just as God commanded them, they lived and stood up…a very great army" (37:1-15). The vision meant where judgment had been pronounced previously, hope is proclaimed. The bones represented the exiles, who, according to v. 11, have given up all hope of reviving the kingdom of Israel because they have been in Babylon ten years. God said, "And I will sanctify My great name, which has been profaned among the nations…and the nations shall know that I am the LORD. I will give you a new heart and put a new spirit within you; I will take the heart of stone out of your flesh and give you a heart of flesh. I will put My Spirit within you and cause you to walk in My statues and you will keep my commandments" (36:23-27). God is bringing restoration, not because of the merits of the exiles, but rather for His namesake. The restoration will vindicate God; He is not powerless, but He is holy and righteous!

AN IMPORTANT AND POWERFUL MESSAGE FROM THE BOOK OF ZEPHANIAH

Zephaniah (which means "The Lord Has Hidden") God's prophet delivered a message of destruction to the people of Judah to shake them out of their complacency and urge them to return to God. This prophecy was written to Judah and all nations in their time (640-621 B.C.) and also meant for our day as well. The people refused to listen. If we too refuse to listen to God's Word, the Bible, we are as shortsighted as the people of Judah.

The key themes in the Book of Zephaniah are, God's judgment, a day of reckoning, is inevitable; it's never too late to seek God and return to Him; God will judge both claim to have faith and those who don't. Zephaniah's writings has three components: 1) the universal judgment for sin; 2) an appeal for repentance because God is righteous and willing to forgive; 3) a promise that the remnant have made God their refuge will be saved.

This message of Zephaniah has future significance. Because of the repeated use of the term "The Day" is either the period of time, or the actual day of God's wrath on our days' end. There are four timeless lessons for both believers and unbelievers in the Book of Zephaniah: 1) God is perfect justice as well as perfect love. If the call to repentance is continually ignored, God's judgment must consequently fall; 2) Punishment is not God's choice, for God loves the world (John 3:16); 3) To settle into complacency or be disobedient to God is tragic and more so if one has no awareness of spiritual emptiness; 4) Even to the rebellious God offers last-minute reprieve; "The remnant who humble themselves and seek righteousness will be hidden in the Day of the Lord's anger" (2:3).

To escape God's judgment we must listen to Him, accept his correction, trust Him, and seek his guidance. The people of Judah had no sorrow for their sins. They were prosperous and no longer cared about God. God's demands for righteous living seemed irrelevant to the people of Judah, whose security and wealth made them complacent. Sadly, there are people of our day now who think and act as the people of Judah. We can never allow material comfort to be a barrier to our commitment to God. We need to be aware that prosperity can produce an attitude of proud self-sufficiency. We must admit that money cannot save us and we can't save ourselves. Only God can save us and our indifference to spiritual matters. Prosperity can hinder people's repentance and it is known to be a false sense of security. Money is not evil, it's the love of money that can trap you and cause evil.

The Day of Judgment will one day come when God will judge all people who mistreated his people and have been disobedient to his Word and way of life. But He will also purify his people, purge all sin and evil. God will restore his people and give them hope. No matter how difficult our experience now we can look forward to the day of celebration when God will completely restore us. Take time and read the short but powerful Book of Zephaniah. You will have a renewed respect for God!

Take Zephaniah's prophecy to heart and the teachings within this Book of Zephaniah: The sin of pride is most often revealed by the words we speak, language becomes unclean with repeated expressions of self-will, or the profane use of God's holy Name. So purify your heart and speech and allow God to purify your lips and language (3:9-13). Remember, complacency is the enemy of spiritual growth; remain zealous for God (1:12). Persevere in following the Lord. Do not turn back. Find your answer in God (1:6). Avoid letting your attitude and character be shaped by the worldliness that surrounds you. Remember, we are citizens of another world! Beg the Lord to save you...all you who are humble...all you who uphold justice. Walk humbly and do what is right (Zephaniah 2:3).

A helpful prayer for someone you care about, or someone you have been praying for their salvation. Just put their name in the blank lines.

Dear Jesus,

I boldly come to the Throne Room of God as you say for all your children to do. I come with a petition for the one you know as ——— Your Word in the Bible says, "...if I dwell in you Jesus and You dwell in me, I can ask whatever I will so I may bring glory to you, and you also said, whatever we ask, believing...it shall be done, and whoever asks will receive..." (Matthew 11:9-10).

Lord Jesus, I ask NOW in love that you would bless ——— all he/she puts their heart, hands and soul to for Your Glory and the Kingdom of God. Bless ——— with wisdom, understanding, guidance, joy, health and the compassion of the needy, lost and hurting. Help ——— to heal you have planned them to be. May he/she always put you first in their life, and be the loving, caring example you want the world to see brightly reflecting from their heart. May their life be as a beautiful picture of your heart.... Lord also, Lord God, help ——— to wall in love and in the Spirit so would not fulfill the "pride" of the world and the flesh.

Dear Jesus, I also ask for the salvation, health, peace and fulfillment of their entire family. Lord, you are so awesome, loving, faithfuls and caring! We are grateful and praise you for the sacrifice you made upon the Cross for us. You took our punishment so we could one day live in eternity with you...THANK YOU!! I pray and believe in this prayer petition in the Holy Name of Jesus Christ our Lord and Savior. AMEN.... So be it!

NAHUM... "COMFORTER" OR "FULL OF COMFORT"

"Nahum," whose name means "Comforter" or "Full of Comfort," is unknown for his brief prophecy. The Book of Nahum pronounces God's judgment on sin and evil, personified in the wickedness of the Assyrians. Nahum pronounced God's judgment on Assyria and comforted Judah with his prophecy. The vision God gave to Nahum, concerning the impending doom of Nineveh is that God is jealous over those He loves; that is why He takes vengeance on those who hurt them. He furiously destroys their enemies. He is slow in getting angry, but when aroused, his power is incredible, and He does not easily forgive. God's patience cannot forever be taken for granted. When God is ready to punish, even the earth trembles.

Often people avoid God because they see evildoers in the world and hypocrites in the church. They don't realize that because God is slow to anger, He gives his true followers time to share his love and truth with evil doers. But judgment will come; God will not allow sin to go unchecked forever. When people wonder why God doesn't punish evil immediately, remind them that if He did, none of us would be here. We can be thankful that God gives people time to turn to Him!

The kingdom of the Assyrians, with their capital at Nineveh, had been a thriving nation for centuries by the time the prophet Nahum appeared on the scene. Ancient documents attest the cruelty of the Assyrians against other nations and they would boast of their savagery, abuse and torture. In 722-721 B.C., the Assyrians acted as God's instrument and conquered the northern kingdom of sinful Israel and also threatened Judah, the southern kingdom. Only a divine intervention prevented the desecration of Jerusalem. But now God would bring destruction on the Assyrian Empire at the capital city of Nineveh. While the judgment of Assyria is the overwhelming theme of Nahum, the book is primarily a message of comfort to the people of Judah. The Book of Nahum focuses on a single concern: the fall of the city of Nineveh. The attempts to defend the city against her attackers will be in vain because the Lord has decreed the fall of Nineveh and the rise of Judah (2:1-3). In the third and final chapter of the book, God's judgment may seem overly harsh, but He is justified in His condemnation. Nineveh was a "bloody city" (3:1), a city guilty of shedding the innocent blood of other people. The city was known for deceit, falsehood. Such sin was an offense to God, so His verdict of judgment was inevitable (3:2, 3, 5-7).

Nahum graphically portrays the seriousness of sin in the sight of God. Though His mercy and patience may cause Him to withhold judgment for a season, God will ultimately announce a day of reckoning! When His righteous judgment is unleashed, no human or superhuman power can withstand its force!

Nahum calls us to seriously self-examination and warns against the subtle sin of believing that life can be lived apart from the will and ways of God. The most frightening words anyone could ever experience are those directed toward Nineveh by the Lord: "Behold, I am against you" (2:13). With such prospects in view, serious self-examination should lead us into wholehearted repentance.

Misuse and abuse of other people is a sin in God's sight. Assyria built an empire by raping and plundering others, but national or personal kingdoms founded on deceit and tyranny also are displeasing to the Lord and will be judged by Him! A life of wickedness eventually will lead to isolation, not only from other people, but also from God. Graciously, His judgment against the sinful is offset by His mercy toward the faithful. To the proud, the arrogant, and the rebellious He comes with condemnation. To the humble, the devoted, and the faithful He comes with comfort. It is also a renewed understanding that vengeance is the work of God, not ourselves. True faith leaves judgment in the hands of God. The truth of God's judgment upon sin and the sinner should prompt believers to a renewed evangelistic mission. Those we fail to reach with the saving message of the gospel will indeed suffer the wrath of God! The prophecy of Nahum to Nineveh was primarily intended for the people of that time, but the judgment which Nineveh suffered will be the inevitable judgment of all men who proudly and arrogantly resist God and do not humble themselves before Him.

God's plan unfolded as a chastisement of Assyria because of its horrific sins, and a lesson to Judah of God's sovereign provisions for her. Assyria was used as a rod of correction against Judah's infidelity in the past in order to bring Judah back to God. Nahum challenges Judah to keep, "His promises are being kept; His sovereignty is vindicated! Keep your feasts, O Judah, fulfill your vows, for never again shall the wicked come against you" (v. 15). Addressing both Nineveh and Judab Nahum asks, "Who do you think God is?" Nahum is virtually saying, "Do you Assyrians think that you can resist God without enduring the consequences? Do you Judeans think that you can protect yourself with alliances and military pacts?" God will make a full end (v. 9) to all who perversely follow their own ways. Heed the warning!

The Book of Nahum teaches us to trust God for He is good and He is a place of safety for us when we are in trouble, and He is faithful to care for those who trust Him to do so. Believe that God is willing and able to deliver us from any bondage. Also know God will eventually stop any attack upon us. God may judge the nation in which we live, but He is able to protect and spare His people from judgment that may fall even on their neighbors.

NEHEMIAH... MEANS "YAHWEH COMFORTS"

Our first glimpse of Nehemiah is in a role as cupbearer at the court of Artaxerxes. A cupbearer had a position of great trust as advisor to the king and the responsibility of keeping the king from being poisoned. While Nehemiah enjoyed the luxury of the palace, his heart was in Jerusalem. Nehemiah is the last of the Old Testament historical books. It records the history of the third return to Jerusalem after captivity, telling how the walls were rebuilt and how the people were renewed in their faith. The book shows the fulfillment of the prophecies of Zechariah and Daniel concerning the rebuilding of Jerusalem's walls.

Nehemiah's prayer and fasting, qualities of leadership, powerful eloquence, inspirational organizational skills, confidence in God's purpose, and quick, decisive response to problems qualify him as a great leader and man of God. Most important, he shows us a self-sacrificing spirit whose only interest is summed up in his repeated prayer, "Remember me, O God, for good."

Nehemiah expresses the practical, everyday side of our faith in God. He was the James of the Old Testament, challenging the people to show their faith by their works. Four lasting principals stand out in Nehemiah. First, compassion is often the springboard of obedience to God's will. Second, cooperation with others is required to carry out God's will. And third, confidence results from fervent prayer and the exposition of the Word of God, which reveals God's will. Forth, courage will manifest itself as sanctified tenacity in refusing to compromise on the conviction that one is doing God's will. Nehemiah typifies Christ by the life he modeled. He was a courageous leader, defying the odds and encouraging the people to do Yahweh's work. Finally, he was dedicated to God's law.

Nehemiah was a proven leader. He left a secure position in the government of Persia to return to his homeland and rebuild the walls of Jerusalem. He succeeded, too, despite incredible obstacles and opposition. We often dream of the glory and praise of leadership, but we tend to forget about the turmoil and difficulty leadership can carry. God uses men and women who show the same tenacity that Nehemiah had. Read the Book of Nehemiah to see true leadership in action.

The wall was finally completed, and the covenant God made with his people in the days of Moses was restored (Deut. 8). This covenant includes principals that are important for us today. Our relationship with God goes far beyond church attendance and regular devotions. It should affect our relationships (10:30), our time (10:31), and our material resources (10:32-40). When you chose to follow God, you promised to serve him. The Israelites had fallen away from the original commitment they had made to follow God. We must be careful not to do the same!

God put the desire to rebuild the walls in Nehemiah's heart, giving him a vision for the work. God still wants his people to be united and trained to do his work. As we recognize deep needs in our world, God can give us the vision and desire to "build."

Nehemiah teaches that living God's way means putting God's priorities first and realizing that they often are different from ours. God still accomplishes all things through His Word. Therefore, the Scriptures are a guide for ordering our lives according to God's will. When we understand and obey them, they bring joy. They also teach us to acknowledge God's hand in all our success.

After the work of the wall began, Nehemiah faced scorn, slander, and threats from enemies, as well as fear, conflict, and discouragement from his own workers. Although these problems were difficult, they did not stop Nehemiah from finishing his work. When difficulties come, it is easy to get discouraged. But remember, there are no triumphs without troubles. When problems arise, we must face them squarely and press on to complete God's work. We do not have to retreat—our God is a God of absolute victory!

Although God had enabled them to build the wall, the work wasn't complete until the people rebuilt their lives spiritually. Recognizing and admitting sin is not enough. Being serious about God must result in a changed life, or it is merely enthusiasm. God does not want halfhearted measures. We must not only remove sin from our lives, but also ask God to move into the center of all we do.

When Nehemiah began his work he recognized the problem, prayed right away, and then acted on the problem. Prayer still is God's way to solve problems. Prayer and action go hand-in-hand. Through prayer, God guides our preparation, teamwork, and efforts to carry out his will. Without prayer, we are limited to our own finite resources.

The Book of Nehemiah is rich with much wisdom to grow on for today's Christian, such as recognizing and facing your fear, spiritual renewal, encouraging and inspiring others in team work, and doing and finishing a task God gives you, learning to face tragic news with prayer, leadership, learning to deal with opposition, taking care of all that God gives us, learning to rely on Scripture, be thankful for God's blessings and putting God first and center in our life. There is so much more treasure in this book, that one will be richly blessed by reading it and study and apply the knowledge to your life. Enjoy!!!!

PHILIPPIANS

The purpose and message of Philippians was to thank the Philippians and to strengthen them by showing that true joy comes from Jesus Christ. It was written about A.D. 61, from Rome, during Paul's imprisonment for the Christians at Philippi and all believers. Paul and his companions founded the church at Philippi on his second missionary journey (Acts 16:11-40). Paul also appealed for a spirit of unity and steadfastness among the Philippians. In addition, he warned against dangerous heresies that were threatening them, probably Judaism and Gnosticism.

In many respects, this is the most beautiful of Paul's letters it is full of tenderness, warmth, and affection. To Paul, Christ was more than an example; He was the apostle's very life. For Paul, true joy is not a surface emotion that depends on favorable circumstances of the moment. Christian joy is independent of outward conditions, and is possible even in midst of adverse circumstances, such as suffering and persecution. Joy ultimately arises from fellowship with the risen, glorified Christ. Throughout the letter, Paul speaks of joy in the Lord, emphasizing that through Christ alone is Christian joy realized.

The joy presented in Philippians involves eager expectation of the near return of the Lord. Paul further describes a joy that springs from fellowship in the spreading of the gospel. Christian joy is an outgrowth of being in the active fellowship of the body of Christ as well. Paul reveals the timeless message that true joy is to be found only in a dynamic personal relationship with Jesus Christ and in the assurance that God is able to turn adverse circumstances to our good and His glory.

For Paul, Christ is the sum and substance of life. To preach Christ was his consuming passion; to know Him was his highest aspiration, and to suffer for Him was a privilege. Paul's chief desire for his readers was that they might have the mind of Christ.

Philippians teaches to conduct our life as a gospel sermon for observers of our life, and develop the heart attitude of unity (1:27). Also we are to live unselfishly, and esteem others as being more important and more worthy than ourselves (2:3, 4). We are to maintain unity with other believers in our thoughts, attitudes, love, spirit, and purpose. We are to adopt Christ's attitude of unselfishness, servanthood, humility, and obedience (2:5-11). We are commanded to rejoice as a constant discipline; to refuse to worry about things and understand that Jesus gives peace to those who trust Him and ask for His help (4:4-7). Death is not to be feared but remembering that dying in God's timing and will is only victory for a believer (1:21-24). Faith eliminates fear and worry and brings the freedom to rejoice evermore.

Character and conduct begin in the mind. Our actions are affected by the things we dwell on in our thoughts. Paul cautions us to concentrate on things that will result in right living and in God's peace (4:8-9).

Rejoice in the Lord always. Again I will say rejoice! Let your gentleness be known to all men. The Lord is at hand. Be anxious for nothing, but in everything by prayer and supplication, with thanksgiving, let your requests be made known to God; and the peace of God, which surpasses all understanding, will guard your hearts and minds through Christ Jesus. Finally, brethren, whatever things are true, whatever things are just, whatever things are pure, whatever things are lovely, whatever things are of good report, if there is any virtue and if there is anything praiseworthy... meditate on these things (4:4-8).

THE MEANING OF THE BOOK OF LEVITICUS FOR THE CHURCH OF TODAY

"You shall be holy, for I the Lord your God am holy"

(Leviticus 19:2)

If after reading the Book of Leviticus you might wonder how this Book concerns us today. This Book describes the sacrificial system and worship ordered by God. The Book teaches the value of blood: it is the "life" of man and animal; therefore, sacrifice is a life for a life. God has provided blood to cover sin. The blood actually makes atonement for a human life. No blood, no atonement. We all are now grateful that Christ's blood fulfills the requirement for redemption! But the Book of Leviticus goes beyond the issue of sacrifice through the sacrificial worship and work of the priests. The concept of holiness affects not only the relationship that each individual has with God, but also the relationship of love and respect that each person must have for his neighbor. God is pure and holy, and He reminds us all through the Book of Leviticus that He is the Lord our God and He wants our devotion. God is entirely holy in His nature, motives, thoughts, words and deeds. He wants us to be holy as He is holy. Holy means set apart, dedicated to sacred purposes, being clean, morally or ceremonially pure, God wants us to have a life that expresses zealous devotion that focuses on knowing and pleasing Him. He does not want a halfhearted devotion for it is unworthy (Rev. 3:16). This Book deals with many issues relating to purity, holiness, the whole priesthood, the sanctity of God, and the holiness in everyday life. The word "holy" appears eighty times in this book. The entire Book of Leviticus is permeated with the sanctity of God, the holiness of his character, and the necessity of the congregation to approach Him in purity of heart and mind. God tells us moral impurity is extremely destructive to spiritual life and personal relationships. Sexual unfaithfulness is often an analogy for idolatry. God tells us avoid all spiritual and moral uncleanness. It will corrupt and defile every aspect of your life (Lev. 11:47; 15:31; 18:1-30). God's attitude about homosexuality is a serious perversion. Though He offers grace to the homosexual offender, He rejects his conduct (Lev. 20:13).

Leviticus can prove helpful for any believer who is serious about learning to live a life that is godly in Christ Jesus. Leviticus makes it clear that godliness is not optional for those who want to live in a way that pleases the Lord. Do not conceal wrong doing that you are aware of; confess it quickly, for it will only harden your heart. Know that you are accountable even for sins you are not aware of. Always confess your sins quickly, frankly, and openly, and make restitution for sins you have committed against others, as a part of genuine repentance. Stay sensitive to the Holy Spirit's conviction. Remember God cannot look upon sin because of his holiness, so we should not overlook it or deal with it lightly.

Although the Book of Leviticus focuses on the life and worship of ancient time, it teaches believers of today to hold God in holy reference and not to take Him lightly, but honor God with your love and a life that is holy, devoted, and pleasing to Him.

THE BOOK OF PHILEMON {BIBLE BOOK}

Anger

Paul is the author and this letter is Paul's personal appeal to Philemon, a wealthy Christian slave owner. Slavery was widespread in the Roman Empire.

Philemon owned a slave called Onesimus who had stolen from him and run away. Paul had asked Philemon not only to forgive his runaway slave who had become a Christian, but to accept him as a brother. As Christians, we should forgive as we have been forgiven… "…and forgive us our sins just as we have forgiven those who have sinned against us" (Matthew 6:12), because "If you forgive those who sin against you, your heavenly Father will forgive you but if you refuse to forgive others, your Father will not forgive your sins" (Matthew 6:14-15). In Christ we are one family. True forgiveness means that we treat the person we've forgiven as we would want to be treated. No walls of race, economic status, or political differences should separate believers. Let Christ work through you to remove barriers between Christian brothers and sisters. Take steps to act out the love of Christ.

Paul was a friend of both Philemon and Onesimus. He had the authority as an apostle to tell Philemon what to do. Paul chose to appeal to his friend in Christian love rather than to order him to do what he wished. He knew when dealing with people, tactful persuasion accomplishes a great deal more than commands.

While the shortest of Paul's epistles, the Book of Philemon is a deep revelation of Christ at work in the lives of Paul and those around him. It reveals how Paul politely yet firmly addressed a central issue of the Christian life, namely, love through forgiveness, in a very sensitive situation. The epistle is an expression of true Christian relationships. Only with Christ's example of forgiveness through the cross are we able to overcome our hurts and mistakes and be reconciled to our brothers and sisters in Christ.

In the Book of Philemon one can see the act of mercy, the spirit of peace and a pure heart of love and gentleness as they were taught at the Sermon on the Mount: "God blesses those who are gentle and lowly (Mat. 5:5), God blesses those who are merciful (Mat. 5:7), God blesses those whose hearts are pure (Mat. 5:8); God blesses those who work for peace (Mat. 5:9).

THE BOOK OF ECCLESIASTES

"Fear God and keep His commandments, for this is man's all.

For God will bring every work into judgment,

including every secret thing, whether good or evil"

(Ecclesiastes 12:13-14).

The name Ecclesiastes is derived from the Greek word ekllesia (assembly) and means "One Who Addresses an Assembly." The Hebrew word so represented is qoheleth, which means "One Who Convenes an Assembly," often being rendered "Teacher" or "Preacher" in English versions.

Ecclesiastes is generally credited to Solomon (about 971 to 931 B.C.) written in his old age. The words in Ecclesiastes 1:1 states: "The words of the Preacher, the son of David, king in Jerusalem," seem to point to Solomon, although he was not mentioned by name as the author. The pessimistic tone of Solomon's spiritual state must have been repented and he came to his senses before his death, and turned back to God. Solomon had it all and did all he could do but in spite of it all, or because of it all, he was restless and hated life. He could not find meaning to life from possessions. He shows how empty it is to do what feels good and don't worry about tomorrow and pursue life's pleasures in place of a relationship with the eternal God. Solomon knew what he was talking about because as a very intelligent and wealthy king he had spent a lifetime experiencing and analyzing everything the world had to offer.

The determination of the Preacher to find what real value in this life is should be a challenge for any true believer in Jesus Christ. The Preacher's failure to find real value in earthly things and comfortable lifestyles challenges the Christian who lives in this age of greed and materialism to concentrate on the things that are above (Col. 3:1) and not to glorify greed and possessions.

The writer of Ecclesiastes wanted to help those who would live after him lead a fulfilling life. He taught the lessons he learned from his own life. The observation proved that without God, all of our work, pleasure, and wisdom are useless. Lasting fulfillment comes from honoring God in all we do. Solomon made it clear that wealth cannot buy happiness and enjoying your work and life is a God-given gift. True happiness does not come from accumulating or attaining honors-we always want more than we can have, and there are circumstances beyond our control that can snatch away all our possessions and achievements. No lasting pleasure or happiness is possible without God.

Nothing in the world can satisfy our longings and restless heart! The cure for emptiness is to focus on God and fill your life with serving God and others. Human wisdom doesn't have all the answers. Knowledge and education have their limits. To understand life, we need the wisdom that can be found only in God's Word to us—THE BIBLE.

Solomon tried to shake people's confidence in their own efforts, abilities, and wisdom. He did this to direct them to faith in God as the only sound basis for living. Without God, there is no lasting reward or benefit in hard work. Work done with the wrong attitude leaves us empty, but work accepted as an assignment from God can be seen as a gift. When we realize that God will evaluate all we do, we should learn to live wisely, remembering that God is with us at each moment. STOP RIGHT NOW…and think…God is with you right this moment! We can have God's wisdom only when we obey him.

God has a plan for human destiny that goes beyond life and death. Life does not seem to be short when a person is young, yet the years pass all too quickly. Because life is short, we need wisdom greater than this world can offer. We need the Words of God, as Solomon feared through a meaningless life without God in his younger years. Solomon learned true enjoyment in life only comes as we follow God's guidance for living and take each day as a gift from God, thanking him for it and serving him in it.

If you are a sincere Christian, and have not yet learned from the Book of Solomon to spare the bitterness of learning through your own experience, that life is meaningless apart from God, it's not too late to learn.

THE BOOK OF COLOSSIANS

No other book of the New Testament sets forth more fully or defends the universal Lordship of Christ more thoroughly. For Paul, the Lordship of Christ in the believer's life is the most crucial and clearest evidence of the Spirit's presence. Paul lifts up Christ as the center of all that exists. The incarnate Son of God, He is the exact revelation and representation of the Father, Christ is the supreme Creator and Sustainer of all things.

Paul had never visited Colosse, a small town in the province of Asia, about 100 miles east of Ephesus. The church was an outgrowth of his three-year ministry in Ephesus about A.D. 52-55. Scholars believe Paul wrote this letter during his first Roman imprisonment, around A.D. 61.

The heresy in the church then was a blend of pagan-occultism, Jewish legalism, and Christianity. The error resembles an early form of Gnosticism, which taught that Jesus was not fully God and fully man, and was merely one of the semi-divine beings that bridged the chasm between God and the world, and was lacking in authority and the ability to meet the needs of the Colossians.

With urgency, Paul wrote this epistle with a fourfold purpose: 1) expose and rebut the heresy; 2) to instruct the Colossians in truth and alert them to the danger of returning to pagan vices; 3) to express personal interest in the others that did believe the truth; 4) to inspire them to promote mutual love and harmony.

Because this is an age of religious pluralism and syncretism (that is, a diluting of truth for sake of unity), Christ's Lordship is deemed irrelevant by many religious groups that believe one religion is as good as the other. The false teachers at Colossae had undercut the major doctrines of Christianity. Colossians sets forth Christ as supreme Lord in whose sufficiency the believers find completeness. Jesus Christ is preeminent in the church as its Savior and Creator. He is its Life and Leader, and to Him alone may the church submit.

Because Christ is supreme, our life must be Christ centered. To recognize Jesus as God means to regard our relationship with him as most vital and to make his interests our top priority. He must become the navigator of our life's voyage. He requires first place in all our thoughts and activities. We should live in constant contact and communication with God. We must not hold on to our own ideas and try to blend them into Christianity like the people did in Colosse. Christ is our teacher, our hope and our true source of wisdom. We must reject any teacher whose message is not based absolutely on the truth of Christ. We are not allowed anything other than the Word of God to control or judge us. We are not judged holy or unholy by external regulations, but by the condition of our heart.

We should heed Paul's warnings against listening to people who pander to the flesh, rather than edifying in the truth. Human relationships were designed to be fueled and filled by righteousness. To the degree we give in to the urging of our flesh nature, we will fail to experience righteousness or fulfilling relationships. Choose peace to govern all of your relationships.

Paul makes it clear in Colossians that Christ alone is the source of our spiritual life. The path to deeper spiritual life is not through spiritual duties, special knowledge, or secrets; it is only through a clear connection with the Lord Jesus Christ. The Christian life is a process, but when we keep listening to God, we will be changing all the time to be like Jesus.

THE BOOK OF…1 PETER

Peter, the encourager, reminds Christians that even persecution need not be feared if we know Jesus Christ. This letter is a manual on how a Christian should live in the fear of persecution, disintegrating relationship, discouragement, and suffering. It is a note of encouragement.

Peter wrote this letter just before the cruel emperor Nero began his intense persecution of Christians in Rome and throughout the empire. Peter knew what it was like to be afraid for his life, for as a disciple of Jesus, he had denied knowing Jesus three times (John 18:15-27). As Christians, even hurting Christians, we must strive for holiness, abandoning ugly sins that choke our, spiritual lives. Even in tough times, Christians should live Christ-like lives, imitating Christ in our relationships—husbands, wives, employers, employees, fellow Christians and neighbors. God promises, "So if your faith remains strong after being tried by fiery trials, it will bring you much praise and glory and honor on the day when Jesus Christ is revealed to the whole world" (1 Peter 1:7).

Peter offers faithful believers comfort and hope. Persecution makes us stronger because it refines our faith. We can face persecution victoriously as Christ did, if we rely on Him. The fact that we will live eternally with Christ should give us confidence, patience, and hope to stand firm even when we are persecuted. Our hope is not only for the future; eternal life begins when we believe in God and join his family.

Peter also tells us to be like our heavenly Father…holy in everything we do. Holiness means being totally devoted or dedicated to God, set aside for his special use, and set apart from sin and its influence. We should not blend in with the crowd, yet we shouldn't be different just to be different. What makes us different are God's qualities in our lives. Our focus and priorities must be his.

Peter told both young and old men to be humble, to serve each other. Young men should follow the leadership of older men, who should lead by example. Respect your elders, listen to those younger than you, and be humble enough to admit that you can learn from each other. Peter also encouraged the wives of unbelievers to submit to the authority of their husbands as a means of winning them to Christ.

Our attitudes toward our mates are governed by our attitudes toward God. God designed marriage to illustrate the relationship He intends to have with His people. The husband is to give his wife honor and understanding, protecting her and acknowledging that she is a fully partnered heir of God. Husbands, be kind and gentle with your wife. Honor her as your best friend. Listen to her and spend time with her. Cherish her and make her feel extremely important (3:7). Recognize that not doing so will hinder your prayer life and obstruct answers. The wife is to accept the care and authority of the husband (3:1-6) living in a manner that honors him. The beauty of character and gentleness of spirit of such a woman will be precious to God and to her husband.

Peter urged all family members to treat others with sympathy, love, tenderness, and humility. Though it's never easy, willingness is the best way to go to influence our loved ones. Relationships with parents, brothers and sisters, and spouses are important aspects of Christian discipleship. As members of God's family, we are all equally loved so we must be devoted, loyal, and faithful to Christ, the foundation of our spiritual family.

God will judge everyone with perfect justice. He will punish evildoers and those who persecute his people; those who love God will be rewarded with life forever in his presence. Because we are all accountable to God, we can leave judgment of others to him.

Ancient tradition suggests that Peter was martyred in Rome in conjunction with Nero's severe persecutions of Christians after the burning of Rome in A.D. 64. This letter was likely written toward the end of Peter's life.

1 Peter is summarized as: 1. suffering for being a Christian, 2. the hope of eternal life, 3. a call to holy living, 4. the honor of your marriage and family, 5. respecting people in authority and, 6. advice for elders and young men.

ZEPHANIAH... (THE LORD HAS HIDDEN)

The meaning of Zephaniah's name ("The Lord Has Hidden") conveys the ministry of Jesus Christ. The truth of the Passover in Egypt, where those hidden behind blood-marked doors were protected from the angel of death. The message of Zephaniah also has future significance. The book of Zephaniah is a good example of people who were complacent. Zephaniah spoke out against the evil and complacency toward sin that permeated society in the nation of Judah. Zephaniah, a true prophet of the Lord, faced a corrupt and godless nation, Judah. The message of prophecy is not a product of Zephaniah's own heart, but is a word, that is, a revelation, which the Lord gave to him. The Lord was to use Assyria as His instrument to bring about the destruction of Judah. This destruction would be a day in which the righteousness of the Lord would be vindicated. It would truly be a Day of the Lord. Sin is serious business and ultimately brings horrible judgment and punishment. We should weep because of the consequences that we see coming from sin and for those who take sin lightly. Zephaniah thundered his warnings against evil pronouncing judgment and punishment upon all who were against the Lord. In order to arouse sinners from their indolence and bring them to repentance, he describes the terrors of the day of the Lord. The entire nation would be destroyed and their survivors would be carried off into captivity. But it was the only way to purge the nation of its sinful way of life which had penetrated into the fiber of society. The people did not listen, either because they doubted God's prophet, or thus did not, however, was not ready to listen to God's Word, and instead of repenting, the nation showed itself more zealous in performing more wicked deeds. When the officials are corrupt, the citizenry itself is likely to be corrupt. When the heart is impure, the lips speak impure things. Does this sound familiar? Look at our nation! The prophet warned that the nation would be destroyed if they did not repent from complacency and sinful ways and turn back to God. The bold attempts of King Josiah of Judah, to reform and turn back to God were probably influenced by Zephaniah. But in the end, however, the evil of Josiah's predecessors had so permeated society that only a succession of good kings could bring lasting revival. That did not happen. Even the priests, who should have taken the lead in the worship of God, perverted the law. They treated holy things as though they were profane, which made the true worship of God practically impossible.

The Lord said, "I will search with lanterns in Jerusalem's darkest corners to find and punish those who sit contented in their sins, indifferent to the Lord, thinking He will do nothing at all to them. They are the very ones whose property will be plundered by the enemy, whose homes will be ransacked. They will never have a chance to live in the new homes they have built. They will never drink wine from the vineyards they have planted! The terrible day of the LORD is near" (Zeph. 1:12-14). There will be no escape from divine punishment! They will be compelled, however, to recognize God's sovereignty, for He will bring judgment upon them. Their gods will be plundered, and they will thus come to learn that God is in control even of their own lives. If we refuse to listen to God's Word, the Bible; we are as shortsighted as the people of Judah. The kingdom of self is a dangerous place to live, for we exclude the God who created us. In that self-centered condition, we don't trust God and don't seek Him or his wisdom. That's what happened to the people of Jerusalem. Since they relied on themselves so much and took God and sin lightly, God could not reach them with normal discipline, He was forced to take drastic measures. When we rely too much on ourselves, we begin to believe that we don't need God. A healthy sense of self-worth and self-sufficiency does not deny our need for God's strength and guidance, but don't become so self-sufficient that you no longer recognize God's discipline when it comes. To escape God's judgment we must listen to Him, and accept his correction, trust Him, and seek his guidance daily. If we accept God as our Lord, we will escape his condemnation.

When we stay sensitive to God, He won't have to take drastic measures to help us. The people of Judah were prosperous and no longer needed or cared about God, and were not sorrowful for their sins. Their wealth and security made them complacent. God's demand for righteous living was irrelevant to them. We can never let material comfort be a barrier to our commitment to God. We have to be aware that prosperity can produce an attitude of proud self-sufficiency. Prosperity is a false sense of security. The answer is to admit that money won't save us and that we cannot save ourselves! We cannot allow ourselves to be shaped or conformed to the world's way of thinking.

Because of the repeated use of the term "The Day of the Lord," the Book of Zephaniah has meaning for the end times. The Day of the Lord is either the period of time or the actual day when God will bring His purpose to culmination for mankind and for the Earth. The righteous will be rewarded with eternal blessing, and the wicked will be condemned to eternal damnation.

Since His coming, the Holy Spirit has been crying out to the world as Zephaniah did, "Gather yourselves...before the decree is issued, or the day passes like chaff, before the Lord's fierce anger comes upon you! Seek the Lord, all you meek of the earth, who have upheld His justice. Seek righteous, seek humility. It may be that you will be hidden in the day of the Lord's anger" (Zeph. 2:1, 3). He is saying don't be stiff-necked and hard hearted as your fathers did (Acts 7:51). Jesus said that one of the works of the Holy Spirit would be to convict the world of judgment because the ruler of the world is judged (John 16:8-11).

Four timeless lessons for both believers and unbelievers are found in Zephaniah: (1) God is perfect justice as well as perfect love, (2) punishment is not God's choice, God loves the world (John 3:16), (3) to settle into complacency and to participate in the ritual of a well-structured religious life without obeying God's voice, receiving correction, or drawing near to Him is an ever-present possibility. Even more tragic is to have no awareness of such spiritual emptiness, (4) Even to the rebellious, God offers last-minute reprieve. "The remnant who humbles themselves and seeks righteousness will be hidden in the Day of the Lord's anger" (2-3). "They will be gathered to Him and healed (3:18), for God dwells in their midst" (3:17). This abiding promise to God's people is the essence of the gospel.

FAITH, LOVE, AND JOY

"Rejoice in the Lord always: and again I say Rejoice"

(Philippians 4:4).

As Christians we know "faith worketh by love." It won't work any other way. Those two decisions...to operate by faith in the Word of God and to walk in love are the most important decisions a believer can make. But we cannot walk in faith and love and leave joy out. The force of joy is too important to leave dormant in your spirit. Joy is an essential part of a life of victory. Without it, one might have an occasional triumph now and then, but then, one wouldn't be able to sustain them. They quickly slip away. Joy is what gives you the strength to hold steady when the circumstances get rough ("The joy of the Lord is your strength" (Nehemiah 8:10)). Joy gives you the ability to laugh in the devil's face when he starts trying to knock you off your faith. It gives you a kind of staying power that will make you a winner again and again.

Make a commitment to not only walk in faith and love but joy as well. Make it a point to rejoice in the Lord always...and there won't be anything the devil can do or say to steal your victory from you!

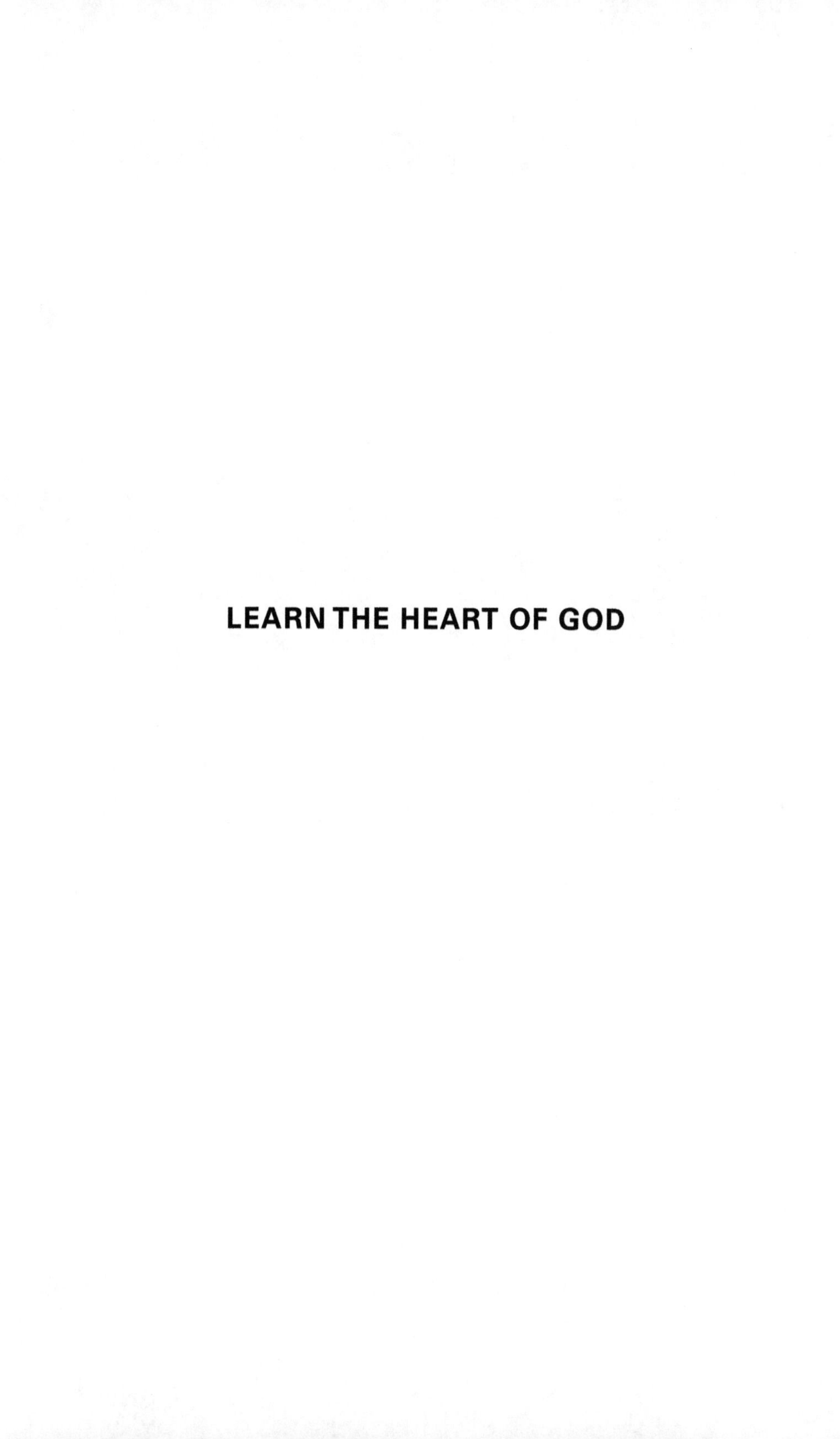

LEARN THE HEART OF GOD

FROM THE HEART OF THE LORD

The Lord tells His children to thank Him for our troubles. When our mind gets snagged on a difficulty, we are to bring it to Him with thanksgiving. We are to depend on Him and ask Him to show us the way to handle the situation. The very act of thanking the Lord releases our mind from a negative focus. As we turn our attention to Him, the problem fades in significance and loses its power to trip us up. Together with the Lord we can deal with the situation, either by facing it head-on or putting it aside for later consideration.

Most of the situations that entangle our mind are not today's concerns; we have borrowed them from tomorrow. In this case, He will lift the problem out of today and deposit it in the future, where it is veiled from our eyes. In its place He gives us His wonderful peace, which flows freely from His Presence.

"Be anxious for nothing, but in everything by prayer and supplication, with thanksgiving, let your requests be made known to God; and the peace of God which surpasses all understanding, will guard your hearts and minds through Christ Jesus" (Philippians 4:6-7).

THE HEART OF GOD

The Lord wants us to be assured how safe and secure we are in His Presence. This is a fact, totally independent to our feelings. We are on our way to heaven; nothing can prevent us from reaching that destination. There we will see the Lord face to face, and our joy will be off the charts by the earthly standards. Even now we are never separated from the Lord, though we see Him in the eyes of faith. He has promised to walk with us now and onward through eternity. Although the Lord's Presence is promised, it doesn't necessarily change our feelings. When we forget He is with us, we may experience loneliness or fear. It is through awareness of His Presence that Peace displaces negative feelings. The Lord tells us to practice the discipline of walking consciously with Him throughout each day.

THE FATHER'S HEART

Each moment we can choose to practice the Presence of the Lord or we could practice the presence of our problems. When we keep focused on the Lord our whole perspective is brighter, more joyful. When we are preoccupied with our problems we feel weighed down and anxious. We seem to have thoughts that flow toward finding what is wrong and trying to fix it. This is a harmful and hurtful pattern in which we need to be free of.

The Lord tells us His grace is sufficient and we need to stop trying to fix things and stop focusing on our failures. He reminds us that we live in a fallen world and right now we are a part of the brokenness. We can't be perfect in practicing His Presence, and we can no way save ourselves. Nonetheless, we are being transformed and renewed by the Holy Spirit.

We must stay in agreement with the Lord and His ways and Word so He can set us free from hurtful ways. When we view each moment as a fresh opportunity to draw near our Lord, He will welcome us with open arms.

"Come to Me, all you who are weary and burdened,
and I will give you rest" (Matthew 11:28).

THE FATHER'S HEART

God's kingdom is not about earning and deserving; it is about believing and receiving. This is good news for many who try to deserve God's kingdom. We actually can never be good enough to deserve His kingdom. Yet so many struggle with a strong desire to earn their way…at least partially…rather than simply receiving everything Jesus has already done for them. In some ways, some Christians find believing and receiving more difficult than earning and deserving. They find themselves wanting to be recognized for their efforts and accomplishments. The Lord knows how vulnerable we are to idolatry. He tells us one of the most prevalent temptations is to idolize ourselves or our good works. For this reason, God will often withhold success until people can handle it. When we have been sufficiently broken by adversity and failure, we are better able to deal with success. So when trials of many kinds come our way, we need to receive them as gifts from God. We need to believe God knows just what He is doing, and His way is perfect. After we suffer a little while (1 Peter 5:10), He will make us what we ought to be, grounded, secure, and strengthen. This is how the Lord, prepares us to share in His kingdom.

"Consider it pure joy, my brothers, whenever you face trials of many kinds, because you know that the testing of your faith develops perseverance" (James 5:10).

THE FATHER'S HEART

God has told us… "Trust in Me with all your heart and mind and do not lean on your own understanding. In all ways acknowledge Me, and I will make your path straight" (Proverbs 3:5-6). Trusting God is our goal. But our mind's ravenous appetite for understanding seems to be the culprit for making better progress, and behind the need to understand everything lays a strong desire to feel in control of our life. But our true desire is to trust God wholeheartedly! God is pleased when we try to please Him. But we must allow the Lord to do His supernatural work in our heart, and many of our difficulties in our life our designed to help this endeavor.

The Lord wants us to trust Him with all of our heart and all of our mind. We have the Holy Spirit to help us think trusting thoughts, but it will require our cooperation. Instead of relying on our own understanding to help us to feel in control, we need to ask the Holy Spirit to control our mind. As we look to God, trusting and talking with Him, He will straighten out our path before us.

"The mind of sinful man is death, but the mind controlled by the Spirit is life and peace" (Romans 8:6).

THE FATHER'S HEART

The Lord commands us to have an attitude of gratitude, for thankfulness opens the windows of heaven. Spiritual blessings then fall freely unto us through those openings into eternity. This seems to be such an easy condition, but yet we stumble over it almost every day. We need to pray and ask the Holy Spirit for help to overcome our ungrateful attitude. Throughout the Bible God repeatedly commands thankfulness because it is vital to our well-being. It is also crucial for a healthy relationship with the Lord, since He is our Creator, our Savior and our King. When we thank God we acknowledge our indebtness to Him: how much He has done and what He is doing, and what He will do for us. This attitude brings joy both to us and to Him.

Giving thanks is similar to priming a pump with water so that it will produce more water. Since thankfulness is one of the spiritual blessings God bestows on us, it will increase along with the others when we "prime" the Lord with thanksgiving.

Remember that He is the God of all grace. When we fail to be thankful, we can simply ask for forgiveness. As we freely receive this priceless gift…remember what it cost Jesus and our gratitude will grow. We should be looking up at Jesus and see the spiritual blessings cascading down on us through the wide-open windows of heaven.

"Enter His gates with thanksgiving and His courts with praise;
give thanks to Him and praise Him" (Psalm 100:4).

"Blessed be the God and Father of our Lord Jesus Christ,
who has blessed us with every spiritual blessing in the
heavenly places in Christ" (Ephesians 1:3).

"Devote yourselves to prayer, being watchful and thankful"
(Colossians 4:2).

THE FATHER'S HEART

"That you may love the Lord your God, that you may obey His voice, and that you may cling to Him, for He is your life and the length of your days..." (Deuteronomy 30:20).

"Jesus replied: 'Love the Lord your God with all your heart and with all your soul and with all your mind. This is the first and greatest commandment'" (Matthew 22:37-38).

God wants us to cling to Him as our lifeline. We need His help continually and He is always eager to provide it! God knows we don't always obey his voice perfectly and God doesn't want us to be anxious. The most important commandment is to love God with all of our heart, soul and mind! We won't do this perfectly either, nonetheless, God still delights in the love we give from our heart. He sees it as a mother would when her loving child brings her a crumbled flower. God also sees our flawed obedience and the desire to obey, and He rejoices! Instead of worrying about the ways we fall short, He wants us to focus on doing what we can; out of love for Him. But at times our inadequacy can actually be a blessing, because it can protect us from becoming self-righteous. It also trains us to depend on God more and more.

When we do relate to God as our lifeline, God is pleased. Plus it is the wisest way to live! God created us to depend on Him, being dependent and clinging to Him. If we don't depend and grasp on to Him, we will be lead to addictions, destructive relationships and other forms of idolatry. So the more we cling onto God, the better our life will be. Our Father God realizes we are weak and our faith-muscles easily tire. However, our weakness and waywardness cannot diminish His love for us. "As a father has compassion on his children, so the Lord has compassion on those who fear Him; for He knows how we are formed, He remembers that we are dust" (Psalm 103:13-14). God's infinite wisdom enables Him to take our errors and weave them into an intricate work that is good.

But when we feel like we are losing our grip, we need to cry out to God, for He tells us "For I am the Lord, your God who takes hold of your right hand and says to you, do not fear; I will help you" (Isaiah 41:13). The Lord tells us that the best strategy for accepting ourselves, even when we make mistakes, is to live close to Him. This nearness helps us see things from His perspective.

SHARING MY PERSONAL ENCOURAGEMENT

BY SANDRA BECKMAN

GOD SHARES HIS HEART

The Lord says, we as His children need Him every moment. Our awareness of our constant need for Him is our greatest strength. Our neediness, properly handled, is a link to His Presence. However, there are pitfalls that we must be on guard against: self-pity, self-preoccupation, giving up. Our inadequacy presents us with a continual choice: deep independence on the Lord, or despair. The emptiness that we feel within will be filled either with problems or with the Presence of the Lord. The Lord says to make Him central in our consciousness by praying continually: simple, short prayers flowing out of the present moment ("Pray without ceasing" (1 Thessalonians 5:17)). We are to use His Name liberally, to remind us of His Presence. The Lord says, keep on asking and you will receive, so that your gladness may be full and complete ("Until now you have asked nothing in My name. Ask, and you will receive, that your joy may be full" (John 16:24)).

YESTERDAY'S SERVANT

There are many road blocks in a Christian's life that they must walk and overcome so they can "die to self and put on the image of Christ." None of us have not arrived to perfection and need to continue on the road to maturity and be refined. Some experiences or circumstances may be painful, or hurtful, which at times is caused because one does not recognize the blessing within these experiences of warning or chastening. But these steps of self denial are necessary if one is serious in following Jesus in their faith walk to becoming all that God has for them and wants for them. This has been one of my lessons I want to share. I was following after a heart's desire I had since I was a young girl. But even though it was a godly thing, God did not have an open door for me there, or the anointing for it. I was struggling with it, and I had no peace or resulting fruit. I did pray about it, but was blinded and deceived by my heart, and did not hear God's voice saying, "This is not what I want you to do." Because it was a heart's desire and it was a good thing, I got involved only to find out, it was my desire and not God's. I had to overcome my fleshly ambition with the help of the Holy Spirit's chastening and the conformation I learned when I read R. T. Kendall's book, "The Anointing," given to me by a caring and spiritual sister in the Lord. We all need to continue in giving and doing good works and uplifting and supporting one another, especially when we are blind and deceived and are heading down a wrong path in the wrong direction, and are not aware of it! With an open mind, teachable and humble, repentive heart, we will be on the right road again! I know I am grateful to my sister's sensitivity and her obedience to the leading of the Holy Spirit and the Lord's chastening for bringing me back on track.

Many of us have admired someone with a great talent or creativity, or a high IQ, and desired to have such a gift. So we may, at times get distracted and open our own door of ambition without realizing we do not have the anointing for such a gift, stepping over our limitations. What we need to realize in our heart is, that God is our Creator and has made each of us in a unique way for a unique purpose, giving us limitations. He gave us unique blessings and the anointing for our personal gift, or talent to fulfill our purpose in the kingdom. We never should question it, or regard it lightly, but be honored and thankful and privileged using it to do the very best to fulfill the advancement of His kingdom. Just think, God has chosen before we were born, our parents, our environment, our childhood peers, plus shaped our interests and determined our I.Q. (Jer. 1:5), preparing us for the very purpose He had planned for us! These anointed gifts and talents are always meant to bless others, not for personal gain or satisfaction.

But because we allow ambitions and at times listen to our selfish heart desires, we over-step our boundaries and limitations God set upon us, allowing us to be governed by unrealistic expectations. We find ourselves struggling in a situation or talent we should not be in, even though it is a not a bad desire but it was not meant for us. There was no anointing upon us to fulfill it. We are then doing this in the flesh and not the Spirit. When we are walking in our own anointing and talents and gifts God gave to each of us, we will not struggle but have peace, joy and fruit from the labor of our hands. It will flow, and doors will open and we will not get weary or struggle.

It's only when we step out of our limits of anointing and into others anointed blessings and purposed gifts that we run into a dead end. Paul reminds us that we should not think of ourselves more highly than we ought to think but to accept the "measure" that was given to us, which means the limit of our faith and the limits of our anointing. At times it may become hurtful to admit one's limits, but to accept them with grace and gratitude for then you will have peace and joy. Plus, when you are walking in your gift you never have to prove yourself. Straying outside of your anointing will surely rob you of your freedom of ever having nothing to prove, and blind your true direction and purpose. It will also put you in a position of having God "chasten" you. The word chasten means "enforced learning." But if it is necessary because you did not turn from this direction of being outside your anointing, God will do what He needs to do to get your attention, because He loves you and wants you to be blessed. Believe me, He got my attention! But I am truly grateful He did! Why put yourself in a situation where there is no fruit flowing from what you are doing? You will never get a reward for wasting God's time, your energy or for walking out of your anointing. You will never hear, "Well done." No, you will only become yesterday's servant!

SHARING WITH YOU:

As a writer I love sharing everything I'm learning with the Lord and my study time. But I think sharing what's on my heart with others also is important because we may be going through the same growing step. So I would like to share a growing moment with you.

I find myself always wanting to be in control and keep order throughout my day by organizing my activities. Although I know the Lord wants me to allow Him to unfold the day and walk me through the steps He has provided; I try but fail many times, even though I know there is peace, and less confusion His way. I do try to walk those steps but as the day progresses, I realize I am again in control and have lost my focus to stay in the boundaries and perspective of the day the Lord provided for me. Tomorrow's tasks creep in, or other problems that need not be solved today are again on my mind and find myself doing things not planned for the day. Can you relate? I know it's time for a brief timeout with the Lord to get refocused! Help me Lord!

So I am in the process of learning when my peace has left me, and I feel anxious, I am out of tune and no longer following the day the Lord had planned for me. I need to take time and reconnect with Jesus! Because we deal with so many distractions in our world it is easy to get out of focus. I am learning the Lord's peace in His Presence need not be shaken by what is going on around us. If you are learning this step of growth then you too will know it will take some effort on our part, but I know you will agree we have to press on if we are to mature in our Christian walk. I know I would have a more successful day if I learned to stay in touch with Jesus throughout the whole day!

Let's keep on growing together! God Bless you... Sandie (founder and author of *Pathway Outreach*)

SHARING WITH YOU: UNDER CONSTRUCTION

So many times my spiritual lesson is about "waiting." The Lord knows I can be a bit impatient. At times I wait for just so long and then I find myself trying to solve my problems, or trying to fix others. I know it's all about trusting, which I have learned to do so much better. I know the Lord has the perfect answers, but when there is a delay to the answer, I seem to try to make things happen myself. I also know when I pray for patience, the Lord will give me more situations involving patience, so I know I better learned this lesson very soon! I also know when I try to do things without the Lord and His guidance; it becomes a disaster, and another mistake. When I am hoping and waiting, I find it connects me closer to the Lord, and strengthens my faith. The more we have the opportunities to have to wait for an answer, the stronger we will grow. So if you are one like me, who finds waiting for an answer from the Lord or hoping something will come to pass sooner, take hold and be patient with yourself, for the Lord knows how to help us when we ask Him. He is patient! As long as we recognize our weaknesses, we can always go to the Lord in prayer, as many times as we like. Remember, we are all "under construction" but we are progressing and growing! You can be sure the Lord will help us pass the test!

God Bless You! Sandie… (Author / Writer of *Pathway Outreach*)

A STRONG STIRRING IN MY SPIRIT

I have felt a strong stirring in my spirit about the vital urgency of the end times, the importance of the Body of Christ and keeping the constant presence of God throughout the day. I truly believe I have been led to share this message as it was laid on my heart during my prayer time and fellowship with the Lord. As a Christian writer, I have always written my articles in the past through the inspiration from the Holy Spirit as He placed them in my spirit. I believe I am to share this message in obedience to the Lord.

God could have chosen to birth each of us in any year, but He purposed for this generation to serve Him in these end time days. I believe as the Body of Christ we have not been considering or taking our important roles seriously enough for this era. We have not been redeeming or being the good stewards of this time God has given us to carry out what He wants done before the return of Christ.

I have felt a strong desire to continually pray for the strengthening, unity, and maturity of the Body of Christ. Church we have to wake up and unite in one heart and one accord, one focus and stir up the hunger for the Kingdom so we can be about the Father's business. Even the Devil knows his time is short so he is about pouring on the heat of his deceptive influence making times tough! But this is the time the "tough" get going! Time is of the essence. We cannot afford to be complacent. Let's start examining our hearts and spirits. We need to ask ourselves, "Where is our daily focus? Are we being self-centered, worldly minded and being deceived by life's issues, allowing the weight of the worlds turmoil overcome us?" Satan has a way of distracting us from our purpose, our given authority through Christ Jesus. God has already equipped us with all the spiritual weapons needed for this time. But the Devil does not want us to exercise our influence or responsibilities as the Church so he causes a diversion and division in our life.

Not only as a member of the Body of Christ, you men have a wonderful privilege, honor and a responsibility and the anointing as the "head of the household" (Eph. 5:22, 23). God has place the husband in the anointed position to lead your wife and family in spiritual wisdom and the knowledge of God; being a strong example. He is expecting you to pray daily for the needs, and protection, discernment and godly strength of your family. He did not choose the woman...but the man. Yes, the wife has her responsibilities to God and the children but she also is to submit to a godly husband and respect his anointed position. God is expecting husbands and fathers to hold their position in high regards, walking in godliness, integrity, sincerity and love; being a Christ-like example. As the head of the family husbands help teach their children the importance of praying together as a family and leading them in the ways of God.

God is telling husbands to take charge...see that your household is praying and putting God's ways into action and walking in love daily. Men don't take your anointed position lightly, for your position effects your whole household, which in turns effects the whole Body of Christ. God takes the family order very seriously. These are critical times which will only worsen and God is depending on a strong Church. Remember, revival starts with the individual and that starts at home. God is building up a strong army for these end times and needs us all to do our part. Also I would like to add, as wives we are "covered from many of the destructive attacks by Satan as our husbands walk and take charge of their anointed position."

As a wife, let me say it's a comforting, secure encouragement to know my husband is understanding the honored position of his anointing and that he is praying for discernment, guidance and wisdom needed for our household. It stirs up my inspiration and hunger for more of the Lord. It also deepens my respect, honor and admiration for my husband. I enjoy our morning prayer study each day which starts our day rolling. But we find without our prayer time together in the morning things seem to fall out of balance and wrong doors get opened. We also have our individual prayer time and fellowship with the Lord daily. We both have so much more to learn spiritually but we want to grow strong in the Lord and be a strength to the Body of Christ.

"Therefore, submit to your own husbands, as to the Lord. For the husband is the head of the wife, as also Christ is head of the church; and He is the Savior of the body. Therefore, just as the church is subject to Christ, so let the wives be to their husbands in everything. Husbands, love your wives, just as Christ also loved the church and gave Himself for her."

(EPHESIANS 5:22-24)

The message to Christians is: "Set your mind on things above, not on the things on the earth. For you died, and your life is hidden with Christ in God" (Colossians 3:2, 3).

Being a child of God requires us to share the love and Word of God. We are his hands, heart and voice. We can make a difference in our families, the work place and in our communities. You can bring salvation and healing to many as the return of Christ draws near. Let God work through you as the opportunities become available. When you care about the lives of others and where their destination is headed, you will step up and share the love of God in a gentle manner and lead them to the Lord in prayer such as:

Dear Lord, I know I am a sinner and need you in my life. I do believe You died for me and that Your blood paid the price for my sins and provided me the gift of eternal life. Please come into my life and help me to live the life You have for me. I now acknowledge You as my Lord and Savior. In the Name of Jesus I pray...Amen.

When you lead someone to the Lord, it is very rewarding and because of you, one day they will stand with you in heaven! God says, we can and will make a difference in this world, one soul at a time... "He who believes in Me, the works that I do he will do also; and greater works than these he will do, because I go to My Father" (John 14:12 NKIV).

I pray Follow the Son has been an inspiration to you, and it has helped you to draw closer to God and has directed your focus more on the kingdom of heaven and the lost souls who need you. God bless you all!

FREE MONTHLY NEWSLETTER

To encourage your spiritual walk
If you are interested in receiving a free newsletter called
"The Pathway Outreach," send your inquiry to:

Pathway Outreach
P.O. Box 3095
Holiday, Florida 34692

Or…send your name and address to db246ok@gmail.com.

PLEASE SEND YOUR TESTIMONIES TO

Sandra Beckman / Author of Pathway
P.O. Box 3095
Holiday, Florida 34692

May the grace of the Lord Jesus,
the love of God and the
fellowship of the Holy Spirit be with you.

www.ingramcontent.com/pod-product-compliance
Lightning Source LLC
LaVergne TN
LVHW011304300925
822322LV00001B/20

* 9 7 8 1 6 4 8 0 4 0 8 9 4 *